S0-BEA-840

The Third World in Global Environmental Politics

The Third World in Global Environmental Politics

Marian A. L. Miller

BOULDER
LONDON

To my mother,
Gloria Miller Craig

Published in the United States of America in 1995 by
Lynne Rienner Publishers, Inc.
1800 30th Street, Boulder, Colorado 80301

Library of Congress Cataloging-in-Publication Data
Miller, Marian A.L., 1950–
The Third World in global environmental politics / Marian A.L. Miller.
Includes bibliographical references and index.
ISBN 1-55587-422-3 (alk. paper)
ISBN 1-55587-423-1 (alk. paper, pbk.)
1. Sustainable development—Developing countries.
2. Environmental policy—Developing countries. 3. Economic development—Environmental aspects. I. Title. II. Series.
HC59.72.E5M55 1995
333.7'09172'4—dc20 94–36484
CIP

Printed and bound in the United States of America

The paper used in this publication meets the requirements of the American National Standard for Permanence of Paper for Printed Library Materials Z39.48.1984.

5 4 3 2 1

CONTENTS

TABLES

ACKNOWLEDGMENTS

Writing this book has been an exciting voyage of discovery, and I have received support and encouragement from a number of colleagues before and during the journey. My interest in environmental politics was kindled during my graduate studies at the University of Southern California; I would like to thank Professor Robert Friedheim for his encouragement of this interest. Nourishment along the way was provided by my colleagues in the Political Science Department of the University of Akron, who created an environment conducive to research and writing. I owe a special debt to Christopher Smith, who has been generous with his time, incisive comments, and expressions of encouragement. Finally, I would like to thank the editors at Lynne Rienner Publishers for their patience.

This book is dedicated to my mother, Gloria Miller Craig. She has been consistent with her encouragement and support throughout the years.

—Marian A. L. Miller

1
INTRODUCTION

The environment looms large on the global political agenda. The increased attention is the result of several factors: increased awareness of the environmental damage caused by economic activity; rapid population growth; the perception of the earth as a single biosphere; and, more recently, the end of the Cold War. During the past few decades, the scientific community has uncovered new information on the environmental consequences of humankind's interaction with the earth. Much of this has found its way into the popular media. As a consequence, the public has some familiarity with issues such as global warming, ozone depletion, nuclear pollution, and hazardous waste disposal. This period has also seen accelerating population growth, growth that has thrown into stark relief the problems caused by the inadequate supply of food and resources in certain localities and by the maldistribution of food on a global level.

In the past, food and resource shortages were perceived primarily as local or national problems and, consequently, as the responsibilities of many different jurisdictions. But this has changed because of the new perception of the earth as a single biosphere. There is an awareness that actions in one part of the world can have implications for resource availability in distant areas. For example, a poorly managed nuclear power plant in one country can damage people and crops thousands of miles away. Similarly, each country's decision regarding the use of fossil fuels will have implications for global warming and for life on earth. As a consequence, many issues that were initially regarded as matters of local concern are increasingly becoming issues of global concern and, therefore, the subject of international politics. Finally, the end of the Cold War has allowed the environment to rise on the global agenda. As military security issues loom less large on that agenda, more attention is paid to issues of environmental security. This change was illustrated by the unprecedented gathering of 118 heads of state at the United Nations Conference on Environment and Development in Rio de Janeiro in June 1992.[1]

As the scientific community has uncovered more about the causes of commons[2] environmental problems such as global warming and ozone depletion, the new findings have highlighted the unified nature of the biosphere. Since an action by one state can have environmental implications for the rest of the global community, it is no longer acceptable for countries to defend their actions with claims of sovereignty. Gaining ascendancy is the perspective that sovereignty as a legal right of states will need to be modified in the light of these new circumstances. Increasingly, it has become obvious that the existing institutional arrangements are inadequate to handle the burgeoning environmental problems, and the global community of states has begun the process of establishing new institutions for global environmental management. For the most part, this process has gone forward in a piecemeal manner, with separate regimes for specific issue areas. Some areas have regimes that include specific control measures, and other areas are yet to be carefully addressed. The formation and evolution of environmental regimes have cast into stark relief the differences between the interests of the Third World and those of the industrialized states, a difference that is linked to the two groups' positions in the world economy.

The Economic Context

It is essential to examine the economic context within which environmental practices and policies evolve. Economic growth is the lodestar for much of the world. Regardless of their economic status and political perspective, a primary objective of nation-states is growth. However, current economic development strategies can have significant consequences for the environment. One important measure of development is per capita energy usage. In the past few decades, the reliability of this indicator has been affected by increased energy efficiency in some states, but economic growth is still an energy-intensive process. Between 1965 and 1990, the commercial energy consumption per capita increased from 936 to 1,316 kilograms of oil-equivalent energy.[3] This does not include energy usage in the noncommercial sector, which is significant in some developing countries.

Two major ecological problems associated with energy consumption are resource depletion and pollution. Fossil-fuel sources of energy, such as oil and coal, are finite; they also pollute the air and water and contribute to global warming. A third fossil-fuel source, wood, also contributes to global warming and atmospheric pollution. Although in theory wood is a renewable source, in some parts of the world wood harvesting has passed the maximum sustainable level. Nuclear power is sometimes touted as the solution to the problems of energy scarcity and global warming, but the use of this form of energy raises concerns regarding public safety and waste disposal. Even a renewable source like hydroelectric power is not without environmental problems. Mega-dam projects sometimes displace thousands of people and destroy ecosystems.

The increasing international trade, which is such a vital component of our global economy, also has important environmental implications.[4] For the past 40 to 50 years, great emphasis has been placed on the desirability of free trade. However, trade is a resource-consumptive process; the more economies become dependent on far-flung trade, the more resource consumptive trade will become. Regional trading blocs seem to be a good idea, but they are being used to supplement, rather than supplant, global trade. The various regimes that manage global and regional trade also impose specific environmental costs. One example of this is the pressure to standardize health and environmental guidelines, often to a level below those already established in many developed and developing countries.[5]

The environmental consequences are inevitable, given the logic of a world economy that relies on infinite growth. At the 1993 Group of Seven[6] Summit, one of the few things the leaders were able to agree on was the importance of economic growth. But in our global economic system, growth results in the use of finite resources, in the pollution caused by the use of these resources, and in the problems associated with the disposal of the hazardous wastes that are often the by-products of industrial growth.

The benefits of economic growth, such as they are, come at great cost in terms of resource depletion and pollution. But these costs and benefits are not shared equally among the world's peoples. Although Third World countries have limited access to these benefits, they pay a disproportionate share of the costs. In large part, developing countries' role in the global economy is rooted in their colonial past; dependency theorists see the development and wealth of the North and the underdevelopment of the South as functions of each other.[7] Patterns of resource exploitation emerged that enabled the colonial power to accumulate capital and assume political hegemony over the subordinate colony, leading to a pattern in which the colony's resources were used in a manner incongruent with local needs. At the same time, these patterns of resource exploitation incorporated new products and technologies from other areas of the globe. Developing countries became very dependent on both export and import trade, and decolonization did not end this pattern.

As a result of the internationalization of economies, developing countries often have only minimal control over the disposition of their resources. In addition, the degree and pattern of use of these resources do not directly reflect the needs of the source country. Outsider interests such as transnational corporations and consumers in other countries often have more influence over resource choices than do the citizens of the particular nation-state. Although foreign and international interests may also be important in developed countries, the size and precarious economic health of many of these countries' economies make them more vulnerable to outside interests.[8]

Because of the Third World's position in the global economy, on a per capita basis these countries are generally less resource consumptive and less polluting of the atmosphere than the industrialized countries.[9] But the Third World countries hope their economic position is temporary. They expect further industrial growth, and, given the available industrial processes, this is likely to have negative ecological implications. In addition, the poverty in many of these countries has created pressures on natural resources, sometimes resulting in the despoliation of natural ecosystems such as forests and coastal areas, with significant implications for biological diversity.

The political and economic context has affected the way in which the developing countries participate in environmental politics, with the end of the Cold War further modifying their participation. During the Cold War, some of these countries used to play First World against Second World interests and were sometimes able to benefit economically from this maneuver; with the end of the Cold War they have lost this leverage, and the interests of the industrialized world have shifted to the development of the resources and markets of the former Soviet bloc countries. The end of the Cold War has put global environmental politics higher on the global agenda, but in this post–Cold War context Third World countries have lost some leverage, calling into question their ability to affect the evolution of global environmental politics.

Global Environmental Politics in the Twentieth Century

Concern about environmental degradation is not a twentieth-century phenomenon. In the second century B.C., Plato talked about the erosion caused by earlier deforestation in Attica,[10] and in the third century B.C., Erastothenes described how governmental land policy, navigation needs, and mining resulted in the deforestation of Cyprus.[11] But for the most part, the concerns expressed throughout the centuries did not generate any widespread alarm. The first vestiges of an environmental movement did not develop until the second half of the nineteenth century. In 1865 the first private group dedicated to environmental protection, the Commons, Footpaths, and Open Spaces Preservation Society, was established in Britain. A few decades later, groups focusing on wilderness preservation and resource conservation developed in the United States.[12]

Environmental Politics, 1900–1960

Rudimentary efforts at international organization took place early in the twentieth century. In Paris in 1909, at a meeting of the International Congress for the Protection of Nature, European nature protectionists proposed the creation of an international nature protection body.[13] When this idea was proposed to the governments of 19 major states, all but two agreed in principle.[14] A Consultative Commission for the International Protection of Nature was established in 1913; its stated purpose was the collection, classification, and publication of information on the international protection of nature. However, this early institutional attempt was killed by the outbreak of World War I.[15]

Many of the early efforts at international cooperation were regional in scope and dealt with issues such as migratory animals and wildlife. They included such agreements as the European Convention Concerning the Conservation of Birds Useful to Agriculture, which was signed by 11 nations in 1902; and the Convention on Nature Protection and Wildlife Preservation in the Western Hemisphere in 1940, which was sponsored by the Pan American Union.[16]

Much of the postwar development of international environmental politics has taken place under the auspices of the United Nations (UN). The United Nations Educational, Scientific, and Cultural Organization (UNESCO), which was established in 1945, and the International Union for the Protection of Nature (IUPN), which was formed in 1948, were important actors in this political process. The postwar activity led to an international conference on the conservation and use of resources, called by the United Nations Economic and Social Council (ECOSOC) for summer 1949.[17]

This first major international conference on the environment was held in the United States. The UN Scientific Conference on the Conservation and Utilization of Resources (UNSCCUR) was organized by the Food and Agriculture Organization (FAO), the World Health Organization (WHO), UNESCO, and the International Labour Organisation and was attended by more than 500 delegates from 49 countries.[18] The delegates represented themselves and were not official representatives of their countries.[19] In the Cold War climate, there were no delegates from the Soviet bloc; in fact, more than half of the delegates were from the United States.[20] It was a meeting of scientists rather than politicians or diplomats, and it was criticized for taking place within a political vacuum.[21] UNSCCUR's mission was to address the problem of nature protection primarily from an economic perspective.[22] The conference had no power to bind governments or make recommendations to them. Although questions of policy did surface, the conference's primary task was to share information on techniques for the conservation and utilization of resources.[23] The scientists were generally confident that the world could support its rapidly growing population.[24] The prevailing opinion was that technology could successfully address any obstacles.[25] The meeting focused on the environment as a resource base; therefore, it addressed global resource rather than pollution issues. The resource areas examined included minerals, fuels and energy, water, forests, land, and wildlife and fish. The conferees also looked at the integrated development of river basins. Although this conference focused on science rather than policy, some policy analysts regard it as the first major event in the development of the international environmental movement.[26]

Work on environmental protection was also proceeding outside of the United Nations within the framework of the IUPN, which was a hybrid of governmental and nongovernmental bodies. Its focus was the preservation of wildlife and the natural environment, education, scientific research, legislation, and the collection, analysis, and dissemination of data and information.[27] Concurrent with UNSCCUR, IUPN held the International Technical Conference on the Protection of Nature (ITC), which was sponsored jointly with UNESCO. Although the conference focused on the protection of nature, it also addressed the conservation of renewable natural resources. Unlike UNSCCUR, ITC had the task of making recommendations concerning national and international legislative measures.[28] The conference agenda also included the matter of technical assistance to less developed countries. It was attended by representatives from 32 countries and 11 international organi-zations, including FAO, WHO, the International Council for Bird Preservation, the International Council of Scientific Unions, and the Organization of American States.[29] At this time there were fewer than 40 independent developing country-states. Most of today's Third World states were still colonies, so many of the conservation issues that related to these areas were addressed by the industrialized countries. Preparatory meetings and the conference itself were dominated by the developed countries; the independent developing states had very little impact on the process.

Between 1948 and 1956, IUPN's agenda gradually broadened to include conservation. This was reflected in its new name—the International Union for Conservation of Nature and Natural Resources (IUCN). Its agenda now included the conservation of representative ecosystems.[30]

Environmental Politics, 1960 to Stockholm (1972)

The early 1960s marked the period of greatest change in both the environmental movement and environmental politics. Books such as Rachel Carson's *Silent Spring* and Rolf Edberg's *On the Shred of a Cloud* mobilized public opinion.[31] The environment moved from being the concern of a few scientists, administrators, and conservation groups to being the focus of a mass movement that affected much of the industrialized world. Consequently, the public began to pressure governments to address issues of pollution and resource mismanagement. Sharpening the focus on the environment was the growing concern about the potential impact of nuclear fallout.

Public concern was heightened by a series of environmental disasters between 1966 and 1972. Among these was the wreck of the *Torrey Canyon* in March 1967. Hundreds of miles of Cornish coastline were polluted when about 875,000 barrels of crude oil were spilled. Two years later, an oil platform blowout off the coast of Santa Barbara, California, polluted miles of

California coastline. Japan was the site of another well-publicized disaster, which had more direct human implications. Local residents were poisoned as a result of decades of mercury discharges into the ocean. Fifteen hundred people became sick, and more than 200 died. Although environmental disasters were not new phenomena, the increased public sensitivity to environmental issues after the early 1960s heightened the impact of these disasters.

In addition, this period also saw an increase in scientific knowledge. It is within this context that the Biosphere Conference (the Intergovernmental Conference of Experts on the Scientific Basis for Rational Use and Conservation of the Resources of the Biosphere) of 1968 was held in Paris.[32] The conference was primarily a UN-sponsored effort; it was organized by UNESCO, with help from FAO and WHO. The International Union for the Conservation of Nature and Natural Resources and the International Biological Programme were also involved in its organization.[33] The Biosphere Conference addressed the human impact on the biosphere, including the effects of air and water pollution, overgrazing, deforestation, and the drainage of wetlands.[34] Conference participants emphasized that environmental deterioration had reached a critical threshold and that methods of developing and using natural resources had to change.[35] This was clearly a change from UNSCCUR's general optimism 19 years before. The conference recommended additional research on ecosystems, human ecology, pollution, and genetic and natural resources; new approaches to environmental education; and assessments of the ecological impacts of large-scale development projects.[36]

Some of the themes explored at the Biosphere Conference were developed further in the United Nations Conference on the Human Environment (the Stockholm Conference) in 1972. However, whereas the Biosphere Conference focused on the scientific aspects of environmental problems, the Stockholm Conference looked at the broader political, social, and economic issues. As a result, nongovernmental organizations (NGOs) were involved at Stockholm to a greater extent than had been the case at the Biosphere Conference;[37] in fact, observers from 258 NGOs were present.[38] Participants at Stockholm had a very broad agenda, reflecting the wide-ranging priorities among the members of the international community.

The Stockholm Conference was the result of efforts to place the protection of the biosphere on the official agenda of international policy. The participation of most of the world's nations and many organizations suggests that these efforts succeeded. There were delegates from 113 nations, 21 UN agencies, and 16 intergovernmental organizations.[39] The conference took place at a time when issues of global inequality were gaining ascendancy on the international agenda; it is not surprising, then, that North-South differences over global economic relations and environmental politics were major elements of this conference. Third World countries played a prominent role in preconference discussions and thus were able to modify the agenda.

The conference had been planned to address the particular set of environmental problems identified by developed countries, but the developing countries were concerned that the conference outcome might have negative consequences for their development prospects. The industrialized countries were persuaded to broaden their environmental agenda to include issues of particular interest to the Third World such as shelter, food, and clean drinking water. The tendency had been to focus on issues such as pollution, population explosion, conservation of resources, and limits to growth. Some Third World countries saw much of this discourse as an academic exercise, with little relevance to their everyday lives. Using their United Nations General Assembly voting power, they were able to press developed countries to embrace a broader vision of environmental issues, one that addressed Third World development needs.[40] Third World countries were beginning to play a role in determining the international environmental agenda.

The most tangible outcome of the Stockholm Conference was the creation of the United Nations Environment Programme (UNEP). This institutional framework would address the issues put forward in the Stockholm Declaration, Principles and Action Plan. In the decades since Stockholm, it has played a vital policy-coordinating role. The developing countries campaigned to have the UNEP secretariat located in a developing country. Their position prevailed, and the secretariat was placed in Nairobi, Kenya.

Environmental Politics, Stockholm to Rio (1972–1992)

The second wave of international environmentalism was spurred by events such as the Bhopal disaster at the Union Carbide plant in India, the Chernobyl explosion, and the *Exxon Valdez* oil spill. On the research front, there was growing consensus among scientists regarding environmental issues such as ozone depletion and climate change. In addition, renewed attention was given to the tension between growth and the environment, one example of which was the 1987 report by the World Commission on Environment and Development.[41] The report concluded that continued economic growth was essential, particularly for the people of the developing world, but it made the point that this growth would not be feasible if traditional growth patterns were pursued and called for a switch to new modes of environmentally sound or sustainable development. It was within the context of this second wave of environmentalism that the UN General Assembly mandated the 1992 UN Conference on Environment and Development (the Earth Summit), which was held in Rio de Janeiro, Brazil.

The Earth Summit was held on the twentieth anniversary of the Stockholm Conference. It was initiated by developed Western nations to deal primarily with the environmental consequences of industrialized society. It followed nearly two years of preparatory work. More than 170 nations sent delegates to the conference; also present were representatives of thousands of NGOs, many major industrial corporations, and nearly 9,000 members of the media. The conference drew 118 heads of state, the largest such gathering ever.[42]

Yet the conference proved that the world was still divided. For Rio, the Third World and the industrialized countries had suggested agendas that reflected their differences at the Stockholm Conference. The developed countries wanted to address ozone depletion, global warming, acid rain, and deforestation, whereas the developing countries were more interested in examining the relationship between developed countries' economic policies and developing countries' sluggish economic growth. Leaders of developing countries insisted that environmental protection alone was not enough; therefore, any agreement about global environmental issues must also include measures for economic development. The sentiment was that an environmentally healthy planet was impossible in a world that contained significant inequities. The North acknowledged the connection between environment and development in many of the conference documents, and some industrialized countries did promise increased monetary aid, but the North refused to commit to specific steps to reduce its own industrial pollution and continued to press the developing countries to protect their forests and wildlife.

The Earth Summit produced new international treaties on climate and biodiversity, a statement on forests, the Rio Declaration, and an action plan for sustainable development, known as Agenda 21. In addition, the meeting produced a consensus that preparations should begin for a treaty to curb desertification. The parties also established a watchdog commission to monitor progress on the pledges made at Rio.

The Purpose of the Study

As nation-states of the global community negotiate global regimes, it becomes clear that their common concern for the biosphere does not necessarily lead to shared interests. Developing countries recognize different priorities from those identified by the developed countries. This book examines the role of the Third World in global environmental politics. Specifically, it examines how these countries have attempted to modify the evolving global environmental regime and assesses the extent to which they have been successful. It addresses these issues within the context of globalization, both economic and ecological. It finds that whereas the former acts as a constraint on developing countries' influence in environmental politics, in certain contexts ecological globalization provides them with some room for maneuver. The focus on globalization of the economy pays particular attention to the constraints imposed on developing countries as a consequence of their role in the world economy. Since the ready assumption is that the industrialized countries hold the preponderance of power, it is easy to assume that the developing countries have little or no influence on the formation of environmental regimes. This would be consistent with the realist perspective of international politics.

For realists, international behavior is based primarily on interests and power. Politics is a struggle for power within a state-centric system.[43] Consequently, the realist paradigm is based on conflict and competition among states. It assumes that states are unitary actors with gradations of capabilities among them and perceives a clear separation between domestic and foreign policy. The regime approach, which is central to this study, makes several modifications to the traditional realist perspective. It assumes that competing, self-interested states can find it in their interest to opt for cooperative behavior. In making this assumption, it modifies the realist perspective regarding the role played by self-interest. The regime concept also embraces a more expansive conception of power. As with realist theory, the regime approach sees states as primary actors, but unlike realist theory, it also recognizes that regimes can be major global actors.

Global and regional environmental problems present challenges that cannot be clearly understood using the state-based theory of realism. Environmental problems often transcend national boundaries, and the institutions and organizations that are emerging as critical for addressing these issues include regimes and international organizations, both of which are neglected in realist theory. Additionally, realist theory does not allow for the focus on cooperation called for by an examination of regimes. Scholars find the regime approach particularly useful because of its focus on the cooperative behavior that is an important part of the evolution of global environmental politics. The study of regimes offers a different perspective on power. The very nature of global environmental problems creates new power dynamics between developed and developing countries and changes the way in which gradations of power among countries are perceived. For example, the fact that the Third World is likely to release immense amounts of greenhouse gases in its efforts to industrialize provides these countries with an important bargaining chip. The globalization of the environment implies that biosphere issues are considered within a commons context, in which situation any actor has the ability to subtract from the welfare of the other actors. This, then, is a potential basis for leverage by the Third World.

Although the globalization of the environment and of the economy both result in interdependence, they represent two different types of interdependence. Economic interdependence is a constructed interdependence since it is a result of the current economic and social system. In a world in which there is globalization of resources, capital, and labor, there is an increasing number of transnational, intergovernmental, and transgovernmental relationships. The resulting interdependence makes all global actors, to a greater or lesser degree, more sensitive to changes in other actors and more vulnerable to external events.[44] Although the multiple linkages are the most pronounced among the industrialized countries, major intergovernmental organizations (IGOs) and NGOs have been instrumental in integrating the Third World countries into the global economy. Because of the power asymmetry, the sensitivity and vulnerability that are consequences of an interdependent world are more likely to be reflected in the Third World as costs rather than benefits. Whereas this interdependence is likely to be a long-term feature, it is not a permanent, unchanging characteristic of the world-system. Ecological interdependence, however, is a consequence of the biosphere within which all human beings live. It is a naturally occurring interdependence, and all of humankind must operate within the constraints of the biosphere.

The concept of a biosphere emerged in the late nineteenth century; however, much of the credit for the development of this concept has been given to Russian mineralogist V. I. Vernadsky, who wrote about it in the first half of the twentieth century. The biosphere is composed of the lower atmosphere, the oceans, and the lithosphere. Vernadsky argued that outside of this "terrestrial envelope" humankind could not live naturally. He also asserted that because of the natural and necessary connections among all living organisms, no organism is truly free of other organisms; there is a natural interdependence.[45]

In a system in which there is economic interdependence, economic asymmetry can be exploited to benefit the more powerful actors. However, the regimes examined in this book illustrate that a general perception of ecological interdependence places constraints on both the powerful and the puny. In situations in which developed country actors perceive this interdependence, Third World actors are able to exercise some modest leverage in environmental politics. This book explores how this power is exercised and how it is modified, and it focuses on the role of the Third World in the formation and evolution of three environmental regimes: the hazardous waste trade regime, the biodiversity regime, and the ozone protection regime.

Each of these regimes has been developed to manage a different kind of environmental problem. Although both the biodiversity and ozone protection regimes address common property resource issues, there are substantial differences between these two commons problems. Since ozone protection is an atmospheric issue, we are dealing with a resource held in an open access arrangement; biodiversity, on the other hand, is held in a mixed property regime with a wide variety of arrangements, including private property, government control, communal property, and open access. The hazardous waste trade regime addresses a transboundary problem rather than a commons problem. Its purpose is to regulate the shipment of wastes from one country to another. These varying property and access arrangements affect how states perceive their interdependence and vulnerability; consequently, they have implications for the leverage of the Third World in international environmental negotiations. This study focuses on the role of the Third World at three stages of regime evolution: problem definition, bargaining, and regime transformation.[46]

This study does not assume that the Third World countries are unitary actors. All the groups and individuals in each country are not assumed to hold the same interests. The interests of the government may or may not be consonant with those of business, the rural poor, or the urban poor; governments may or may not transcend vested interests in favor of more general public interests. However, since the focus is on the Third World in the global arena, the emphasis is on the role and influence of the Third World governments and the interests they represent.

Organization of the Book

Chapter 2 defines the term *Third World* and discusses the Third World's position in the context of the global economy. It focuses on the links between global inequality and environmental policies and politics. In so doing, it examines the structural constraints of the global economy and the roles played by the industrialized countries, intergovernmental organizations, and nongovernmental organizations. In the course of covering these issues, the chapter addresses the impact of distributive issues on environmental cooperation and examines the domestic sources of Third World environmental politics. Domestic factors such as the tax and subsidy structure, the distribution of resources and power, population pressures, and the status of women all affect the nature of environmental politics in Third World societies.

Chapter 3 deals with the Third World's role in environmental regime formation and evolution, summarizing some of the literature that addresses these issues. It then focuses on the role of power and discusses how the globalization of the economy and the environment might affect the use and impact of power in regime formation and evolution. It examines how this might be played out at the stages of problem definition, bargaining, and regime transformation.

In Part 2, Chapters 4 through 6 address the ozone protection, hazardous waste trade, and biodiversity regimes, respectively. Each chapter describes the particular environmental problem and then outlines the evolution of the regime. This is followed by an analysis of the interests various sets of actors bring to the process. The problem definition, bargaining, and regime transformation stages are then described. Each chapter concludes with an evaluation of the Third World's role in the process.

Part 3 focuses on the implications of the findings for conflict or cooperation in global environmental politics. Chapter 7 assesses the formation and evolution of the three regimes and discusses how the context of economic and ecological interdependence has affected the Third World's influence in global environmental politics.

Chapter 8 concludes the study with an assessment of the implications for environmental governance and sustainable development. It examines the ramifications for global environmental politics, looking specifically at the issue of structural inequality and the prospects for sustainable development.

Notes

1. World Resources Institute, *The 1993 Information Please Environmental Almanac* (Boston: Houghton Mifflin, 1993), 9.

2. Commons refers to common property resources, such as air and water, regarding which exclusion or control of access is difficult or impossible. The concept is discussed in detail in Chapter 3.

3. United Nations Development Programme, *Human Development Report 1993* (New York: Oxford University Press, 1993), 185.

4. The bulk of international trade moves by sea. In 1991 the total volume of international seaborne trade reached 4.05 billion metric tons, the highest level ever recorded. This was up from a volume of 2.6 billion metric tons in 1970. Total ton-miles reached 17,390 billion. See United Nations Conference on Trade and Development, *Review of Maritime Transport 1991* (New York: United Nations, 1992), 2.

5. The link between trade policy and the environment was among the many issues addressed during the debates on, and preparations for, the North American Free Trade Agreement and the Uruguay Round of the General Agreement on Tariffs and Trade.

6. The Group of Seven consists of the following major industrialized countries: Canada, France, Germany, Italy, Japan, the United Kingdom, and the United States.

7. Variations on this perspective are presented by several scholars, including Paul Baran, *The Political Economy of Growth,* 2d ed. (New York: Monthly Review Press, 1956); Andre Gunder Frank, *Capitalism and Underdevelopment in Latin America* (New York: Monthly Review Press, 1967); and Walter Rodney, *How Europe Underdeveloped Africa* (London: Bogle-L'Ouverture, 1973).

8. Marian A.L. Miller, "Balancing Development and Environment: The Third World in Global Environmental Politics," *Society and Natural Resources* 5 (1992): 298.

9. United Nations Development Programme, *Human Development Report 1993,* 185. In 1990 per capita commercial energy consumption for developing countries was 517 kilograms of oil-equivalent energy. If we were to focus on the least developed countries group, this per capita figure would be 63 kilograms. For the industrialized countries the corresponding per capita figure is 4,937 kilograms.

10. Plato, *Critias.*

11. Strabo, *Geography* xiv, 6.5.

12. John McCormick, *Reclaiming Paradise: The Global Environmental*

Movement (Bloomington: Indiana University Press, 1989), vii–viii.

13. Robert Boardman, *International Organization and the Conservation of Nature* (Bloomington: Indiana University Press, 1981), 27, cited in ibid., 22.

14. The governments approached were Argentina, Austria, Belgium, Britain, Denmark, France, Germany, Hungary, Italy, Japan, the Netherlands, Norway, Portugal, Romania, Russia, Spain, Sweden, Switzerland, and the United States. Japan and Romania were the two that did not agree in principle.

15. McCormick, *Reclaiming Paradise,* 22.

16. Lynton Keith Caldwell, *International Environmental Policy: Emergence and Dimensions,* 2d ed. (Durham: Duke University Press, 1990), 32–33.

17. McCormick, *Reclaiming Paradise,* 27.

18. "Conservation and Utilization of World Resources," *Nature,* November 12, 1949, 813.

19. Ibid.

20. Leonard Engel, "Science Notebook," *The Nation* 169, September 3, 1949, 226.

21. James Rorty, "Growing into World Order," *Commonweal,* October 7, 1949, 623.

22. International Union for the Protection of Nature, *Preparatory Documents to the International Technical Conference on the Protection of Nature, August 1949, U.S.A.* (Paris: UNESCO, 1949), 94.

23. "Conservation and Utilization of Resources," 813.

24. Engel, "Science Notebook," 226.

25. Robert K. Plumb, "Seas Held Source of Food Reserves," *New York Times,* August 25, 1949, 25.

26. McCormick, *Reclaiming Paradise,* 37.

27. Ibid., 35.

28. International Union for the Protection of Nature, *Preparatory Documents,* 94.

29. McCormick, *Reclaiming Paradise,* 37.

30. Ibid., 40.

31. Caldwell, *International Environmental Policy,* 29.

32. McCormick, *Reclaiming Paradise,* 88.

33. Caldwell, *International Environmental Policy,* 27.

34. McCormick, *Reclaiming Paradise,* 89.

35. Caldwell, *International Environmental Policy,* 27.

36. McCormick, *Reclaiming Paradise,* 89–90.

37. Ibid., 90.

38. List of NGO observers, UN Doc. A/Conf. 48/Inf. 6 (1972).

39. *Report of the United Nations Conference on the Human Environment Held at Stockholm, 5–16 June 1972.* List of Participants, UN Doc. A/Conf. 48/Inf. 5 (1972).

40. McCormick, *Reclaiming Paradise,* 92–105.

41. World Commission on Environment and Development, *Our Common Future* (Oxford: Oxford University Press, 1987).

42. World Resources Institute, *1993 Information Please,* 9.

43. Realist work of the twentieth century includes George F. Kennan, *Realities of American Foreign Policy* (Princeton: Princeton University Press, 1954); Hans J. Morgenthau, *Politics Among Nations,* 5th ed. (New York: Knopf, 1978); Reinhold Niebuhr, *Christianity and Power Politics* (New York: Charles Scribner's Sons, 1940).

44. See Robert O. Keohane and Joseph S. Nye, *Power and Interdependence: World Politics in Transition* (Boston: Little, Brown, 1977).

45. V. I. Vernadsky, "The Biosphere and the Noosphere," *American Scientist* 33 (January 1945), 4, cited in Caldwell, *International Environmental Policy,* 355.

46. The three stages selected here draw upon the work of Gareth Porter and Janet Welsh Brown, *Global Environmental Politics* (Boulder: Westview Press, 1991); and Oran R. Young, *International Cooperation: Building Regimes for Natural Resources and the Environment* (Ithaca: Cornell University Press, 1989). Two of the processes identified by Porter and Brown were issue definition and bargaining. Instead of using their third process, regime strengthening, I have instead used Young's term, *regime transformation,* because it allows for the weakening, as well as the strengthening, of regimes.

PART 1

THE ECONOMIC AND POLITICAL CONTEXT

2
The Third World in the Global Economy

Defining the Third World

Since the 1950s, the term *Third World*[1] has been applied to a group of countries otherwise referred to as developing, underdeveloped, or backward. The term was originally intended to capture the idea that these countries were excluded from power in the world, and that they aspired to a role in history independent of the superpowers.[2] Over time, however, this characterization has been criticized for suggesting a nonexistent unity among a disparate group of countries; and more recently, analysts have argued that the term has outgrown its usefulness since there is no longer a Second World.

In spite of the current political context, and regardless of the economic, political, cultural, and social differences among them, the countries of the Third World "share a set of historically determined socio-economic characteristics"[3] that result from their experiences with colonialism and imperialism. The term *Third World,* then, is not merely a geographic term referring to specific continents and countries; rather, it describes the common experiences shared by the societies and peoples of these countries. These same experiences also place a qualitative dividing line between the Third World and the countries of the developed world and are the bases for their different experiences with regard to development. As a result, both capitalism and socialism exhibit different characteristics in a Third World country than in a developed country. Whatever political and economic approach these countries adopt, it will have to address problems that have resulted from the distortion of their societies and economies by colonialism and imperialism.[4]

Exploring Third World Diversity

As the term is used in this study, the Third World consists of the independent countries of Central and South America, the Caribbean, the Middle East,

Africa, and Asia. It does not include Israel, the newly autonomous Asian republics of the former Soviet Union, and South Africa. For decades, Israel and South Africa have been regarded as pariah states by Third World countries; consequently, they were not included in the Group of 77.[5] Although some of the former Soviet republics and South Africa may eventually be included in the Third World group, during the period covered in the study they were not regarded as members. Some definitions of the Third World exclude China, but this study includes China, which has been one of the Third World's more assertive members in the negotiations addressing global environmental politics.

Although these countries often work as a bloc in international politics, they have many political, cultural, economic, and social differences. The group includes huge states, such as China and India, and tiny states, such as Singapore. With an area of more than 9.5 million square kilometers, China is larger than the United States; and India's area is approximately 3.3 million square kilometers.[6] At the other extreme, the area of the city-state of Singapore is about 1,000 square kilometers. Some Third World countries have been independent actors in the world community for more than 150 years,[7] whereas approximately 50 percent of the group's members have achieved this status only since 1960. Although there is increasing economic diversity within the group, many countries still have economies that depend on agriculture; others draw their wealth from the export of oil or other mineral resources. The following section focuses on the differences within the Third World in the two interrelated areas of income and major export category, areas that have particular consequences for the nature of these countries' interactions in the global arena.

Divisions Based on Income

When developing countries are being categorized, one of the more immediate bases of division is income levels. Based on this distinction, the Third World is sometimes further divided, with the poorest of these countries placed into a group of nations called least developed or Fourth World. Forty-three percent of Third World countries are in the low-income group, and 37 percent are in the lower-middle-income range; only 5 percent are high-income countries. Most mem-bers of the high-income group are either oil-exporting countries or exporters of services.[8] Although these high-income economies are still at a disadvantage vis-à-vis the developed countries, they generally have more economic and political options than do the majority of the Third World countries.

Many Third World countries are dependent on income earned from the exploitation of natural resource capital. In the prevailing economic logic, the depletion of resources—which is, in fact, the loss of wealth—is regarded as net income. The poorest countries are usually the most vulnerable in this regard because lack of both capital and trained manpower restricts their ability to make the transition to other economic activities. Additionally, in a poor country the poorest citizens suffer the most from environmental degradation. This context of limited options increases dependence on such practices as overgrazing, mining, commercial logging, fuelwood harvesting, deforestation, and the burning of crop residues and dung. The consequences can include soil erosion, water pollution, sedimentation, flooding, and salinization.

The countries' status is directly related to the options available to them in the global economy and is enhanced if they possess goods that are in high demand or cheap enough to be competitive in the global marketplace. In this context, then, it is useful to explore the divisions based on major export category.

Divisions Based on Major Export Category

Whereas some Third World countries have a niche in the manufacturing and service sectors, others are still largely dependent on extractive industries. In the former group are the newly industrializing countries (NICs), such as Singapore and the Republic of Korea, which have successfully developed particular sectors and industries that are globally competitive. At least two explanations have been proposed for the evolution of NICs. One holds that their emergence is part of a changing economic structure that corresponds to shifts in the economic division of labor among countries. As a result, advanced developing countries are vacating more basic industrial sectors in which the next tier of developing countries has a relative advantage. This perspective suggests that the number of NICs will continue to increase. The alternate perspective sees the evolution of NICs as a process of concentration of industrial capacity in selected countries that are characterized by special circumstances that make high-volume dynamic expansion of manufactured exports flexible, which would lead to the concentration occurring in a limited number of countries.[9] In fact, both processes seem to be occurring at the same time, so it is unlikely that there will be as many NICs as the first perspective suggests, or as few as the second indicates.

The NICs have had high levels of growth in output and exports, as well as a significant level of industrialization; consequently, there are substantial economic differences between them and the bulk of the Third World states. Yet despite these differences, the NICs do belong in the Third World category. As with the other Third World states, their political, social, and economic landscape has been conditioned and distorted by the cumulative impact of colonization, imperialism, and foreign domination.[10]

Only four Third World countries—a mere 3 percent of the group—have manufactures as their major export category; they are China, the Republic of Korea, Lebanon, and Singapore. About 26 percent (32 countries) are primarily service exporters, involved in activities such as tourism, data processing, and merchant shipping. Most of the service exporters are in the middle- and high-income categories.

Among those Third World countries that are still dependent on extractive industries, the petroleum-exporting countries enjoy a special status. Because oil is such a vital input in the industrialization process, it has the potential to be a valuable political and economic tool. The oil embargoes of the 1970s demonstrated the clout of oil, and the 1991 Gulf War emphasized its continued importance. Third World fuel exporters include Algeria, Angola, Brunei, the Congo, Gabon, Iran, Iraq, Libya, Nigeria, Oman, Qatar, Saudi Arabia, Trinidad and Tobago, the United Arab Emirates, and Venezuela—approximately 11 percent of the Third World group.[11]

About 35 percent of Third World countries depend principally on the export of nonfuel primary products, such as agricultural products and ores. These countries are more vulnerable than are other groups to the vicissitudes of the global marketplace because they often produce goods that are readily available elsewhere and that can be easily replaced with substitutes. It is not surprising that more than half of the members of this group are in the low-income category and are also severely indebted.[12] Finally, another 25 percent (31 countries) have diversified economies, since no single category accounts for more than 50 percent of their exports.

Since income and export characteristics condition a country's political participation, these differences may be expected to result in divergences among Third World actors in international politics. However, when the states participate in global forums, their differences do not generally take center stage. In spite of the distinctions, the countries are linked by their common position in the world-system.

The Third World and the Global Economy

Since the 1980s, increasing attention has been paid to the constraints a globalized economy imposes on the industrialized nation-states. Such constraints have long been the experience of Third World countries. Because of their inferior position in the economic and political system, they have long been aware of the limits imposed on them by the nature of the global economy. Beginning in the 1960s, dependency analysts—many from the Third World—attempted to explain the economic stagnation in the developing countries and the widening gap between the rich and the poor. One of the characteristics they emphasized was the vulnerability of the Third World countries, particularly vis-à-vis the developed world. These scholars offered an external explanation for Third World problems.[13] They saw the problems originating in the experience of colonialism and foreign domination, with the economic surplus being transferred from the Third World to the industrialized countries, and argued that the same processes that generated development in the Western metropolises simultaneously generated underdevelopment in the Third World.

Later, world-systems analysts developed a more holistic perspective, focusing not just on the Third World but on both developing and developed states. The unit of analysis became the world-system rather than the nation-state. Viewed from a world-systems perspective, there is one single world-economy;[14] consequently, no state is really autonomous, although some states have greater autonomy than others.

There are three categories of states. Industrialized countries, such as the United States, Britain, France, and Japan, comprise the core states. These states have a strong state apparatus with which to advance the interests of their bourgeois. The core constitutes the most technologically advanced states of the world-system, in which the focus is on technologically sophisticated production activities. At the other extreme are the periphery states, which are depicted primarily as providers of raw materials and unskilled and semiskilled labor for the system. Profits from the periphery are extracted by the core countries. The third group makes up the semi-periphery states. They play an intermediate role and have a mix of production activities. Semi-periphery countries play the role of core states to the periphery countries while remaining periphery countries to the core states. What we have, therefore, is a global division of labor. A country's role in the world economy depends on its position in the world-system. It is in the interest of the core countries to maintain the relative power relationship since the affluence of the core is based on the exploitation of the periphery and the semi-periphery. In the context of the present world-economy, the Third World countries are in the periphery and semi-periphery groups.

One set of linkages tying together the core, periphery, and semi-periphery countries is the harmony of interests between certain powerful groups in the core and the national elites of the periphery and semi-periphery. The national elites tend to identify more with powerful interests in the core and less with the people of their own countries. This linkage ensures the continuation of the division of labor not only within the world-system but also within individual Third World countries. As a consequence, when we talk about global inequality, we are talking about two levels of inequality: the inequality between the core states on the one hand and the periphery and semi-periphery states on the other, and the inequality between national elites and the mass of the population of each state. The developing states' elites often share strong social and economic interests with the elites of the core states, which can work to the detriment of the masses of the population of the developing countries. Policy decisions often reflect elite interests rather than the public interest. Elites have generally accepted the development myth, which holds that the only way to proceed economically is to follow the path of the developed countries, and this myth informs many of their decisions.

Both the dependency and world-systems approaches underline the periphery's dependency. The awareness of being a part of a global economic system and therefore subject to its constraints is not new to the Third World in either experiential or analytical terms; however, it has only recently been widely acknowledged as a part of the experience of industrialized countries. The decline of hegemony and the expanding network of technological, social, and economic linkages emphasize the connections among the components of the world-system. Still, the Third World countries, because of the nature of their economies and their relative lack of power, are much more vulnerable and constrained by the world-system than are the developed countries. This difference has significant implications for environmental policy.

As economies in the industrialized countries stall, these countries attempt to stave off decline by increasing their exploitation of the Third World. As the population of the Third World grows and as these countries try to industrialize, they have a greater domestic demand for their own resources; however, the industrialized countries want to prevent a growing Third World from using up resources and waste sinks they are used to regarding as theirs. Third World leaders try to satisfy the interests of both Northern capital and themselves by extending the boundaries of their economies. For some developing countries, this means exhausting soil, removing old-growth forests, or overexploiting fisheries. More resources such as land, water, and forests are becoming factors in their industrial development. The emphasis on growth by both the North and the South places increased strains on resources and waste disposal capacity. This situation is exacerbated by structural problems at the global level, which produce a devastating combination of economic forces for the Third World: oppressive debt burdens, declining terms of trade, and rising capital flight. An examination of the Third World's interactions with industrialized world actors demonstrates some of these forces at work. Although they are addressed singly, these forces often act in concert, with a resultant exponential increase in their impact on the Third World.

The Third World and the Industrialized Countries

Despite decades of "development," the gap between the industrialized countries and the Third World is growing rather than decreasing. An examination of the widening gap in real gross domestic product (GDP) per capita[15] for developing countries and the industrialized countries is illustrative. Using data for 86 developing countries,[16] the United Nations Development Programme compared the average income for industrialized countries and the Third World for 1960 and 1990. In 1960 the average income for a Third World country was 17 percent of the industrialized world average; 30 years later it had declined to 15 percent. Only 20 of the 86 states showed a relative increase in income, whereas some experienced a precipitous decline.

For example, Venezuela was on par with the industrialized country average in 1960; by 1990 it was down to 43 percent of that average. In 1990 Singapore was the only Third World country to exceed the industrialized country average. Only four other states[17]—Barbados, Cyprus, Saudi Arabia, and Oman—exceeded 50 percent of the industrialized country average, although Saudi Arabia experienced a slight decline over the 30-year period. But most telling is the fact that in 1990 40 countries—almost half the group—had per capita GDPs that were 10 percent or less of the developed country average; in 1960 only 25 of the 86 countries were in this group. The disparities appear even greater if we compare individual countries. A comparison of GNP per capita for Switzerland and Mozambique shows a ratio of 408:1.[18]

Major structural differences still constrain Third World development. One example of this is the uneven terms of trade with which these states are faced. Many still depend heavily on the export of raw materials, such as copper, iron ore, and timber, and cash crops such as sugar, cotton, and coffee. But since 1980 the prices of many of these products have fallen sharply. This decline has been a function of a number of factors: dependence on primary products, structural adjustment program provisions, the changing tastes of importing countries, technological advances, availability of new suppliers, and the protectionism of the industrialized states. Table 2.1 illustrates the trade performance of developing countries from 1980 to 1990. These countries had increases in exports over this period, but this was countered by the declining terms of trade, with the most significant declines occurring in Africa and the Middle East. Commodity export prices fell significantly during this period, whereas the prices of imported manufactured goods rose significantly. Increasingly, developing countries have had to rely on loans to make up the difference between income and expenditures. But with the declining commodity prices, they are caught in a scissor squeeze of rising debt and falling earnings.

Another measure of the Third World's weakness in the economic system is its vulnerability to the imposition of economic pressure. An examination of the use of economic sanctions between 1949 and 1990 reveals that they were used most often by the developed world against the developing world. In this period countries were the targets of sanctions by the developed world a total of 69 times; in 65 cases—94 percent—the targets were developing countries. Developing countries have used this tool sparingly. During the same period, they employed sanctions 18 times; developed countries were the targets 8 times, or 44 percent of the time.[19] The industrialized states' use of sanctions primarily against the developing states is a demonstration of unequal power. Since the industrialized countries realized that these countries were unable to retaliate in kind, the Third World states provided easy targets for economic sanctions.

The structure of relations between the core interests and the Third World is reflected in many of the organizations that serve both the developed and the

Table 2.1 Trade Performance, 1980–1990 (Average Annual % Change)

Country Group and Indicator[a]	1980–1990
Low- and middle-income countries[b]	
Import volume	0.8
Export volume	3.9
Terms of trade	–3.6
Sub-Saharan Africa[c]	
Import volume	–4.1
Export volume	2.3
Terms of trade	–5.3
Asia	
Import volume	7.1
Export volume	9.7
Terms of trade	–1.6
Middle East and North Africa	
Import volume	–4.0
Export volume	–1.8
Terms of trade	–7.4
Latin America and the Caribbean	
Import volume	–2.5
Export volume	2.9
Terms of trade	–3.0
Memorandum item	
World export volume	4.2

Source: World Bank, *The Annual Report 1993*.

Notes: a. Trade volumes are measured in constant 1987 prices and exchange rates. Terms of trade reflect the ratio of export price to import price.

b. Excludes the republics of the former Soviet Union.

c. Excludes the Republic of South Africa.

developing states and in institutions such as the General Agreement on Tariffs and Trade (GATT), the International Monetary Fund (IMF), and the World Bank. Nongovernmental organizations, such as multinational corporations and environmental organizations, also reflect this divide.

The Third World and Intergovernmental Organizations

Third World relations with intergovernmental organizations (IGOs) reflect the nature of the world-system within which these countries operate. The industrialized countries' structural advantage is reinforced by the actions of institutions such as the IMF and the World Bank that are critical to the operation of the international economic system. When these international economic institutions were established after World War II, their major purpose was to facilitate transactions among the industrialized countries. As a consequence, their focus was on such issues as exchange rate regulation, loans to cover balance-of-payments difficulties, reconstruction loans, and a liberal trading system.

Developing countries had other concerns, including access to capital for development, access to the markets of developed states, and equitable prices for the commodities they were selling internationally. The international institutions, which were tailor-made for the industrialized countries, are still run by those countries; therefore, from the beginning their decisionmaking and voting procedures were heavily weighted toward the wealthier states. Developing country membership in these institutions seemed almost incidental. They were not recognized as equal participants or partners, which is clearly reflected in their relations with the major intergovernmental organizations. This section examines Third World relations with institutions such as the World Bank, the IMF, and GATT and also looks at UNEP, the major intergovernmental environmental organization.

The World Bank group. The World Bank is important because it is the principal single source for Third World development funding. It promotes economic development by lending the governments money to fund their development projects. The World Bank Group is an umbrella organization that includes the International Bank for Reconstruction and Development (IBRD), the International Finance Corporation (IFC), and the International Development Association (IDA). IBRD lends funds to governments (or to private enterprises if the governments guarantee repayment), usually for specific projects. IFC makes loans to private corporations without government guarantees. IDA provides interest-free "credits" to the world's poorest countries for a period of 50 years, with a 10-year grace period.[20] In fiscal year 1993, IBRD and IDA approved assistance to the Third World totaling more than US$19.8 billion.[21] The World Bank has 152 country members, with the United States providing approximately 16 percent of the Bank's capital replenishment. This is the greatest share provided by any single state; therefore, the United States wields the most influence over World Bank affairs. However, it can no longer act alone as the blocking minority, since 20 percent is needed in order to effect a block.

Because of its role in development projects, the World Bank can have a profound impact on environmental policy in developing countries. Its initial development model emphasized large-scale schemes such as water management, power generation, and transport infrastructure. Many of these projects, especially the large dams and power-generation plants, almost invariably result in serious disruptions of local ecosystems, in environmental stress, and in the displacement of thousands of people.[22] Yet despite the high social and environmental costs that are often exacted by these projects, the World Bank economists have consistently preferred to fund large development projects. Their assessments of these projects have not adequately addressed environmental degradation and the costs of resettlement. Increasing pressure over the years has caused the World Bank to pay more attention to environmental issues.

In 1970 the World Bank established an Office of Environmental Adviser, but this had little impact on formal policies. In the late 1970s and the early 1980s, the Bank began to receive pressure to implement formal environmental assessment procedures. Much of this pressure was the result of an aggressive campaign by environmental NGOs, which publicized the high social and environmental costs of many World Bank projects. Responding to the pressure, the World Bank created a new Environmental Division in 1985.

The World Bank took this restructuring process further in 1987, when it committed itself to a major program of environmental reforms. The intent was to prevent or mitigate the environmental damage caused by its projects and to focus more on funding environmentally sound development projects. A central environmental department was established, and environmental units were assigned to each regional bureau. More money was devoted to free-standing environmental loans: an increase from a total of $400 million in the period up to 1990 to $1.6 billion in 1991. The Bank also required environmental impact assessments for all its projects.[23] Borrowing governments were to provide environmental impact reports for projects for which they sought funding, and the governments were to guarantee the resettlement of all people who were forcibly displaced by any Bank-funded projects.

In the wake of the 1992 Rio Conference, the World Bank further reorganized its environmental management process. A new vice presidency of Environmentally Sustainable Development was established. Its responsibility includes an Environmental Department, an Agriculture and Natural Resources Department, and a Transport, Water, and Urban Develop-ment Department. The unit is designed to help the Bank provide assistance to member countries. During fiscal year 1993, the World Bank developed regional strategies for Asia, Central and Eastern Europe, and the Sahelian countries of Sub-Saharan Africa and expanded its program of environmental research. It also made plans to assist its borrowers and aid recipients with the preparation of national environmental action plans.[24]

Whether the World Bank reorganization will mean a sea change in the preparation and implementation of World Bank–funded development projects is unclear. In the past, substantive changes have been resisted by both the Bank and the recipient countries. Some countries saw environmental requirements as an imposition of the environmental concerns of the industrialized countries on the Third World. Additionally, the World Bank has often lacked the political will to enforce its own regulations.

The Sardar Sarovar Projects in India present an example of the World Bank's failure to implement its own guidelines. The dam and canal complex being built on the Narmada River would displace more than 240,000 people,[25] ruin the lives of thousands more, and destroy land, forests, and fisheries. In June 1992 an independent review found that neither the World Bank nor the Indian government had done an adequate impact assessment of Sardar Sarovar. They had failed to consult local people and were facing heavy resistance from villagers. An Environmental Work Plan was already six years overdue. Faced with this information, some of the Bank's executive directors wanted to suspend funding for the project, but in October 1992 the majority of the board voted to approve continued funding.[26] The only concessions made involved loosely worded benchmarks for the Indian government to meet, but these were generally disregarded.[27] In March 1993 the government told the World Bank to cancel the undisbursed portion of the loan for the project. In spite of mounting pressure, India planned to complete the project on its own.[28] But by June 1993 the government bowed to local, national, and international pressure and agreed to discuss and review the issues connected with the Sardar Sarovar Dam.[29]

The World Bank process with regard to projects like Sardar Sarovar leads to failures in environmental planning and management. According to a report by the Bank's Portfolio Management Task Force, more than one-third of Bank-supported projects fail, largely because the pressure to lend takes precedence over other considerations. This rush to lend money has occurred for several reasons, including both the Bank's desire to grow and expand and pressure from the United States. Some analysts feel the United States has found making multilateral loans to the Third World preferable to forgiving much of Third World nations' commercial debt; therefore, it encourages multilateral institutions such as the World Bank to give money to heavily indebted nations.[30] As a result, the Bank is inclined to place quantity before quality and thus to bypass its own environmental regulations. It is also more likely to fund development plans that will earn foreign exchange for Third World countries. As one example, it has invested in the Tropical Forestry Action Plan (TFAP), which has opened up large areas of forest for exploitation.[31] The World Bank has justified these projects by saying that without the Bank's involvement the projects' implementation would have been even more destructive.

A strong commitment to implement and enforce the regulations seems to be missing. Obstacles to implementation include internal resistance and conflicting external pressures. Whereas some personnel within the World Bank feel sustainable development is a necessary strategy for halting Third World environmental degradation, others focus on economic logic.

An internal memorandum from Lawrence Summers, then vice president and chief economist of the World Bank, illustrates this point. His memorandum consisted of editorial comments on the draft of a World Bank report, comments that reflected the neoclassical economic logic that drives much of international development policy. Summers asked whether the World Bank should not be encouraging dirty industries to move to developing countries. He offered a number of reasons such an approach would make economic sense: Less income and gross national product (GNP) would be lost as a result of the illness and untimely death of a Third World worker than would be the case with a worker in the First World; the marginal, incremental cost of dumping waste in uncontaminated places was lower than it would be in heavily polluted places; and concerns such as clean air were luxuries the poor could forgo.[32] The memorandum drew the ire of many in the international community, particularly those in the Third World.

With this attitude prevailing at the highest levels of the World Bank, it is no wonder that the implementation of environmental reforms has been slow. In this context, staff appraisals of projects are often seen as marketing devices for ensuring loan approval, and little attention is given to the governments' implementation capacity or to the actual distribution of benefits within a country. Scant effort is put into assessing the sustainability of projects during their operational phase.[33]

The fact that some Third World countries are unwilling to cooperate with World Bank guidelines only complicates matters. Several developing country governments have resisted "environmental conditionality," arguing that this concern for the environment is merely another imposition of the goals and objectives of the industrialized nations on the poorer countries.

The World Bank is in a unique position to influence development in the Third World. Of all of the multilateral financial institutions, it has the greatest ability to assist the movement toward sustainable development. However, its efforts at environmental reform have been largely limited to bureaucratic changes that have been ineffective in implementing the stated policy of funding sustainable, environmentally sound development projects.

The International Monetary Fund. The International Monetary Fund provides technical assistance and financing to countries that are experiencing balance-of-payments difficulties. Whereas the World Bank and regional development banks have received considerable criticism in recent years for their role in environmental policy, the IMF's role has been largely overlooked. The IMF was originally created to provide short-term balance-of-payments support for needy countries in order to help stabilize the world economic system. During the 1980s it played a central role in efforts to resolve the international debt crisis.

In 1991 the Third World owed more than $1 trillion—nearly half of its collective GNP—to developed country banks and governments.[34] If we examine specific cases, Argentina, with a debt of $63.7 billion, owed approximately $1,950 for every man, woman, and child. The burden of debt is most severe on some of the poorest countries. Brazil's $116.5 billion debt was about 27 percent of its GNP. Panama, in contrast, had a debt of "only" $6.7 billion; however, that figure was 127 percent of its GNP.[35] Of real concern for the Third World is the fact that more money actually moves from the developing world to the developed world than vice versa. The massive diversion of resources to the developed countries has taken a toll not only on the people but also on the land, which is often ruthlessly logged, mined, and ploughed in the effort to pay off foreign bankers.

In fiscal year 1991, the Fund loaned $20 billion. In return for access to IMF financing, the Fund requires recipient countries to adopt structural adjustment programs that include a range of policy measures intended to restore creditworthiness. The harsh terms of these programs have hurt the economies and, consequently, the environments of the developing countries. Program prescriptions include drastic cuts in government expenditures, reductions in subsidies, currency devaluation, curbing of fiscal deficits, and reduction of trade barriers.

Structural adjustment is supposed to be shock treatment for the economy; however, it is usually ineffective and has negative domestic socioeconomic impacts. Third World governments and development experts charge that the prescriptions of structural adjustment programs hurt the poor disproportionately. Although devaluation may increase the volume of exports, it usually means basic commodities are less affordable for the poor. Curbing fiscal deficits often means governments must lay off public-sector employees and remove subsidies from basic necessities such as food and fuel. Rising interest rates may mean increased savings, but they also mean loans are less accessible to small businesspeople and first-time homeowners. Structural adjustment can cause severe socioeconomic dislocations in developing countries. The resulting economic turmoil has discouraged investment by residents of rich countries and encouraged national elites to invest their money in foreign banks.

In addition, these programs can have a disastrous impact on the environment. The emphasis on boosting exports to earn foreign exchange can result in the destruction of natural resources such as forests, wetlands, and mangroves and in the excessive development of ecologically damaging industries such as mining. The pressure for countries to drastically reduce government expenditures can cause the elimination or postponement of crucial environmental programs such as management of wildlife or enforcement of environmental laws. Finally, structural adjustment programs that hurt the poor will often also hurt the environment. For instance, unemployed laborers might increasingly engage in slash-and-burn agriculture in the tropical rainforest.

Unfortunately, the IMF is resisting even the most basic environmental reforms. The U.S. Congress passed a bill in 1989 directing the U.S. Treasury Department to use its influence with the IMF to promote a range of reforms. These were to include creating an environmental department, implementing procedures for more consultation with the public, and weighing environmental considerations in policy framework papers prepared jointly by the recipient country, the IMF, and the World Bank.[36]

In early 1991 the IMF executive board considered the creation of an environmental department but decided against establishing one, opting instead to tap the environmental expertise and resources of other institutions such as the World Bank, the Organization for Economic Cooperation and Development (OECD), and the United Nations Environment Programme. This expertise would help IMF missions prepare for informed discussions with governments that were addressing the environmental implications of macroeconomic policy choices. However, the IMF would not impose environmental conditionality.[37]

As was the case with the World Bank, the Rio Conference prompted some activity at the IMF. As a result, in May 1993 it hosted its first conference exploring the relationship between macroeconomic policies and the environment. Participants included 20 environmentalists from all over the world as well as staff members from the World Bank and the IMF. The seminar was seen as the continuation of a dialogue between the IMF and the NGOs that had begun in Rio. The environmentalists urged a paradigm shift that would make environmental concerns a central focus. Although the IMF representatives acknowledged the need for greater environmental awareness, they emphasized fulfilling the IMF's mandate, which they saw as helping members "adopt policies to stabilize their economies and promote sustainable growth."[38]

General Agreement on Tariffs and Trade. The General Agreement on Tariffs and Trade was established in 1947 as part of the post–World War II effort to manage the international economy. It is a multilateral regime that establishes norms and rules for international trade and provides a forum for their further elaboration.[39] Since its establishment, it has espoused a liberalized trading system. Standards are set and revised by way of periodic multilateral negotiations, called rounds. The most recent, the Uruguay Round, was launched in September 1986 and wound up negotiations in December 1993.

The Uruguay Round continued the emphasis on free trade; however, free trade obligations and environmental protection are on a collision course. The reconciliation of these two objectives has been receiving increasing attention. It has been addressed by the European Community and was one of the major issues in the debate over the North American Free Trade Agreement (NAFTA). The potential conflict between free trade and environmental protection was also addressed in the Uruguay Round of GATT.

Much of the attention in this round focused on four areas: trade in services, intellectual property rights, international investment flows, and agriculture. Once ratified, the Final Act would liberalize trade in agricultural products and establish a formal international organization called the World Trade Organization (WTO). On average, tariffs on industrial goods would be cut by more than one-third. The WTO would also cover intellectual property, trade in agricultural products, services, textiles, and clothing. Other provisions include reducing the use of subsidies, countervailing measures, and technical barriers; tightening antidumping rules and eliminating specific restrictive trade-related investment strategies; strengthening measures to open up government procurement opportunities to foreign suppliers; and regulating the use of restrictive safeguards.[40] Although some analysts argue that the agreement will benefit both the Third World and the industrialized world,[41] others feel the Uruguay Round will have disastrous consequences for the Third World.[42]

Those who can keep wages low and minimize social and environmental regulations will benefit from the largest profits. The major beneficiaries are likely to be the powerful transnational corporations that control 80 percent of world trade. Although there might indeed be a boost in world trade, it is not likely to benefit the citizens of the Third World. It is estimated that Indonesia and the African and Mediterranean countries will lose approximately $7 billion per year in earnings.[43]

Both industrialized and Third World countries are required to reduce domestic support and export subsidies, but this requirement exempts payments not directly connected to the farmers' level of agricultural output. As a result, European Community farmers will still benefit from their income support payments, as will U.S. farmers from their deficiency payments. This will allow the big-grain companies to dump cheap grain in Third World countries and will discourage domestic production of food staples. This undercutting of local farmers is likely to increase Third World poverty and exacerbate the associated environmental consequences.[44]

Some GATT provisions have more direct implications for environmental regulations. One of GATT's objectives is to limit most restrictions on trade; therefore, GATT could be used to challenge the rights of nations to use import and export controls to conserve threatened resources such as forests and fisheries. The new trade provisions also discourage the use of strong environmental protection by states, since these could be judged as being in violation of GATT rules. An additional concern is the fact that some environmental treaties require restrictions; as a consequence, two sets of international agreements could potentially conflict with one another. Under international law, when the parties to a dispute are members of both agreements, the most recent treaty generally takes precedence. This would tend to protect most environmental treaties; with a successful conclusion to the Uruguay Round, however, GATT, as the most recent agreement, might supplant the environmental treaties.[45] This could threaten the implementation of existing international agreements, some of which use trade sanctions as enforcement tools. Even before the conclusion of the Uruguay Round, the GATT rules were used to challenge environmental restrictions. In September 1991 a GATT dispute resolution panel ruled that the use of trade sanctions for environmental purposes was at odds with GATT rules.[46]

The United Nations Environment Programme. The United Nations Environment Programme was established by the UN General Assembly in 1972, following the Stockholm Conference; and UNEP reports to the General Assembly. Its basic functions are to disseminate information, cultivate understanding, and collaborate with the environmental programs of other agencies. Because its secretariat is in Nairobi, Kenya, it was the first UN agency to be headquartered outside of the industrialized world. The siting decision can be seen as a move toward modifying the lopsided relationship between the First and Third Worlds. UNEP has also established offices in Thailand, Switzerland, Mexico, and Bahrain.

UNEP provides more of an opportunity for the Third World countries to assert themselves than does any of the other three intergovernmental organizations examined in this section. It provides a forum in which Third World countries can examine mutual problems and has also been useful with issues that require a North-South dialogue. In this context, Mostafa Tolba, UNEP's executive director from 1976 to 1992, sometimes acted as an advocate for Third World interests. However, UNEP has not been a major forum for environmental problems that are primarily developed country issues. These countries have generally preferred to take care of their environmental objectives through other organizations such as OECD and the European Community.

UNEP is divided into several program areas, including environment and development, environmental awareness, Earthwatch, the arms race and the environment, regional and technical cooperation, and the regional seas program. Since 1980 UNEP has become increasingly active with regard to the issues of stratospheric ozone depletion and climate change. It was instrumental in bringing about the Montreal Protocol. Since 1982 UNEP has served, through its Clearinghouse, as a mediator and facilitator of funding between developing countries with specific environmental problems and donor nations. Tolba believed UNEP's most important achievement has been to raise the level of environmental awareness of policymakers.[47]

However, UNEP's effectiveness has been constrained by a number of factors. Throughout much of its existence it has been plagued by financial shortfalls and late contributions. These complications have made planning difficult and have limited the scope of UNEP's activities. UNEP's location in Nairobi has also been a source of problems. Although this location fulfilled the function of siting a UN agency in the Third World, some argued that it isolated UNEP from the industrialized world in which political and economic power is centered. The location also made it more difficult to recruit qualified staff; since it was distant from other UN agencies, it could not draw from a common personnel pool. An additional problem involved other UN agencies' cooperation with UNEP. Since it had no executive powers, UNEP had to depend on other specialized agencies to carry out its programs. Well-established UN agencies, such as WHO, FAO, and the World Meteorological

Organization, were already addressing environmental issues and did not welcome UNEP interference. Facing this reality, UNEP focused on activities that did not conflict with the programs of the other agencies. UNEP has a mixed record of achievement, but it has been successful in alerting governments to national and international environmental issues. However, its progress has been hampered by its limited financial and technical resources.[48]

The Third World and Nongovernmental Organizations

Nongovernmental organizations, such as transnational corporations and environmental interest groups, are major actors in global environmental politics. The relationship between these two sets of institutions and the Third World is generally reflective of the global economic power structure.

Transnational corporations. Transnational corporations (TNCs) are powerful business enterprises controlled by centralized hierarchies. Most are based in the industrialized countries, but subsidiaries operate in both industrialized and Third World countries. These corporations are dominant actors in the world division of labor, and they play a central economic and political role in the countries in which they operate. They owe loyalty to no community, government, or people; as a consequence, they are free to pursue their own interests. Because of their pursuit of power and influence, they play a pivotal role in the world capitalist system. Five hundred corporations control 70 percent of world trade, 80 percent of foreign investment, and 30 percent of world GDP.[49]

These corporations are able to influence or modify the policies of large industrialized states, and Third World states are even more vulnerable to their effects. An illustration of the potential influence of these enterprises is seen by looking at Cargill, which controls 60 percent of the world trade in cereals; consequently, it wields significant political and economic influence.[50] The income of individual TNCs dwarfs that of many Third World countries. For example, Shell Oil's 1990 gross income ($132 billion) was more than the combined GNPs of Tanzania, Ethiopia, Nepal, Bangladesh, Zaire, Uganda, Nigeria, Kenya, and Pakistan—countries that represent almost one-tenth of the world's population.[51]

Because they control the bulk of world trade and investment, transnational corporations are major environmental actors. They can affect the environment in Third World countries, both directly and indirectly. In order to attract investment by these corporations, a Third World country might adopt inadequate environmental regulations or choose not to enforce existing policies. Virtually all commercial enterprises have direct environmental impacts as producers, managers, and distributors of goods and services; and their activities can result in process and product pollution. The former includes pollution generated by the chemical, iron and steel, petroleum, and paper industries. The latter variety is found in the agriculture industry.

It is important to focus on transnational agribusiness, since agriculture is the primary economic sector for many developing countries. Transnationals control 80 percent of the land used for export crops worldwide. Twenty transnationals account for more than 90 percent of pesticide sales and control the bulk of the world's genetic seed stocks.[52]

One important sector of this business is the agrochemical industry. It is economically powerful, but its influence depends on more than this. Over time, agrochemical interests have made alliances with research institutes, agricultural colleges, regulatory agencies, government ministries, and aid agencies. Because of these alliances, they are able to significantly determine agricultural practices and policies. Many agricultural research institutions in the industrialized world receive funding from agrochemical or farm machinery companies, which are then able to exercise control over the content of research projects and can retain the power to suppress research that might prove controversial or harmful to their interests.[53] Through the strategic placing of grants, the industry can also influence the research agenda, directing research within universities and other public institutions into areas that best serve its own ends. These research orientations inevitably affect the curricula of training colleges and the programs of agricultural extension services. There are similar ties at the international level, with the industry working primarily through alliances with international development agencies.

The UN Food and Agriculture Organization has consistently discouraged traditional methods of agriculture. In its quest to modernize farming in the Third World, it has worked closely with the agrochemical companies. In the 1960s the FAO and an agro-industry lobbying group set up a joint program called the Industry Cooperative Programme (ICP), under which representatives from agrochemical companies worked hand in hand with technicians from the FAO. ICP seminars that promoted pesticide distribution were organized in Third World countries. Criticism of the relationship between the FAO and the agrochemical industry forced the FAO to dispense with the most obvious example of this collaboration, the ICP, in 1978; however, the alliance continues. FAO programs encourage the use of pesticides, and the agro-industry group still provides personnel and training material for FAO workshops. The agrochemical industry, therefore, derives much of its clout from its involvement in the network of institutions, individuals, and industries that have a stake in industrialized agriculture.[54]

Agribusiness companies will find their interests well served by the Uruguay Round of GATT. Grain companies such as Cargill, Continental Grain, Louis Dreyfus, Bunge, Andre and Company, and Mitsui/Cook can benefit from the subsidy system retained for farmers in the United States and Europe, which will allow the corporations to buy grain cheaply and dump it in the Third World. Some of these companies already dominate the economies of various Third World countries. In Brazil, as one example, transnational corporations own more acreage than the amount owned by all of the country's peasants combined. As farmers are driven off the land by cheap, imported grain, they may find themselves growing crops under contract for the transnational corporations. In India, for example, the richer farmers are growing maize and sunflowers for Cargill and tomatoes and potatoes for Pepsi.[55]

Creating a network of alliances has been very important for the strategies of transnational corporations, which have been able to identify political and personal contacts with similar interests. Financial institutions such as the World Bank have helped in the cultivation of Third World factions and interests that were sympathetic to those of the industrialized world. World Bank funds assisted the creation of autonomous agencies that would be somewhat insulated from domestic pressures and be responsive to the World Bank and its affiliated interests. The Bank has controlled the staffing of these agencies, and their personnel's transnational outlook is further encouraged through training at the World Bank's Economic Development Institute.

When the cultivation of personal and political interests has failed to ensure the establishment or maintenance of transnational regimes, more direct action has been taken. Brazil is one example that has particular relevance for environmental politics. In Brazil a transnationalist faction under General Castello Branco came to power by way of a coup that removed the nationalist government of Joao Goulart in 1964. After the coup, the IMF resumed loans under conditions that hastened Brazil's shift to export-oriented industrialization.[56] Plans for land reform were abandoned, peasants were suppressed, and the military regime began to court foreign industry. With the backing of the World Bank, Operation Amazonia encouraged occupation and development of the forest interior, with subsidies, cheap land, and new roads being used as incentives.[57] This is just one instance of the conglomeration of forces at work and of the asymmetry of power and influence affecting the Third World in environmental politics.

Criticism of the environmental consequences of the corporate culture grew during the 1970s and the 1980s, spurred by evidence of the ozone hole, dying lakes, vanishing forests, and toxic dumps. TNCs could no longer deny their connection to environmental degradation. They therefore launched a public relations campaign that adopted the language of the environmental movement. Increasingly, they have claimed to be helping developing countries achieve sustainable development. Their strategy has included restructuring their corporate organizations to include environmental officers or departments, implementing programs such as reducing waste and labeling toxic products, using environmental themes in advertising and public relations, and establishing environmental codes of conduct. However, in spite of these changes, the basic characteristics of the corporate culture remain unchanged. For example, corporations still depend on a cost-benefit analysis that marginalizes most environmental costs and also try to avoid responsibility for the problems caused by their products.[58]

TNCs gained access and influence at the Rio Conference through the Business Council for Sustainable Development (BCSD), a group of about 48 chief executive officers or chairpersons of corporations from such industrial sectors as energy, chemicals, forestry, and pesticides. The BCSD leadership is also a part of the International Environment Bureau of the International Chamber of Commerce (ICC), which has observer status at the United Nations, where it lobbies on behalf of business interests. Both the ICC and BCSD pressed hard to keep language regulating TNCs out of the United Nations Conference on Environment and Development (UNCED) documents. They argued that free trade was essential to sustainable development.[59]

Environmental interest groups. The two decades following the 1972 Stockholm Conference have seen the rapid growth of environmental NGOs. Although these organizations do not wield the clout of the TNCs, they are able to call upon a strong core of public support as they attempt to affect national and global environmental politics. Eighty-five percent of the environmental NGOs registered with the UNEP Environmental Liaison Center in the 1980s were based in developed countries, but the number of Third World–based environmental NGOs has been growing rapidly.[60] These NGOs have not acquired the international influence of major industrialized country–based NGOs, but they are learning the strategies that are useful in affecting both domestic policies and their governments' input into international environ-mental policies.

NGOs have performed a number of functions. They have been outspoken national and international critics of government, TNC, and intergovernmental organization policies; they have worked in concert with IGOs; they have been important components of epistemic communities; and they have worked as independent monitors of agreements.

NGO strategies vary: Some focus on traditional lobbying, and others use confrontational tactics. The more traditional approach includes working with intergovernmental organizations such as UNEP in developing and implementing international environmental arrangements. For example, environmental NGOs were able to influence the structure and policy of the International Whaling Commission (IWC) by convincing nonwhaling states to join the IWC. Because these new members were more susceptible to conservationist arguments, it was then possible to get the three-quarters majority necessary for a moratorium.[61]

Environmental NGOs have also had some limited success in their campaign for structural and policy changes at the World Bank. Pressure in the 1980s by environmental groups such as the National Wildlife Federation and the Natural Resources Defense Council resulted in the substantial enlargement of the World Bank's environmental section. In what could be an attempt either to address NGO concerns or to co-opt these organizations, the

World Bank is encouraging greater NGO participation in Bank-financed projects. Although the relationship between the NGOs and the World Bank is still largely adversarial, the two sides have established a working relationship. In 1982 an NGO–World Bank Committee was established; it is composed of senior bank managers and 26 NGO leaders from a variety of countries.[62]

Environmental interest groups also provide forums for networking and the gathering and dissemination of data. At both Stockholm and Rio, the NGOs' parallel conferences offered a wider spectrum of information and viewpoints than did the formal UN-sponsored meetings. The credibility of some major NGOs is enhanced by the fact that they are usually perceived as being independent of any particular nation-state.

Environmental NGOs can affect environmental behavior by initiating formal legal proceedings against states they perceive to be out of compliance with environmental law. One well-publicized instance involved the Earth Island Institute. A 1990 suit by the institute asked the U.S. District Court to compel the executive branch of the U.S. government to comply with the 1972 Marine Mammal Protection Act (MMPA). The MMPA's objective was to address the problem of dolphins being harmed when purse-seine nets were used for tuna fishing. The court ruled in the Earth Island Institute's favor, banning U.S. imports of tuna from offenders. Mexico, one of the offending states, claimed the ban was a violation of GATT, and GATT's three-member panel agreed that the court's action was in conflict with GATT's trade principles.[63]

Two environmental organizations that have activist international agendas are Friends of the Earth and Greenpeace, both of which have primarily targeted issues related to the activities of the industrialized countries. Friends of the Earth believes the focus of environmental policy should be on fundamental social change rather than on temporary remedies. Its strategy is to draw maximum publicity to activities that are inimical to the environment. Over the years, Friends of the Earth has addressed the issues of alternative energy sources, wildlife, ozone depletion, transportation, and pollution.[64]

Greenpeace has been the most confrontational of the direct action groups. Its creation was spurred by the atmospheric nuclear tests conducted after World War II. In the 1970s, activists began sailing fishing boats into the testing areas in an effort to force postponement of the tests. These interventions sometimes led to physical confrontations, as was the case in 1973 when French commandos roughed up Greenpeace volunteers. Twelve years later, members of the French intelligence service blew up the Greenpeace ship *Rainbow Warrior* in the harbor at Auckland, New Zealand. One crew member died during the incident.[65] Greenpeace campaigns have also targeted whaling and hazardous waste disposal. The organization tracks the toxic waste trade and publishes an inventory.[66]

Since 1987, several environmental NGOs have begun to invest in conservation in the Third World. Conservation International, the Nature Conservancy, Rainforest International, and the World Wildlife Fund are among the institutions that have used debt-for-nature swaps to encourage conservation in developing countries. Creditor banks doubt they will ever recover all the money owed to them by developing countries; therefore, they sell some of these debts at a discount. This has allowed Western conservation NGOs to purchase some of these discounted debts and then write them off in exchange for the debtor country putting local currency and effort into conservation. Many such swaps have involved countries in Central and South America.

Some see this plan as a novel way of dealing with two problems: the massive Third World debt and the need for conservation of natural resources. But critics consider the industrialized countries' banks to be the only beneficiaries of these transactions since they manage to get some of their money back. In this scenario, a developed country environmental group gives money to a developed country bank, and a Third World country provides money to its environmental groups or institutions to manage the protected area. The environmentalists use the money to create or enlarge national parks, and rangers are assigned to protect the areas. But this method of imposed conservation is apt to fail in the long term unless other societal and political changes are made to support it. Government policies that would be productive include ending policies that subsidize destructive activities, discouraging the predation of some of the economic elite, and addressing the basic needs of the poor. The case of Ecuador is instructive. Several parks have been established there, but the rangers have to contend with poachers, illegal loggers, foreign oil companies, large-scale plantation owners, and landless farmers.[67]

A 1991 seminar sponsored by the Brazilian Institute for Economic and Social Analysis (IBASE) focused on debt-for-nature swaps. It concluded that (1) the mechanisms used are inconsistent with democratic management of natural resources; (2) because of the budgetary pressure on the government, debt-for-nature swaps penalize the local population; (3) the swaps legitimize the debt at a time when some countries are taking the position that the debts were incurred illegally; (4) the strategy merchandizes and privatizes natural resources; and (5) the strategy diverts attention from the issue of the extraction of resources and wealth from the Third World.[68]

Domestic Sources of Third World Environmental Policy

Although Third World countries are constrained by their position in the world-system, this constraint is not the only determinant of their environmental politics. Their environmental agenda is also influenced by a variety of domestic factors, including tax and subsidy instruments, distribution of wealth and income, population pressure, the status of women, and the political power structure.[69] Although these factors are partially a response to these countries' position in the world-system, they are also conditioned by the unique circumstances of the individual countries.

Agricultural or natural resource pricing policies are intended to encourage specific behaviors. Governments sometimes intervene in agricultural markets in order to keep prices low, which can reduce agricultural incomes and investment in conservation. Subsidies can also have negative consequences for the environment; for example, they can encourage increased pesticide use, with all its negative impacts on human health and long-term agricultural well-being. They can also encourage a level of agricultural production that is not justified in economic or environmental terms. In the case of forest resources, the provision of government subsidies can result in overexploitation.

Another factor that conditions developing countries' environmental policies is the skewed distribution of income and wealth. In some Third World states, this asymmetry is particularly extreme: For example, in Brazil the population decile with the highest per capita income controls more than 50 percent of the national income.[70] In many of these countries, the bulk of the arable land is controlled by a small group of families. In some cases an extremely skewed distribution of land is exacerbated as those with large amounts of land expand their acreage for primary commodity export crops by seizing land from indigenous people or small landowners. This situation may be an obstacle to sound natural resource management. The landless may move onto ecologically sensitive areas such as erosion-prone hillsides or the fragile soils of tropical forests.[71] In Brazil, the poor farmers are often blamed for Amazonian deforestation. However, they have cleared farmland in the forests because they were uprooted from their small farms by businesspeople who wanted to grow more soybeans for the export market.[72]

Because of the decisionmaking structures in developing countries, this situation is difficult to change. Relevant decisions are frequently made by a small elite. This group, or its close associates, might have interests in commercial logging, ranching, plantation cropping, and large-scale irrigated farming operations. Consequently, investment incentives, tax provisions, credit and land concessions, and agricultural pricing policies are likely to favor this elite. The results are often disastrous for the economy and the environment.

Also relevant to resource policymaking in developing countries is the fact that the elites of those countries often have more interests in common with the elites of the industrialized core than with the masses of the people within their own countries. Because of their attachment to core values, these groups' policy decisions do not necessarily reflect the interests of the majority of the country's population.

A related factor is the way in which power is reflected in private and public institutions, which can affect the way the costs and benefits of development projects are distributed. For example, indigenous peoples may bear the majority of the costs of a hydroelectric scheme that benefits another group. These people might lose their homes, farms, and fishing grounds; yet little or no effort might be made to mitigate the environmental and social impacts of the project.

Rapidly increasing populations can exacerbate poverty and natural resource degradation. The fastest rates of population growth are in the countries of Africa and Latin America.[73] The high growth rates in developing countries can be credited to high fertility and increases in life expectancy, but they are also a function of the demographic profile. Thirty-six percent of the Third World's population is under 15 years old. For Sub-Saharan Africa this figure is 46 percent.[74] The relative size of the young population means there are growing demands for food, shelter, education, health care, and employment. All of these basic needs increase pressure on limited resources and make development policies even more critical. This age distribution assures a continued large population growth in developing countries, even if total fertility rates suddenly dropped to replacement levels. Economic considerations and education also play roles in individual decisions about family size and spacing, because women with more educational and economic options tend to have smaller families.[75]

In many developing countries, women have a significant impact on natural resource policy. They carry the major burden of supporting the household and doing agricultural work. In Africa, for example, women are responsible for about 80 percent of the subsistence agriculture, whereas men are more likely to work on cash crops. However, because women do not usually have title to land or adequate access to credit, they may be unable to take the actions needed to protect the land and water resources under their control.[76] In some areas, communities have depended on common property resources to help support the growing population. Women have traditionally had access to these resources, but these commons have increasingly been privatized. This strategy has been encouraged by governments, aid agencies, and transnational corporations. Often, these commons resources are converted to production for export; consequently, women's job of providing food for domestic consumption becomes more difficult. To exacerbate the situation, financial and technical support for agriculture usually targets cash crops that are being produced for export.[77]

Since the 1970s, the environment has become a political issue in the Third World as a result of both internal and external pressures. Within Third World countries, citizens are becoming aware of the damage being done to the environment as a result of internally and externally initiated policies. Environmental NGOs have sprung up in developing countries, and women have become a significant force in some of these groups. One example of this is the Chipko Movement in India, where people stopped the cutting of trees by standing between the trees and the machinery. Although some of these environmental groups have a narrow conservation focus, others have a broader focus, incorporating issues of economic justice. This constitutes a recognition of the connection between economic inequities and environmental degradation.

China and India: A Look at Two Major Third World Actors

China and India are two of the principal Third World actors in global environmental politics. They emerged as major actors at the Stockholm Conference in 1972 and have retained that status. These states have become key actors both by choice and because of geographic and demographic circumstances. They have chosen to play major roles in environmental politics, but regardless of this choice, circumstances such as large territories and large populations have given them a major role in determining the fate of the global environment. In terms of potential environmental impact, not all countries are equal. In negotiations on environmental regimes, it is more important to secure the cooperation of China and India than that of a small state such as Vanuatu.[78]

Both China and India are categorized by the World Bank as low-income countries. In terms of major export category classification, China is primarily a manufacturer of exports, and India is a diversified exporter since no single category accounts for more than 50 percent of its exports.[79] Both countries have embarked on a program of economic growth, a fact that has potentially significant environmental repercussions.

China

With an area of 9.5 million square kilometers, China is the world's third largest country, and its population of more than 1.1 billion people—more than 20 percent of the world's population—makes it the most populous.[80] Although China has been able to reduce its rate of population growth, its population is projected to reach 2 billion by the year 2050.[81] As a result, there will be a growing need for a larger share of the world's resources and greater use of waste sinks. Continuing modernization and industrialization will further increase this demand. The growth rate of the Chinese economy averaged 9.7 percent between 1978 and 1988 and was almost 13 percent in 1992.[82]

Of particular concern is China's dependence on coal and the resultant implications for global warming. China is the world's third largest consumer of energy; therefore, its energy choices have significant repercussions for the global environment. In 1990 it consumed approximately 10 percent of global energy and accounted for almost 11 percent of global carbon dioxide emissions.[83] This reflected a low per capita energy usage, with a Chinese household consuming less than 0.03 percent of the energy used in the average U.S. home. As the usage of modern appliances increases, energy consumption will soar.

Major environmental problems include both environmental pollution and degradation of the natural resource base. The latter includes declining water supplies in the north; the loss of ecosystems such as forests, coastal wetlands, and wildlife habitats; the loss of arable land; and the degradation of cropland. In spite of the scope of the country's natural resource problems, Chinese officials believe environmental pollution is a more pressing concern, with the major problems related to urban air and water quality, rural industrial pollution, and noise.[84]

China's attempts to address environmental problems in a systematic manner were influenced by its involvement in the Stockholm Conference. In preparation for the 1972 conference, China formulated a statement on environmental policy. This led to the creation of an environmental office that a decade later became the National Environmental Protection Agency (NEPA), China's principal environmental agency.[85] Environmental policy is governed by the Environmental Protection Law, first implemented in 1979 and amended in 1989.[86] NEPA shares authority with many other agencies. For example, marine environmental affairs are overseen by the State Oceanographic Administration and the Ministry of Agriculture and Fisheries; energy issues are under the jurisdiction of the Ministry of Energy.[87] NEPA is also supported by a network of provincial, municipal, and county environmental protection agencies.

Although China has an Environmental Protection Law and a network of institutions and organizations that address environmental protection, this circumstance does not necessarily result in environmental protection. Obstacles preventing adequate policy implementation include an emphasis on economic growth, limited resources, and a lack of skilled personnel. For example, a 1980 assessment found a significant shortage of trained ecologists in China.[88]

China has maintained a high profile in global environmental politics. At the 1972 Stockholm Conference it took a militant and activist stand, blaming pollution and exploitation on imperialism and attempting to include language to that effect in the Stockholm Declaration.[89] The Chinese delegate also brought before the conference the issue of the Vietnam War and U.S. ecocide.[90] However, when the conference tried to restrict nuclear testing, China resisted this move vigorously.[91]

Although its rhetoric no longer emphasizes the evils of imperialism, China strongly supports the Third World agenda. It insists on linking accession to environmental treaties to assistance in making the transition to alternative technologies. China's size and population give it substantial leverage. It faces the substantial challenge of cutting its carbon dioxide emissions in the face of its dependence on coal and its rapidly growing demand for energy. Still, it was among the first 10 countries to ratify the UN Framework Convention on Climate Change.[92] China emphasizes its willingness to cooperate in the evolution and implementation of global environmental regimes, provided it receives the requisite financial and technical assistance.

India

Although it is only one-third the size of China, India is the world's seventh largest country. With a population nearing 1 billion, it contains about 16 percent of the world's population. India's rapidly growing population, projected to reach 1.4 billion by the year 2025,[93] is a major concern. The fact that about one-third of the population lives below the poverty line is likely to have continued environmental consequences. Problems of poverty have been linked to the status of women, who have limited access to educational and material resources. Women's 1991 literacy rate was estimated at 39 percent, compared to 52 percent for the general population.[94]

As with China, India's environmental problems include resource degradation and pollution. Both rural and urban populations have inadequate access to clean water and sanitation. Particular concerns in rural India include land degradation, loss of soil nutrients, forest and groundwater depletion, and diminishing biodiversity. Urban India also suffers from air pollution from vehicles and industrial sources.

India has been a major beneficiary of World Bank funding for large dam projects, and the Indian government has drawn domestic and international criticism because of the way the projects have been administered. For example, the Sardar Sarovar Project was allowed to go forward without proper environmental or engineering appraisals.[95] These enormous projects displace local population and destroy ecosystems. Of particular concern to some domestic constituents is the distribution of the projects' costs and benefits. Costs are being borne disproportionately by those least likely to benefit from the projects; additionally, local people have been excluded from the planning process.[96] Local organizations have been developed to address such problems. India has a wide range of NGOs, with an estimated 10,000 organizations involved in development and environmental issues.[97]

Officially, India recognizes the need to balance the environment and development, and it has instituted laws and formed organizations to help in this effort. A Department of the Environment, created in 1980, takes direct responsibility for monitoring and regulating pollution.[98] In addition, the 1986 Environment Protection Act and Rules gives the central government the authority to address issues of pollution and environmental quality. India also has central and state pollution control boards that are responsible for setting and monitoring water quality and protecting air quality.[99]

As with China, despite the environmental laws and organizations, environmental degradation continues. Obstacles include problems with implementation,[100] as well as competition for scarce resources and a focus on development.

As did China, India made its presence felt at Stockholm. One reason was the presence of Prime Minister Indira Gandhi at a conference that had few heads of state or government in attendance. As the environmental regimes have evolved, India has been a strong supporter of the linkage strategy and was also one of the countries blocking the formulation of a forestry convention. For Rio, the UNCED planners had envisioned a forestry convention, along with the biodiversity and climate conventions. But India, as well as Malaysia and Indonesia, opposed this. Kamal Nath, India's minister of environment and forests, spoke out in opposition to what he perceived as the globalization of India's forest resources.[101]

Conclusion

The Third World is made up of a diverse group of actors. In the domestic sphere, they have moved toward formalizing environmental policies with new laws and organizations. The tension between development strategy and environmental policy is sometimes reflected in the contrast between the leaders' rhetoric and environmental reality in these countries. As the cases of India and China show, for these nations the linkage of treaty accession to financial and technical assistance is not merely political posturing; it is a pragmatic move that is necessary in helping these countries manage the demands of both growing populations and growing economies.

Their position at the periphery of economic power constrains the actions of Third World countries. A realist perspective of international relations focuses on the relations between the Third World countries and the industrialized world, and the asymmetry is apparent. However, this would present only a partial picture. Asymmetry is also reflected in the relations of other international actors, both governmental and nongovernmental, with the Third World. For the most part, these actors are closely identified with the developed world, yet none can be said to have an identical set of interests with any state or group of states. Rather, they can be described as having interests that overlap those of the states. The governments of industrialized countries have sometimes been described as proxies for transnational corporations, but that is too facile a description. There *are* large areas of overlap, but these TNCs often have interests and options that conflict with those of their home countries.[102] Some of the actors discussed do have significant interests in common with the Third World states. An NGO like Greenpeace, which is involved in tracking the movements of toxic wastes, finds that this interest supports the objectives of some Third World states.

On average, however, the interests of the NGOs and IGOs discussed are more consistent with those of the industrialized state governments than they are with those of the developing state governments. They reflect the interests of the core rather than those of the periphery.

Notes

1. French economist and demographer Alfred Sauvy is credited with being the first to use the term *Third World* to describe developing countries in an article published in 1952.

2. Kofi Buenor Hadjor, *Dictionary of Third World Terms* (London: I. B. Tauris & Co., 1992), 3.

3. Ibid., 8.

4. Ibid., 8–10.

5. This term originally referred to a group of 77 developing countries that in the 1960s identified common interests and campaigned for changes in the international economic system. Although this group has expanded to include more than 125 Third World countries, it is still known as the Group of 77, and it still represents its members' interests in international forums such as the United Nations.

6. One square kilometer is the equivalent of 0.386 square mile.

7. The list includes Argentina, Chile, Costa Rica, the Dominican Republic, Ecuador, Guatemala, Honduras, Mexico, Paraguay, Peru, and Uruguay. Ethiopia, which had a brief bout with Italian colonialism in the early twentieth century, also has a long history as an independent actor.

8. World Bank, *World Development Report 1993* (New York: Oxford University Press, 1993), 326–327. The World Bank has established the following annual per capita income categories: low income, $635 or less; lower-middle income, $636 through $2,555; upper-middle income, $2,556 through $7,910; and high income, $7,911 or more.

9. Colin I. Bradford, Jr., "The Rise of NICs as Exporters on a Global Scale," in Louis Turner and Neil McMullen, eds., *The Newly Industrializing Countries: Trade and Adjustment* (London: George Allen and Unwin, 1972), 11.

10. Hadjor, *Dictionary of Third World Terms,* 9.

11. World Bank, *World Development Report 1993,* 328–329.

12. Ibid.

13. See Samir Amin, *Unequal Development: An Essay on the Social Formation of Peripheral Capitalism* (New York: Monthly Review Press, 1976); Theotonio Dos Santos, "The Structure of Dependence," in K. T. Kan and Donald C. Hodges, eds., *Readings in U.S. Imperialism* (Boston: Extending Horizons, 1971), 225–236; Andre Gunder Frank, *Capitalism and Underdevelopment in Latin America* (New York: Monthly Review Press, 1967).

14. For more information about the world-systems approach, see Christopher Chase-Dunn, "Interstate System and Capitalist World-Economy: One Logic or Two?" *International Studies Quarterly* 25: 19–42; Immanuel Wallerstein, *The Capitalist World-Economy* (New York: Cambridge University Press, 1979); Immanuel Wallerstein, *The Politics of the Capitalist World-Economy* (Cambridge: Cambridge University Press, 1984); Immanuel Wallerstein, "World-System Analysis," in Anthony Giddens and Jonathan H. Turner, eds., *Social Theory Today* (Stanford: Stanford University Press, 1987), 309–324.

15. Although GDP and gross national product (GNP) are crude measures of

well-being, they are regarded as useful indicators of economic progress.

16. United Nations Development Programme, *Human Development Report 1993* (New York: Oxford University Press, 1993), 148–149.

17. There would no doubt be several more had comparative data been available for countries such as Kuwait, the Bahamas, and Brunei.

18. World Bank, *World Development Report 1993*, 238–239. In 1990 Mozambique had a GNP per capita of US$80, whereas Switzerland's GNP per capita was US$32,680.

19. John M. Rothgeb, Jr., *Defining Power: Influence and Force in the Contemporary International System* (New York: St. Martin's Press, 1993), 77–79.

20. John Tessitore and Susan Woolfson, eds., *A Global Agenda: Issues Before the 46th General Assembly of the United Nations* (New York: University Press of America, 1991), 327.

21. World Bank, *Annual Report 1993* (Washington, D.C.: World Bank, 1993), 166–167. The total amount approved for 1993 was $23.6959 billion, but approximately $4 billion of this was assigned to projects in Turkey and the former Soviet bloc countries.

22. For analyses of the environmental impacts of various World Bank loans, see Bruce Rich, "The Multilateral Development Banks, Environmental Policy and the United States," *Ecology Law Quarterly* 12 (1985): 685–688; Stephan Schwartzman, *Bankrolling Disasters: International Development Banks and the Global Environment* (San Francisco: Sierra Club, 1986); and Bank Information Center, *Funding Ecological and Social Destruction: The World Bank and International Monetary Fund* (Washington, D.C.: Bank Information Center, 1990).

23. Hilary F. French, *Worldwatch Paper 107: After the Earth Summit: The Future of Environmental Governance* (Washington, D.C.: Worldwatch Institute, 1992), 39.

24. World Bank, *Annual Report 1993*, 45–47.

25. Bruce Rich, *Mortgaging the Earth: The World Bank, Environmental Impoverishment, and the Crisis of Development* (Boston: Beacon Press, 1994), 250.

26. "Lies, Fantasy, Cynicism," *The Ecologist* 22, no. 6 (November–December 1992): 259–260.

27. "Campaigns," *The Ecologist* 23, no. 1 (January–February 1993): 38–39.

28. World Bank, *Annual Report 1993*, 49.

29. "Narmada Review," *The Ecologist Campaigns*, July–August 1993, 4.

30. Bruce Rich, "The Emperor's New Clothes: The World Bank and Environmental Reform," *World Policy Journal* 7, no. 2 (Spring 1990): 319.

31. Ibid., 310.

32. Rich, *Mortgaging the Earth*, 247–248.

33. "Lies, Fantasy, Cynicism," 259.

34. World Bank, *World Development Report 1993*, 278–279.

35. Ibid., 238–239, 278–279.

36. French, *Worldwatch Paper 107*, 40–42.

37. "The IMF and the Environment," *IMF Survey*, June 14, 1993, 188.

38. "Seminar Explores Links Between Macro Policy and the Environment," *IMF Survey*, June 14, 1993, 177 and 187.

39. Tessitore and Woolfson, eds., *A Global Agenda*, 327.

40. "Trade Agreement Mandates Board Changes," *IMF Survey*, January 10, 1994, 2.

41. See comments of IMF managing director Michael Camdessus in "Camdessus Hails Conclusion of Uruguay Round Negotiations," *IMF Survey,* January 10, 1994, 1; also remarks of Lewis Preston, president of the World Bank, in "Global Changes Require Quick Response," *IMF Survey,* October 11, 1993, 296–297.

42. See Lori Wallach, "Hidden Dangers of GATT and NAFTA," 23–64; Herman E. Daly, "From Adjustment to Sustainable Development," 121–132; and Martin Khor, "Free Trade and the Third World," 97–107; all in *The Case Against Free Trade: GATT, NAFTA, and the Globalization of Corporate Power* (San Francisco: Earth Island Press, 1993).

43. "Cakes and Caviar? The Dunkel Draft and Third World Agriculture," *The Ecologist* 23, no. 6 (November–December 1993): 219–220.

44. Ibid., 220.

45. Hilary F. French, *Worldwatch Paper 113: Costly Tradeoffs: Reconciling Trade and the Environment* (Washington, D.C.: Worldwatch Institute, March 1993), 48.

46. French, *Worldwatch Paper 107,* 42.

47. John McCormick, *Reclaiming Paradise: The Global Environmental Movement* (Bloomington: Indiana University Press, 1989), 124.

48. Ibid., 110–124.

49. "The Power of the Transnationals," *The Ecologist* 22, no. 4 (July–August 1992): 159.

50. See Robert Gilpin, *U.S. Power and the Multinational Corporation* (New York: Basic Books, 1975). Gilpin makes the point that transnational corporations can dominate and modify the policies of host countries.

51. "The Power of the Transnationals," 159.

52. See "Transnational Corporations and Issues Relating to the Environment: The Contribution of the Commission and UNCTC to the Work of the Preparatory Committee for the United Nations Conference on Environment and Development," United Nations Centre on Transnational Corporations, February 28, 1991.

53. Henk Hobbelink, *Biotechnology and the Future of World Agriculture* (London: Zed Books, 1991), 39.

54. "Power: The Central Issue," *The Ecologist* 22, no. 4 (July–August 1992): 157–164.

55. "Cakes and Caviar?" 220–222.

56. R. Broad, *Unequal Alliance, 1979–1986: The World Bank, the International Monetary Fund, and the Philippines* (Quezon City, Philippines: Ateneo de Manila University Press, 1988), 26–31; cited in "Power: The Central Issue," 160.

57. N. MacDonald, *Brazil: A Mask Called Progress* (Oxford: Oxfam, 1991), 52; cited in "Power: The Central Issue," 160.

58. Kenny Bruno, *The Greenpeace Book of Greenwash* (Amsterdam: Greenpeace International, n.d.), 2–3.

59. Ibid., 6–8.

60. Karen Mingst, "Implementing International Environmental Treaties: The Role of NGOs," paper prepared for the annual meeting of the International Studies Association, Acapulco, March 24–27, 1993.

61. Patricia Birnie, "The International Organization of Whales," *Denver Journal of International Law and Policy* 13 (Fall–Winter 1984–1985): 309–333.

62. World Resources Institute, *World Resources 1992–1993* (New York: Oxford University Press, 1992), 14.

63. David Phillips, "Dolphins and GATT," in *The Case Against Free Trade:*

GATT, NAFTA, and the Globalization of Corporate Power (San Francisco: Earth Island Press, 1993), 133–136.

64. McCormick, *Reclaiming Paradise,* 144.

65. Ibid., 144–145.

66. Greenpeace U.S.A., *The International Trade in Wastes: A Greenpeace Inventory* (Washington, D.C.: Greenpeace U.S.A., 1990).

67. World Wildlife Fund, *Amended and Restated Debt-for-Nature Agreement Between WWF (US) and Fundacion Natura,* April 4, 1989 cited in Rhona Mahony, "Debt-for-Nature Swaps: Who Really Benefits?" *The Ecologist* 22, no. 3 (May–June 1992): 103.

68. "Debt Swaps: A Southern View," *The Ecologist* 22, no. 3 (May–June 1992): 102.

69. Jeremy J. Warford, "Environmental Management and Economic Policy in Developing Countries," in Gunter Schramm and Jeremy Warford, eds., *Environmental Management and Economic Development* (Baltimore: Johns Hopkins University Press, 1991), 13.

70. World Bank, *World Development Report 1993,* 297.

71. See Rhona Mahony, "Debt-for-Nature Swaps: Who Really Benefits?" *The Ecologist* 22, no. 3 (May–June 1992): 97–101 and 103. This article illustrates the link between landlessness and damage to natural resources in Ecuador, the Philippines, Madagascar, and Costa Rica.

72. Robin Broad and John Cavanagh, "Beyond the Myths of Rio," *World Policy Journal* 10, no. 1 (Spring 1993): 67.

73. World Bank, *World Development Report 1993,* 288–289.

74. Ibid., 200–201.

75. See Jodi L. Jacobson, *Gender Bias: Roadblock to Sustainable Development,* Worldwatch Paper 110 (Washington, D.C.: Worldwatch Institute, September 1992).

76. Warford, "Environmental Management," 19–20.

77. Jacobson, *Gender Bias,* 23–25.

78. Vanuatu has an area of 12,000 square kilometers. In 1991, its population was 151,000.

79. World Bank, *World Development Report 1993,* 326–329.

80. Ibid., 238–239.

81. H. Yuan Tien et al., "China's Demographic Dilemmas," *Population Bulletin* 47, no. 1 (1992): 5, 38–39; cited in World Resources Institute, *World Resources 1994–95* (New York: Oxford University Press, 1994), 62.

82. World Resources Institute, *World Resources 1994–95,* 60.

83. Ibid., 65.

84. Ibid., 70.

85. Lester Ross, *Environmental Policy in China* (Bloomington: Indiana University Press, 1988), 204.

86. World Resources Institute, *World Resources 1994–95,* 64.

87. Ibid.

88. V. Smil, "Environmental Degradation in China," *Asian Survey* (August 1980): 787; cited in H. Jeffrey Leonard, ed., *Divesting Nature's Capital: The Political Economy of Environmental Abuse in the Third World* (New York: Holmes & Meier, 1985), 156.

89. "The Chinese Foiled," *The Economist,* June 24, 1972, 28.

90. Christopher C. Joyner, "Stockholm in Retrospect: Progress in the International Law of the Environment," *World Affairs* (Spring 1974): 356.

91. Ibid.

92. World Resources Institute, *World Resources 1994–95,* 78.

93. United Nations, *Long-Range World Population Projections* (New York: United Nations, 1992), 22.

94. World Resources Institute, *World Resources 1994–95,* 85–86.

95. Rich, *Mortgaging the Earth,* 250.

96. William Ascher and Robert Healy, *Natural Resource Policymaking in Developing Countries* (Durham: Duke University Press, 1990), 118–119.

97. World Resources Institute, *World Resources 1994–95,* 84.

98. Leonard, *Divesting Nature's Capital,* 145.

99. World Resources Institute, *World Resources 1994–95,* 88.

100. Leonard, *Divesting Nature's Capital,* 148–150.

101. Adam Schwarz, "Back Down to Earth: Global Summit Fails to Live Up to Ambitions," *Far Eastern Economic Review,* June 25, 1992, 62.

102. See "The 'Stateless' World of Manufacturing," *Business Week,* May 14, 1990, 103. Many major corporations have foreigners in their top ranks, a factor that affects their identification with any single state. They also have a high proportion of their sales outside of the home country. For example, in 1989 more than 80 percent of the sales of Nestle, Sandoz, SKF, Hoffman–La Roche, Phillips, Smithkline Beecham, ABB, Electrolux, Volvo, and ICI occurred outside the home country. For Nestle the figure was 98 percent, and an estimated 95 percent of its assets were outside of Switzerland.

3

Globalization and Environmental Regime Formation

Although few analysts insist that power is the sole determinant in regime formation and evolution, many take the position that it is an important factor in the regime process. Some modelers of international behavior posit that international actors realize that in a context of interdependence, status maximizing can produce suboptimal results. Environmental regime formation takes place in a context of interdependence, which is a function of the globalization of both the economy and the environment. Each type of globalization is likely to result in a different set of constraints and to have different consequences for the nature of the interdependence among actors in the global community. Therefore, globalization is likely to affect how those actors exercise power or coercive pressure and respond to such pressure.

Regime Formation and Evolution

Regimes represent efforts within the international system to develop collaborative or coordinating arrangements. Since the 1970s, extensive research has been conducted on this kind of collective action in the international community.[1] The term *regime* has been used in international relations to describe functions as well as institutions. For the purposes of this study, I use Oran Young's definition of regimes as "social institutions governing the actions of those involved in specifiable activities or sets of activities."[2] Young goes on to say that regimes consist of "recognized roles linked together by clusters of rules or conventions governing relations among the occupants of these roles."[3] A regime is characterized by complex interdependence.[4] Its purpose is to establish a particular order that is intended either to ensure a mutually beneficial result or to avoid a mutually costly one.[5] Order refers to the benefits—such as equity, efficiency, justice, or survival—the regime is supposed to provide.[6] In the case of environmental regimes, survival is an underlying objective, but equity and efficiency are concerns as well.

Regimes may be formal or informal. In informal regimes, consensus and mutual interest may form the basis for ad hoc arrangements. Formal regimes usually result from legislation in international forums. Regimes can be created (1) spontaneously, (2) through negotiations among interested states, or (3) through imposition by one or a few strong states.[7] The creation and evolution of international regimes depend on the interests represented by individual governments, the distribution of power among these governments, and the relative salience of the issue involved. A regime's formation could be initiated by a hegemonic actor that sees benefits accruing from such a development or by a coalition of weaker states. A large enough coalition of individual states needs to possess the resources necessary to protect agreements from nonparticipants. Consensus and power, however, are not enough. A regime will not be created unless the issue is so salient for likely participants that they believe the effort required is worthwhile.

Regimes develop in order to deal with dilemmas of common interests and common aversions. In both cases, joint outcomes are preferable to those that could be achieved independently. Regimes provide the institutional framework within which actors can work collectively to achieve a desired end or avoid an unwanted outcome. But each kind of dilemma requires a different response.

A dilemma of common interests requires a regime of collaboration. In such a context, there are strong incentives to defect from established patterns of cooperation, since defection results in short-term gains. This situation creates the need for both centralization and the establishment of formal organizations. Mechanisms need to be in place for monitoring and compliance, and states must be assured that their short-term costs will be rewarded in the long term.[8] In a collaboration regime, each actor agrees that if it were to follow its own most rational strategy, all of the actors would eventually be worse off. Such a regime requires strict monitoring to ensure that no one cheats; therefore, this process of collaboration is usually greatly formalized in order to ensure each actor that the other will also forgo its rational option.[9]

The metaphor of the "tragedy of the commons" illustrates some of the issues involved in a dilemma of common interests.[10] In this example, herders are free to add livestock to the common pasture. This arrangement is satisfactory until the carrying capacity of the land is reached. Herders continue to act in their own self-interest, and the inevitable result of unrestrained individual action is overgrazing of the common pasture. Each actor is aware of the impact of his action but feels individual restraint would hurt him disproportionately. Although the actor would share in the costs resulting from the degraded commons, it would be excluded from the short-term or medium-term benefits accruing from the addition of more animals to the pasture. For him, that outcome is worse than depletion of the common pasture; consequently, he would prefer to proceed with the exploitation along with the other actors, even if this leads to the eventual depletion of the resources. If they can all be assured of joint restraint, the actors have a common interest in moving from this likely outcome to one in which they can collaborate in managing the resources.[11] The actors, therefore, can opt for a collaborative policy under which they agree to abstain from certain behavior, to work together for certain purposes, and to give the regime's institutions power to monitor and mediate conflicts. This kind of collaborative regime is appropriate for commons environmental issues such as ozone depletion.

A dilemma of common aversions requires a different response—a regime of coordination rather than collaboration. The only purpose of this type of regime is to avoid certain outcomes. If there is great conflict of interest, coordination can be difficult. Once a regime of coordination is established, it is usually self-enforcing; there is no need for strong mechanisms for surveillance and enforcement. The regime can provide an efficient means of collecting and distributing information, but it will not make provisions for monitoring. Because states would have little incentive to cheat, there is no need to devote resources to the prevention of defection. However, formal institution building is still useful under these circumstances because of the transaction-cost savings on the collection of information.[12] The regime that manages international civil aviation, for example, addresses a dilemma of common aversions. There is no requirement for policing in such a regime. Defection in this case is not usually surreptitious cheating but is, rather, an attempt to change the regime.[13]

No matter how widely supported and carefully matched to international conditions, no international regime is perfect, and none operates in a static environment. Global conditions, the interests of individual states and other actors, and policymakers' ideas about proper conduct and organization all change. In time, the issue around which the regime was created is likely to regain salience as problems arise. These changes put pressure on the regime that, if great enough, can threaten the regime's survival.

Regime transformation can occur in several ways. Internal contradictions can spur regime change; these contradictions may be built into the regime, or they may develop over time. In either case, they can threaten the success of the regime and create pressure for change or modification. Sometimes change results from exogenous factors, including shifts in the distribution of power away from states whose interests are served by regime prescriptions to states whose interests are frustrated by these prescriptions. In such cases, modifying the regime through amendments that better serve the rising states' interests, replacing it with a new regime, or simply overturning it all seem possible. Problems may also arise because participating states redefine their interests. This might happen as a result of changes in government or because of the adoption of different ideas by those in power. In addition, regime participants may redefine their interests in response to changes in technology or patterns of economic interaction.

The environmental regimes being considered fall into the category of negotiated regimes; as such, they therefore involve high transaction costs and significant constraints on the freedom of individual actors.[14] Central to the regime concept is the idea of interdependence among all the constituent elements. It has been hypothesized that the common interest in collaboration and cooperation will increase as interdependence becomes greater, thus providing actors with a greater incentive to use existing regimes or to create new ones.[15] The global environment and the global economy are areas in which there is a growing perception of the level and scope of interdependence.

Power in the Global Context

Regime formation is sensitive to the distribution of power among states. Although the term *power* is used with great frequency in international politics, it is subject to definitional confusion. Power has been variously defined as resources, as a goal, and as the ability to control.[16] A resource-based definition encompasses such factors as territory, population, economy, and defense structure. Although these factors are easy to measure, there are problems with this approach. The potential power inherent in resources does not always translate to actual power in international politics; consequently, countries with a smaller store of resources are sometimes more influential than resource-rich countries. There are also problems inherent in analyzing power as a goal. This definition does not address the nature of power, and it tends to focus on the pursuit of power as an end in itself. This again can result in a focus on the buildup of resources and capabilities.[17]

Of more use is a definition based on the concept of power as the ability to control either others or the circumstances of others. Robert Keohane and Joseph Nye described power as "the ability of an actor to get others to do something they otherwise would not do."[18] This definition has several implications. First, it assumes the existence of an interaction and an interdependence between the actor and the target. Second, perception plays an important role in the exercise of power. It affects the assessment of the benefits to be gained by the actor and the target's views of the actor's resources and reputation. Third, the exercise of power is based on conflict between the actor and the target. Important aspects of conflict assessment include the preferences of both actor and target, communication between them, how much the target understands and conforms to the actor's preferences, and how much the target's behavior changes.[19]

Although state power and interests are not necessarily the determining factors in regime formation, they can "condition" regime evolution.[20] In addition, states are not the only actors attempting to influence regime formation and evolution; domestic factions and other major global actors also become involved in the process. The parochial interests and ideologies of domestic elites sometimes act as modifying influences in the regime formation process. In addition, the state is just one of the institutions used by classes to represent their interests in the world-economy. Other dominant actors, such as transnational corporations and environmental NGOs, establish their own networks of power and influence and have interests that transcend those of the home state. Although their roles cannot always be clearly traced, the interests of these actors are relevant to the formation and transformation of environmental regimes.

Once regimes have been formed, they change the relationships among the participant states and modify the way other actors wield power. Regimes play the role of intervening variables so that outcomes do not always reflect the relative power of states. "Moreover, regimes may contribute to strengthening or weakening the capabilities of their members—for example, by transferring resources from one unit to another."[21]

Power has been identified as a major variable in the relations between the industrialized world and the Third World, with the Third World more often the object than the subject of power. An examination of that group's economic status emphasizes this vulnerability. In spite of talk of global interdependence, in economic terms the Third World is more dependent than interdependent. However, as Chapter 1 suggests, global ecological interdependence is qualitatively different from the interdependence engendered by the global economy. The former is a natural rather than a constructed interdependence. Actors are interdependent because they are similarly constrained by their common experience of the limits of a single biosphere. This interdependence does not necessarily result in the same kind of asymmetrical sensitivity and vulnerability that are consequences of the world-economy; it might, in fact, provide the Third World with some leverage in environmental politics. This leverage can translate into negative power that can be used to pressure the developed countries to make concessions in environmental negotiations. But in order for the Third World to exercise this leverage, the core countries must share with the Third World the perception of ecological interdependence.

Globalization and Regime Formation

Globalization—of the economy and of the environment—forms the context for this examination of regimes. Because globalization is likely to create interdependence among the actors, the resulting sensitivity and vulnerability are likely to affect the patterns of interests and the distribution and use of power. Given the nature of the global economy and the structural differences between developing countries and the industrialized countries, there is likely to be a divergence of interests on many procedural economic issues. The two groups' ultimate goals—primarily growth—may be similar, but the strategies are likely to be different. Many of the key global economic institutions were established by the major industrialized countries to serve their particular interests; therefore, these institutions are not necessarily in the best interests of the developing countries.

In the economic sphere, no single power is operating as a global hegemon. There has been a diffusion of power, particularly among the industrialized states group, and economic interdependence exists. But the relationship between the Third World and the developed states is best characterized as one of dependence in a variety of areas, including trade, finance capital, and technology. This power imbalance is further exacerbated by the association of major IGOs, such as the IMF, and NGOs, such as transnational corporations, with the developed world. These actors definitely affect both the regime process and the prospects for regime implementation.

The picture changes when we look at power within the framework of a single biosphere. In the area of the ecology, the economic differences between the Third World and the industrialized states result in a divergence of short-term interests. Their long-term interests converge, however, because they have a common interest in planetary survival. Because of the premise of the ultimate interconnectedness of all organisms in the biosphere, a perception of interdependence leads to a diffusion of power among all the actors in the world-system. Because of the nature of the biosphere, the Third World countries have the power to deny the industrialized countries their environmental objectives, which potentially gives the Third World some bargaining leverage.

International environmental politics affords states a number of avenues by which to exercise power. Each state can exercise power by threatening to withdraw from negotiations or by refusing to abide by the rules of the regime. Some participants in the negotiation process may have the power to link issues in order to coerce or persuade other states to comply. In addition, states that are serious contributors to a particular problem may have a power advantage since the success of the regime is dependent on their cooperation. An important consideration in the environmental regime process is that those who place less value on environmental protection may be able to exercise power because they have less interest in change than do the other actors.

A concern here is not only with why states cooperate on certain issues but also with why they do not cooperate on other issues. In spite of their relative economic weakness, the Third World countries have the power to deny the developed world its environmental objectives. This negative power can be exercised by the strong as well as the weak. On particular issues, small groups of developing countries can form effective blocking coalitions. Third World demands have to be considered because, as a group, these countries have the potential to accelerate the processes of global environmental change. Although they will also be gravely affected by these processes, they are less able to provide the resources needed to implement policies to slow or halt the changes. If they receive no help in making the transition to alternative technologies, they may make rational short-term decisions to address their immediate needs, thereby contributing to a global tragedy of the commons in the long run. The vulnerability resulting from ecological interdependence might help the Third World effectively bargain for a change of norms. In global environmental politics, the Third World countries strongly support such norms as equity and justice; different norms such as efficiency and market liberalization are favored by the industrialized actors.

This study assesses whether the globalization of the environment is likely to counter or reinforce the Third World vulnerabilities that are a consequence of the nature of the world-economy. It examines and assesses the Third World's use of leverage and linkage politics in regime formation and evolution. In the process of this exploration, the study focuses on three stages of the regime evolution process: problem definition, bargaining, and regime transformation.

Problem definition. In the regime evolution process, the definition of the problem determines the agenda for the negotiations; it not only frames the question but also sets limits on what is to be explored. This stage often involves an exposition of available scientific knowledge, and it determines the range of options and alternatives. The process can also have a considerable impact on public awareness and opinion. Obviously, a wide range of actors can have input at this point: state actors, transnational corporations, epistemic communities, environmental organizations, and the broad spectrum of intergovernmental organizations. In addition, the information provided in this process helps these actors assess an issue's salience.

Epistemic communities can be particularly influential at this stage. These are defined as "transnational networks of knowledge-based communities that are both politically empowered through their claims to exercise authoritative knowledge and motivated by shared causal and principled beliefs."[22] Membership in an epistemic community does not necessarily involve belonging to a single scientific discipline. The participants may belong to different disciplines; however, they share common values and a common body of facts, and they also interpret information in a similar manner.[23] Their influence is significant only when there is considerable scientific consensus on an issue. Oran Young has argued that scientists can play an important role in agenda-setting when they are able to achieve consensus among themselves and to overcome their tendency toward caution "in the interests of avoiding any appearance of overstating the inferences to be drawn from the available evidence."[24]

Epistemic communities can have a major impact on an issue's perceived salience and can play a powerful role at the problem definition stage. However, this power is more likely to be wielded by developed country actors than by Third World actors. Even when epistemic communities are transnational, given the unequal distribution of scientific and technical resources and skills, their members are usually drawn from developed country institutions. This increases the role of developed country actors in defining environmental problems and setting the environmental agenda.

In defining environmental and resource problems, transnational corporations are also important forces. They lobby nation-states and wage public relations campaigns in the attempt to affect the international environmental agenda. Even though states determine the final outcome of any decisionmaking process, transnational corporations can influence the process at any stage. By affecting the conception of relative salience, they effectively help to decide the agenda and the alternatives to be considered.

Bargaining. Interactions among participants in the regime-building process are likely to be a complex mix of conventional bargaining and coercive pressure applied by the more powerful actors. In many multilateral negotiations there are significant differences in effective power, influence, and bargaining strength. When relevant parties differ substantially in bargaining strength, the stronger ones are likely to have greater influence on the regime's provisions; consequently, coercion may be an element of the regime bargaining process.[25] States that wield significant economic, political, or military power can use such power to induce other states to support or reject a regime.

At the bargaining stage, the convergence and divergence of interests among the states can play a major role. This is the point at which veto power and bargaining leverage become important. If the support of a particular actor or group of actors is essential to the desired collective outcome, that actor or group of actors can act to block the regime's progress. For example, in the case of the ozone protection regime, major producers as well as major users were potential veto coalitions. Over time, these coalitions sometimes fall apart as a result of a variety of factors, such as new information, change of interests within the coalition, or pressure from other parties. Although the negotiation process could be finalized without winning over key members of the veto coalition, the resulting regime would likely be ineffective.

Regime transformation. Regimes are dynamic, and they can become stronger or weaker over time. These changes may occur because of endogenous as well as exogenous factors.[26] However, with its focus on the role of power and influence in the regime transformation process, this study emphasizes the role of exogenous factors.

Shifts in power within the international system may lead to regime transformation, but there is no direct relationship between the power shifts and regime changes. Much depends on the direction of the power shift and the nature of the regime. If the shift in power is away from those whose interests are served by the regime, the impact on the regime is likely to be significant. In the case of an imposed regime, if the dominant actor suffers a significant loss of power, the regime might disintegrate; at the very least, its configuration is likely to change. Other exogenous factors that can lead to regime transformation include changes in the nature and distribution of technology, shifts in domestic priorities, and changes in demands.[27] At any of the three stages examined here, the regime formation and transformation processes can emphasize integrative or distributive issues.

Property and Access Relations

Management regimes depend to a large extent on the associated property and access relations, factors that have likely consequences for regime evolution. Although all of humankind lives within the unity of one biosphere, not all environmental issues are regarded as common-property issues. Two important variables in environmental regime formation are property relations and access.

Property relations address whether a common-property resource problem is being addressed. These resources have two principal characteristics: First, exclusion or control of access is difficult or impossible; in addition, each user has the ability to reduce the welfare of the other users.[28] Common-property resources are held in a variety of property rights regimes. Global commons such as the oceans and the atmosphere are held in open access regimes. Some other commons resources are held as private property. Still others are held as communal property for the exclusive use of a specific community. Finally, the state controls access to some commons resources such as, for example, marine parks.[29]

Property and access issues are likely to affect the formation and transformation of environmental regimes. If the subject of the negotiation is a common-property resource, interdependence becomes an issue, but the sense of agency and vulnerability is more likely to be shared by all if the resource is held in an open access regime. When the issue is not a common-property problem, interdependence is not a major factor, and it is likely to be more difficult for the Third World countries to secure cooperation from the developed countries.

The three cases under study here offer a mix of property and access relations. The ozone protection case deals with the atmosphere, which is a common-property resource since exclusion of potential users is difficult, if not impossible. This is also a resource to which there is open access.

Biodiversity is also a common-property resource, but it is held in a mix of property arrangements. Biodiversity exists in a wide array of ecosystems such as the oceans, forests, and mangroves. Consequently, it can be found in each of the four basic property arrangements: open access, private property, communal property, and state control. The third regime, which addresses the hazardous waste trade, does not involve a common-property issue. Because it is a transborder environmental problem, the issues of global interdependence relevant to commons problems are unlikely to be major factors in the evolution of this regime.

Conclusion

Although interdependence is not a new characteristic within our world, it is one that is receiving increased attention. A focus on interdependence broadens the analytical perspective from one of power-based state-centric politics to one that brings into view a wider variety of major actors and interstate relations that are less constrained by gradations of power. Regime theory attempts to capture this complexity in its analysis of states' cooperation. Since this study focuses on globalization, interdependence is an important factor in the analysis. Regime theory, therefore, is an appropriate analytical tool with which to address the implications of this globalization for the Third World's role in the formation and transformation of environmental regimes.

Notes

1. Analysts in this area include Ernst B. Haas, "On Systems and International Regimes," *World Politics* 27 (1975): 147–174; John Gerard Ruggie and Ernst B. Haas, eds., *International Responses to Technology,* special issue of *International Organization* 29 (1975); Robert O. Keohane and Joseph S. Nye, *Power and Interdependence* (Boston: Little, Brown, 1977); Oran R. Young, *Resource Management at the International Level: The Case of the North Pacific* (London: Pinter and Nichols, 1977); Seyom Brown, Nina W. Cornell, Larry L. Fabian, and Edith Brown Weiss, *Regimes for the Ocean, Outer Space, and Weather* (Washington, D.C.: Brookings, 1977); Stephen D. Krasner, ed., *International Regimes* (Ithaca: Cornell University Press, 1983); and Oran R. Young, *International Cooperation: Building Regimes for Natural Resources and the Environment* (Ithaca: Cornell University Press, 1989).

2. Young, *International Cooperation,* 12.

3. Ibid., 12–13.

4. Ernst B. Haas, "Words Can Hurt You; or, Who Said What to Whom About Regimes," *International Organization* 36, no. 2 (Spring 1982): 211.

5. Arthur A. Stein, "Coordination and Collaboration: Regimes in an Anarchic World," *International Organization* 36, no. 2 (Spring 1982): 324.

6. Haas, "Words Can Hurt You," 211.

7. Oran R. Young, "Regime Dynamics," *International Organization* 36, no. 2 (Spring 1982): 282–285.

8. Lisa L. Martin, "Interests, Power, and Multilateralism," *International Organization* 46, no. 4 (Autumn 1992): 766.

9. Stein, "Coordination and Collaboration," 312.

10. Garrett Hardin, "The Tragedy of the Commons," *Science* 162 (December 13, 1968): 1243–1248.

11. Stein, "Coordination and Collaboration," 304–308.

12. Martin, "Interests, Power, and Multilateralism," 776.

13. Ibid., 129–130.

14. Young, *International Cooperation,* 93.

15. James E. Dougherty and Robert L. Pfaltzgraff, Jr., *Contending Theories of International Relations* (New York: Harper and Row, 1990), 171.

16. John M. Rothgeb, Jr., *Defining Power: Influence and Force in the Contemporary International System* (New York: St. Martin's Press, 1993), 19–22.

17. Ibid., 20–21.

18. Keohane and Nye, *Power and Interdependence,* 11.

19. Rothgeb, *Defining Power,* 45.

20. Stephen D. Krasner, "Structural Causes and Regime Consequences: Regimes as Intervening Variables," in Krasner, ed., *International Regimes,* 357.

21. Dougherty and Pfaltzgraff, *Contending Theories,* 172.

22. Peter M. Haas, "Obtaining International Environmental Protection Through Epistemic Consensus," *Millennium: Journal of International Studies* 19, no. 3 (Winter 1990): 349. See also Peter M. Haas, *Saving the Mediterranean: The Politics of International Environmental Cooperation* (New York: Columbia University Press, 1990), 55–56.

23. Haas, *Saving the Mediterranean,* n. 18, p. 55.

24. Oran R. Young, "Science and Social Institutions: Lessons for International Resource Regimes," in Steinar Andresen and Willy Ostreng, eds., *International Resource Management: The Role of Science and Politics* (London: Belhaven Press, 1989), 10.

25. Young, *International Cooperation,* 201.

26. Ibid., 96–97.

27. Ibid., 99–100.

28. F. Berkes, D. Feeny, B. J. McCay, and J. M. Acheson, "The Benefit of the Commons," *Nature* 340 (July 13, 1989): 91–93.

29. Ibid.

PART 2

THE THIRD WORLD AT THE BARGAINING TABLE

4
The Ozone Layer Protection Regime

Air pollution, global warming, and ozone depletion are transforming the earth's climate and atmosphere. These changes are among the most far-reaching environmental problems people face today. Nation-states have attempted to address these issue areas at the national and international levels. Of the three areas, ozone depletion is the one in which there has been the most significant progress in regime building. UNEP established a committee to examine the ozone depletion problem in 1978, and the process culminated in a framework convention in 1985. Two years later, this convention was strengthened by the Montreal Protocol, which was amended in 1990; the amendment entered into force in August 1992.

The Ozone Depletion Issue

Ozone limits the amount of harmful solar ultraviolet radiation that reaches the earth. Without it, life on earth would be impossible. Under normal conditions, chemical reactions triggered by sunlight continuously destroy and replenish ozone. But with the introduction of chemicals that contain chlorine and bromine, the balance has been upset; the earth's ozone shield is being depleted by chemicals such as chlorofluorocarbons (CFCs), which contain chlorine, and halons, which contain bromine. These chemicals can survive intact in the atmosphere for more than a century, and each chlorine and bromine atom can destroy tens of thousands of ozone molecules.

The stratospheric ozone layer first became a matter of international concern in 1970, when there was a fear that the supersonic transportation system could damage it significantly.[1] This concern resurfaced in 1974, when two scientists argued that the chlorine in CFCs could destroy the ozone molecules and deplete the ozone layer.[2]

The use of CFCs has become widespread because of their versatility. In the short time since the discovery of this class of chemicals in 1931, they have become a key part of the industrialization process. They have been used in aerosol spray cans, artificial cooling, seat cushions, computer chips, and foam insulation, and, in the 1970s, they began to be used as solvents in the electronics industry. CFCs have been particularly attractive because they have been found to be nontoxic, noncarcinogenic, and inert. The United States and the European Union are the two major producers of these chemicals. In 1986 these two areas accounted for more than 70 percent of world production and more than 50 percent of the world's consumption of CFCs.[3]

In addition to allowing more ultraviolet radiation into the earth's atmosphere, CFCs and halons also prevent infrared radiation from leaving it; thus, they are also factors in global warming. Because of the time lag between the release of the gases and the impact on the ozone layer, even if the production of all ozone-depleting chemicals were to stop now, the gases already rising to the stratosphere and those contained in millions of appliances would continue to erode the ozone layer for many years.

Stratospheric ozone depletion is occurring everywhere except over the tropics, although it is most extensive at high latitudes in both hemispheres. Some of the most significant depletion has been observed over the Antarctic region. But ultraviolet radiation will have negative impacts on people all over the world; these effects include increased incidence of melanoma and nonmelanoma skin cancer, eye disorders, and suppression of the immune system. Because ultraviolet radiation is damaging to some plants and ecosystems, ozone depletion will also reduce the long-term productivity of agriculture and fisheries, thereby exacerbating the problem of hunger in areas where food shortages already exist.[4]

Evolution of the Ozone Layer Protection Regime

In the early 1970s, when scientists began to explore the theory that chlorofluorocarbons might be damaging the ozone layer, their findings were initially greeted with some skepticism. But the issue began to elicit such concern that by the late 1970s and early 1980s, some industrialized countries took steps to limit the use and production of CFCs. In 1978 the United States banned the principal CFCs for most uses; in 1980 European Community countries placed a limit on production of CFCs and cut their use in aerosol products by 30 percent. Sweden, Norway, and Canada also placed limits on CFC use.

This concern at the national and regional levels was also reflected at the global level. UNEP expressed serious concern about ozone depletion in 1975. At that time, it funded a study by the World Meteorological Society to explore the hypothesis that ozone depletion was caused by CFCs. But the definition of the issue did not begin until 1977, when the United States, Canada, Finland, Norway, and Sweden urged UNEP to consider international regulation of ozone.[5] A UNEP conference during that year developed a World Plan of Action on the Ozone Layer, but ozone depletion was not yet seen as an urgent problem. In order to ascertain the extent of the ozone depletion problem, the governing council of UNEP established the Coordinating Committee on the Ozone Layer, composed of government and industry representatives involved in research on ozone depletion. It met eight times between 1977 and 1986.

Because there was little consensus on the seriousness of the problem, the fact-finding and consensus-building process was prolonged. In May 1981 the governing council of UNEP decided to start work on a global convention for the protection of the ozone layer. The council set up the Ad Hoc Working Group of Legal and Technical Experts for the Elaboration of a Global Framework Convention for the Protection of the Ozone Layer. Its task was to prepare a draft convention; in so doing, it met seven times between 1982 and 1985.[6]

At the beginning of the negotiation process, the issue was not yet clearly defined, and nations brought disparate viewpoints to the negotiations. Some were in favor of a complete ban; others were reluctant to dispense with useful, inexpensive chemicals, especially when they were not convinced of their danger by the scientific evidence against CFCs.

The negotiating parties met eight times over a period of three years, but they failed to achieve consensus on the ozone issue. Consequently, they had to be satisfied with a framework convention, which was primarily an agreement to cooperate on monitoring, researching, and exchanging data. The 1985 Vienna Convention for the Protection of the Ozone Layer imposed no specific obligations to reduce the production of ozone-depleting compounds and did not even identify the compounds that were ozone depleting. The parties did agree to resume negotiations on a binding protocol on ozone protection, which provided an opportunity for regime strengthening. UNEP executive director Mostafa Tolba's projection was that a protocol stipulating control measures would be adopted in April 1987.

By the time negotiations for the Montreal Protocol began in December 1986, there were more data confirming that CFCs were damaging the ozone layer. In 1985 the Antarctic hole had made dramatic headlines, as scientists discussed the thinning of the ozone layer over Antarctica. In addition, increases in the use of CFCs meant the scenarios on which projections were based had to be revised. These new data informed an Environmental Protection Agency (EPA)–UNEP atmospheric ozone study that became the scientific basis for the ensuing negotiations.

Although nations were still divided about the validity of the scientific evidence against CFCs, the recent evidence was more persuasive. By 1987 most nations realized some controls were necessary; the major disputes were over the extent and the timing of those controls. Lead states advocated a freeze, followed by a gradual 95 percent reduction in the production of CFCs and other ozone-depleting substances over a period of 10 to 14 years.[7] However, other states were in favor of a production cap rather than a freeze or a reduction.

As a result of the new scientific evidence and the pressure from lead states, the parties successfully negotiated the Montreal Protocol on Substances That Deplete the Ozone Layer. Industrialized countries pledged that by 1999 they would cut CFC production by 50 percent of the 1986 level. During the first decade of the agreement, developing countries were permitted to increase their CFC use up to 0.66 pound per capita annually. This exception was made because these countries had been major contributors to ozone layer damage; the derogation gave them the opportunity to receive some of the industrial and social benefits of CFCs and halons.[8] In addition, developing nations were entitled to receive technical assistance to make the transition to technologies that were not ozone depleting.

The agreement would result in a net reduction of CFCs of 35 to 40 percent, far less than the 85 percent reduction some analysts regarded as necessary to stabilize the level of ozone depletion.[9] The parties agreed to control five CFCs (numbers 11, 12, 113, 114, and 115) and three bromine compounds (halons 1211, 1301, and 2402). As stated earlier, by 1999, production and consumption of CFCs would be cut back to 50 percent of their 1986 levels; production and consumption of halons would be frozen within three years, except for uses in which no satisfactory substitutes were available.

The Montreal Protocol allowed the continued production of ozone-depleting substances, such as methyl chloroform and carbon tetrachloride, and it did not prohibit the use of CFC and halon alternatives that could deplete the ozone layer. It had no provisions for monitoring production and consumption of ozone-depleting chemicals; furthermore, there were no provisions for a fund to defray the costs of CFC substitutes in the developing countries.

In September 1987, 24 nations and the European Economic Community signed the Montreal Protocol on Substances That Deplete the Ozone Layer.[10] Within months of the accord, new scientific evidence indicated that more ozone damage had already occurred than the negotiators had assumed would happen in the next 100 years. New measurements by the National Aeronautics and Space Administration indicated that even with the agreement, ozone loss could result in 5 to 20 percent more ultraviolet radiation reaching populated areas within the 40 years following the accord. Exposure resulting from a 10 percent ozone loss would affect the planet's food chain, both on land and in the ocean. Human health would also suffer, as more people would have skin cancer, cataracts, and depressed immune systems.

Consequently, even before the Montreal Protocol came into force on schedule on January 1, 1989, a major working group had begun the process of strengthening the protocol's control measures. In March 1989 a ministerial conference in London examined developing nations' involvement in the protocol. This was followed by the Helsinki Meeting of the Parties to the Montreal Protocol in May 1989, which took place in an atmosphere of urgency. Many of the parties wanted to accelerate the schedule for the reduction of the production and consumption of CFCs and halons. Although time did not permit a formal amendment of the Montreal Protocol at Helsinki, the delegates adopted a declaration that called for phasing out the production and consumption of the five CFCs listed in the protocol by the year 2000. The agreement also addressed the phaseout of halons and reduced dependence on other ozone-depleting substances. In addition, the parties agreed to help developing countries acquire information, research, and training and to assist them in their attempts to devise ways of financing technology transfers and retooling.

In June 1990 there was a second meeting in London to amend the protocol. The attendees addressed an extensive agenda of amendments, which widened the scope of the protocol considerably. The amendments addressed timetables for phasing out ozone-depleting chemicals not included in the original protocol. The five CFCs and three halons already covered by the Montreal Protocol were to be completely phased out by the year 2000. In addition, the 93 nations would phase out 10 other fully halogenated CFCs and carbon tetrachloride by the year 2000 and methyl chloroform by 2005. A review of the phaseout schedule for the original five CFCs and methyl chloroform was planned for 1992.

An associated resolution addressed the phaseout of 33 partially halogenated CFCs by no later than the year 2040 and perhaps even by 2020. The parties also resolved not to authorize the production or use of 46 other halons. In addition, in order to ensure the Third World's participation, the amendment provided them with financial incentives, including technical cooperation and a fund that would help them make the switch to alternate technology. Developed countries would contribute to the fund. This amendment entered into force in August 1992.

A few months later, spurred by new scientific information, the regime was further strengthened. It was clear that even if the control measures of the amended Montreal Protocol were implemented by all nations, there would still be a significant increase in stratospheric chlorine that would not peak until around the turn of the century. Significant ozone losses were expected throughout the 1990s, and there was the possibility of widespread losses in the Arctic region.[11] With new information coming in on ozone losses, 87 countries met in Copenhagen in November 1992 and agreed to accelerate the phaseout schedule to January 1, 1996.[12]

As Table 4.1 indicates, 13 years elapsed between the definition of the ozone depletion issue in 1977 and the agreement on a binding protocol in 1990. Much of that time was spent reducing scientific uncertainties and building consensus. Because of the strategy of incrementalism, it took five years to negotiate a framework convention, a protocol, and an amendment that contained explicit information on the financing mechanism for the transfer of ozone technology. If it were not for the momentum inspired by the convincing new scientific evidence that surfaced after the Montreal Protocol, the ozone layer protection regime would have been a relatively weak response to the problem.

Table 4.1 International Policy Actions On Ozone Protection

1977	UNEP Coordinating Committee on the Ozone Layer established.
1985	Vienna Convention for the Protection of the Ozone Layer adopted.
1987	Montreal Protocol on Substances That Deplete the Ozone Layer adopted. This required signatory governments to regulate consumption and production of CFCs and halons. Developing countries that are parties to the Montreal Protocol have a 10-year exclusionary period.
1988	Entry into force of the Vienna Convention.
1989	Entry into force of the Montreal Protocol.
1990	Montreal Protocol on Substances That Deplete the Ozone Layer amended in London. The amendment required signatory governments to regulate consumption and production of CFCs, halons, carbon tetrachloride, methyl chloroform, and other fully halogenated CFCs.
January 1991	Establishment of the Interim Multilateral Fund to provide financial assistance to developing countries in order to facilitate compliance with the control measures of the Montreal Protocol.
May 1992	20 states have ratified the amendment to the Montreal Protocol, triggering the mechanism to bring it into force.
August 1992	Entry into force of the amendment.
November 1992	At Copenhagen, parties agree to accelerate phaseout schedule to January 1, 1996.

Actors and Interests

Both state and nonstate actors played major roles in the regime-building process. To a large extent, their roles were determined by their position in the global economic system, but policy choices were also conditioned by the nature of the environmental problem and by unfolding scientific information. Ecological interdependence also modified the resistance of the industrialized countries to financial assistance being given to the developing countries. This section focuses on the interest of four sets of actors: the Third World, the industrialized states, corporations involved in the production of CFCs, and environmental lobby groups.

The Nation-States

All of the nation-state actors embraced the same long-term goal—to protect the ozone layer. But as the regime evolved and as more scientific information became available, significant differences in short- and medium-term interests made the negotiation process difficult.

The Third World. Developing countries were slow to identify a separate set of interests on this issue. In the early stages of the process, they did not emerge as a distinct interest group; in fact, most showed no significant interest in the issue until 1987. In the beginning, ozone depletion was primarily the concern of the nations that were the major users and producers of CFCs and other major ozone-depleting chemicals. Consequently, Third World countries' input at the Vienna Convention was limited. However, as the regime evolved, these countries realized they had significant interests at stake; therefore, when a freeze was suggested, they expressed their concerns.

CFCs are important ingredients in the industrialization process, but their fastest growing use in the developing world is for cooling. China and India, with about 40 percent of the world's population, consume only about 5 percent of all CFCs.[13] As they continue to industrialize and as the use of refrigerators and air conditioners becomes more widespread, their need for CFCs or chemicals with similar properties will increase. The Chinese government estimated that the 1991 production of ozone-depleting substances was approximately 48,000 metric tons. This was projected to increase to 117,000 metric tons by the year 2000 if no measures were taken to control the demand.[14]

Developing countries' key interests, then, were in retaining access to CFCs or in getting assistance in acquiring substitutes. They wanted free or low-cost access to the technologies or, failing that, financial assistance to help them acquire those substitute technologies. India and China argued that it was unfair for the industrialized countries to expect the Third World to incur the costs of switching to CFC substitutes in order to solve a problem they had little part in creating. This perspective was widely held by the Third World group, with Argentina, Brazil, Egypt, Kenya, Mexico, and Venezuela prominent in representing the group's position.[15] Some of the Third World nations pressing hardest for help in making the technological switch were countries whose industrial sectors had already begun to explore alternatives, including Brazil, China, Egypt, and Mexico. Mexico has adopted alternate propellants for use in aerosol sprays, Brazil's researchers have developed a more efficient refrigerator compressor, and China has been working on substitute refrigerants.[16]

The Third World position also received some support from UNEP executive director Mostafa Tolba. Although Tolba wanted the conference delegates to agree on a strong treaty, he also supported the establishment of a fund to help the Third World countries find and buy substitute chemicals.[17] Tolba is an Egyptian, and he saw himself as a representative not only of UNEP but also of the interests of developing countries. Because of concerns that Third World interests be represented, under Tolba UNEP financial assistance allowed delegates from about 10 developing countries to attend the ozone negotiations in February 1987.[18]

Industrialized nation-states. At the beginning of the negotiating process, there were divergent interests within the industrialized countries' group, interests that were put forward by two major groups: the Toronto Group and the European Community (EC). The Toronto Group was composed of the United States, Canada, Sweden, Norway, Finland, and later New Zealand, Australia, and Switzerland.[19] The EC group included its member nations, loosely allied at various stages with Chile, Japan, and the Soviet Union.[20] These two groups had different objectives: The Toronto Group wanted to move more quickly on the ozone matter, and so it was in favor of controlling consumption; the EC group preferred to use production controls. As the major producer and consumer state, the United States might have been expected to side with the EC group; however, it had been forced by domestic pressure to control some CFC uses, and it wanted to reduce the competitive advantage of other nations in this area. The EC included four major CFC-producing states: the United Kingdom, France, the Federal Republic of Germany, and Italy. Because of these countries' production capacities, they had an economic interest in continuing production.

By the time of the London meeting on the Montreal Protocol, the differences between the Toronto Group and the EC had diminished significantly. Although there was some disagreement about the phaseout schedule, both groups agreed that ozone-depleting substances should be completely phased out. In addition, the Toronto Group and the EC initially found common ground in their resistance to the developing countries' requests for financial assistance.

Nongovernmental Organizations

As the ozone protection regime evolved, the role of interest groups in the process increased. According to the rules of procedure, nongovernmental organizations with expertise in fields related to the protection of the upper atmosphere could participate as observers at the meetings.[21] The chair would ask for their perspectives after the participating nations had presented their positions.

The two major NGO groups represented were environmental interest groups and industrial groups. Their representatives made brief statements at the negotiating sessions, focusing their efforts on briefing the press and lobbying ministers and legislators in individual countries. Their tactics differed. The industry group focused on lobbying the relevant government ministers, whereas the environmental groups focused more on press briefings. Although the lobbies operated in a low-key fashion during the negotiation sessions, the presence of these NGOs did put pressure on the negotiators, either because of the press scrutiny gained by the environmentalists or because of industrial lobbies' access to governments.[22]

Corporate interests. The small group of CFC producers had a marked interest in the evolution of the ozone protection regime. At the time of the negotiations, 17 ozone-producing companies were operating in 16 countries. The leader was the U.S.-based DuPont, which produced CFCs for the major markets of North America, Europe, and Japan. The company produced more than 25 percent of the global output of CFCs and controlled 50 percent of the U.S. market.

The CFC manufacturers saw regulation of the chemicals as inimical to their interests; consequently, DuPont and the other U.S. manufacturers and European manufacturers such as Imperial Chemical Industries tried to block the process of regime evolution. As part of this effort, the U.S. manufacturers formed a lobbying organization, the Alliance for a Responsible CFC Policy. In the initial stages of the evolution of the ozone regime, industry representatives denied there was any scientific basis for linking ozone depletion to CFCs, and scientific dissension in the early stages of the negotiations helped to support their position. The industry group also did not want the United States to implement a unilateral freeze, since this move would make its members less competitive in the world market.[23] The industry position was weakened, however, in September 1986, when DuPont issued a statement favoring a protocol to limit CFC emissions.[24] DuPont's change of position can be seen more as a function of the global economy than one of the unfolding scientific knowledge. The company envisioned a globally competitive position in the market for CFC substitutes, and this perspective motivated the change in its stand on the issue. Because DuPont had been engaged in the search for CFC substitutes, it was better suited to make a fast switch to a CFC-restricted market than were its competitors; consequently, international restrictions on CFCs gave the company an initial advantage.[25]

Environmental NGOs. The general objective of these groups was to persuade decisionmakers to implement policies that would halt and reverse the ozone depletion process. They also supported the establishment of a fund to assist developing countries with technology conversion, which they felt was a necessary incentive for an effective regime.

Environmental groups involved in the evolution of the ozone protection regime included Friends of the Earth (FOE), Greenpeace, the Environmental Defense Fund, and the Natural Resources Defense Council (NRDC). The NRDC got involved in the regime process in 1986 when it made the first proposal for a complete phaseout of CFCs and halons over a period of 10 years.[26] But the bulk of the NGOs' input occurred following the signing of the Montreal Protocol in 1987.[27] Three weeks after the signing, the affiliates of FOE International made ozone layer protection their top priority in a campaign that targeted both industry and consumers. These nongovernmental organizations used national lobbying, international lobbying, and consumer boycotts as tools.[28]

Although the environmental NGOs did not have direct input into the negotiation process, through their continued pressure they did affect the process of regime evolution and were also instrumental in their support of a technology transfer fund for developing countries. A statement to that effect, representing the viewpoints of 93 NGOs worldwide, was presented at the First Meeting of the Parties to the Montreal Protocol in Helsinki in May 1989.[29]

The Third World in the Regime's Evolution

The Third World countries were slow to assume active roles in the development of the ozone layer protection regime; consequently, they did not try to affect the definition of the problem. But their interest and efforts increased as the negotiation process evolved.

Defining the Problem

At the beginning of the problem definition process, there was scientific uncertainty about the gravity of the ozone depletion problem. The definition process reduced this uncertainty by accomplishing three major tasks: It confirmed that ozone depletion was occurring; it confirmed the connection between the use of CFCs and halons and the damage to the ozone layer; and it estimated the extent and rate of depletion.

The ecological epistemic community, which played a major role in defining the problem, was a transnational one. It was made up of atmospheric scientists and policymakers, including officials of UNEP, the U.S Environmental Protection Agency, and the U.S. State Department's Bureau of Oceans and International Environmental and Scientific Affairs (OES). The epistemic community used a variety of channels to affect the decisionmaking process. In the process of drafting documents and reports, gathering data, organizing scientific panels, and lobbying delegates, it was able to substantially define the issue and modify the agenda for the negotiations.[30] Significant components of the epistemic community participated in UNEP's Coordinating Committee on the Ozone Layer, in which they were able to share information.[31]

The incorporation of the epistemic community into the UNEP process enhanced the community's ability to define the ozone depletion problem. The expertise of the community was accepted; consequently, it was able to suggest the policy implications of the scientific developments. The group's perspectives gained wide credibility within the political community.[32] Because of this, the policymakers were willing to move ahead with the negotiations, even in the face of some scientific uncertainty.

Corporations involved in the production of ozone-depleting chemicals were initially opposed to the epistemic community's definition of the problem, and they tried to modify that definition. By questioning the evolving body of knowledge about ozone depletion, the corporations were able to slow the process of problem definition, but they could not substantially modify that definition.

As a group, developing countries had little to do with the definition of the ozone depletion problem. Developing country interests were not substantially represented within the epistemic community. Although the ecological epistemic community was transnational, its major components were based in the industrialized world. Much of the research was done and supported by Americans, but atmospheric scientists in Belgium, Britain, France, Japan, and Norway were also at work on the problem. Consequently, epistemic communities based in the industrialized countries defined the problem and set the scientific context for the negotiations.

Bargaining

The bargaining process over the ozone protection regime actually began before the issue was clearly defined. In the beginning, the Third World countries played a minor role in the negotiations, primarily because they did not have clearly defined interests. Nations with economic interests, however, as well as industries involved in CFC production, did have a clear understanding of the interests at stake.

Nations brought dissimilar viewpoints to the negotiations. Some favored a global ban on CFCs 11 and 12 in aerosols (except for essential purposes) and a limit on CFC emissions in nonaerosol uses. The United States, which accounted for 30 percent of worldwide production, was prepared to be the lead state. However, other nations were reluctant to undertake such sweeping actions until they felt the scientific evidence against CFCs was compelling. The latter group would have been satisfied with a framework convention.[33]

The European Community accounted for 45 percent of world CFC output, and by the mid-1980s it was exporting a third of its production to developing states. Because of the major producer states' interests in continuing production, the EC member states constituted a veto coalition.[34] Since these states' participation was necessary for a strong ozone protection regime, their cooperation was important. The large developing states, such as India, China, Indonesia, Brazil, and Mexico, also appear to have had some potential as a veto coalition. Their bargaining leverage was based not on their consumption of CFCs but on their potential as producers and consumers of CFCs. These countries were already producing on a small scale; although they were providing less than 5 percent of the world's CFC production, their production was increasing by 7 to 10 percent each year.[35] However, in the negotiations on the Vienna Convention, these states did not take advantage of their veto power. At this stage, no Third World country played an active role.

The Toronto Group took the lead, pushing for simultaneous negotiation of a framework convention and associated protocols that would obligate states to reduce CFC use. However, the veto coalition would not support the negotiation of regulatory protocols, taking the position that the state of scientific knowledge was insufficient to support such a protocol. The lead states remained on the offensive, proposing a worldwide ban on nonessential uses of CFCs in spray cans in 1983. But the veto coalition offered a counterproposal: Total CFC production would be capped at a level that would allow EC producers to increase production by 30 percent beyond the anticipated 1985 level.[36]

Over a three-year period there were eight negotiating sessions, but the groups failed to achieve consensus on the ozone issue. In 1985, after three years of negotiation, the United States began to define ozone depletion as an urgent issue, but still the veto coalition would not yield. As a result, the parties had to be satisfied with the Vienna Convention, which was a framework convention.

The Montreal Protocol began the process of strengthening the ozone layer protection regime. Because of new findings, most nations accepted the idea of some controls. However, the extent and the timing of the controls were contentious issues. Lead states argued for a freeze, followed by a gradual reduction in the production of ozone-depleting substances over a period of 10 to 14 years, whereas the veto coalition wanted a production cap.[37] The Toronto Group still pressed for a cut, but as a compromise its members suggested a 50 percent cut. As late as April 1987 the EC insisted it would agree to a reduction of no more than 20 percent, but at the Montreal Conference later that year, the EC representative agreed to a 50 percent reduction.

The EC veto coalition was beginning to disintegrate. Some of its members (the Federal Republic of Germany, Denmark, Belgium, and the Netherlands) now felt it was necessary to implement stronger regulation. In addition, the United States was exerting continued diplomatic pressure on the Community. The EC realized that, by remaining inflexible, it risked being blamed for the failure of the negotiations. With the change in the EC position, the parties were able to successfully negotiate the Montreal Protocol on Substances That Deplete the Ozone Layer. By 1999 industrialized countries were to cut CFC production by 50 percent of the 1986 level.

Developing countries successfully pressed for some concessions; they obtained a derogation that would allow them to increase their CFC use for the first decade of the agreement. They were also to receive technical assistance as well as information and advice on CFC recycling and conservation. The fear was that without some concessions Third World countries would set up their own CFC production plants.

But these concessions did not address all of the developing countries' major concerns regarding the evolving regime. Of particular concern was the fact that there were no provisions for a fund to help them make the switch to CFC substitutes. The fund was not established because the United States, Japan, and the EC countries opposed it. Because there were no provisions for financial assistance, three major developing countries—China, India, and Brazil—refused to sign the protocol.[38] These were important holdouts, because they had the potential to become major producers and consumers of CFCs. They refused to participate in the regime until the industrialized countries agreed to provide financial and technological assistance.[39] UNEP's Tolba supported them in their calls for the establishment of the fund.[40]

Scientific revelations about ozone depletion continued to unfold, and they spurred the regime strengthening process. The Montreal Protocol came into force on January 1, 1989, and the negotiations on its amendment began promptly. At a meeting to amend the protocol in Helsinki in May 1989, the veto coalition began to shift its position dramatically. The EC members were among 80 nations voting for a complete CFC phaseout by the year 2000.

At the London meeting in June 1990, a new coalition of 13 industrialized states pushed for a 1997 deadline for the final elimination of CFCs. However, the four leading CFC-producing states—the United States, the United Kingdom, France, and Italy—joined by the Soviet Union offered an alternate phaseout date of the year 2000.[41] The push by some industrialized states for a 1997 deadline caused the United States to change from a lead to a veto role.

When the London Conference began, the industrialized countries were still opposed to the establishment of a fund to assist the developing countries in their transition from CFC technologies. The United States was strongly opposed to the inclusion of this provision, not only because it meant funds would have to be provided by developed countries, but also because of the precedent that would be established. The implications could be significant for subsequent agreements, such as the Climate Change Convention. But the environmental NGOs and some nation-states saw the establishment of a fund as crucial to winning developing countries' cooperation. Continued unrestricted CFC use or production by Third World nations would make any agreement on a reduction or a phaseout meaningless. These countries have the power to invalidate any negotiated regime.

The switch from negotiating control measures to discussing financial mechanisms resulted in a realignment of the major actors. Initially, developing nations had not been significantly involved in the negotiation of this regime, but they identified a funding mechanism as crucial for their transition to substitute technologies that would not be ozone-depleting. Very few of these countries had been involved in the development of the Vienna Convention, but as the regime evolved, they became increasingly immersed in it and began to realize its implications for their own industrial development. In spite of their reluctance over, and resistance to, the establishment of a fund, the developed nations realized that the developing nations' cooperation was essential to the long-term success of the Montreal Protocol. After intensive bargaining and a last-minute policy reversal by the United States, participants agreed to provide developing countries with financial incentives and technical cooperation; in return, developing countries would subscribe to the amendments by becoming parties to the protocol.

Developing countries were concerned that developed countries would try to pass off current assistance as a part of this new fund, and they were largely successful in preventing such a move. Some bilateral cooperation could be included as part of a nation's contribution, but this was not to exceed 20 percent of the total. Only developed countries would be levied for contributions to the fund, but payments by developing countries, nongovernmental organizations, and international organizations were also encouraged.

From this new multilateral fund, grants and concessional disbursements would be made to developing countries, provided the parties agree to the specific expenditures. Fund policies would be the responsibility of the Annual Meeting of the Parties, and its operation and administration would be handled by an executive committee working with agencies such as the World Bank.[42] The agreement on financing arrangements paved the way for the support of major Third World countries such as China and India.

During the course of the negotiations, some of the participants and all of the interested NGOs tried to increase their leverage through use of the media. As regime negotiations progressed, it became easier to gain increased media coverage since there was increasing public interest in the issue of protecting the world's atmosphere. By the time the Montreal Protocol negotiations began, media attention was significant.

Developing countries were usually at a disadvantage with respect to the size and makeup of their delegations. A developing country was likely to be represented by a single generalist, whereas the industrialized countries were more likely to have a team of specialists. Countries that had a strong economic interest in the process were usually represented by large delegations. But most delegations fell between these two extremes. They had, on average, two to four members, usually representing scientific, industrial, economic, legal, and political disciplines. The delegations that had specialists had an advantage since these people usually had special knowledge of, or experience regarding, the ozone issue.[43]

Regime Transformation

The initial controls provided in the Montreal Protocol have been substantially strengthened as a result of two major changes. One is the acceleration of the CFC phaseout schedule in the new agreements made in London and in Copenhagen. The other major change involves the establishment of the fund for developing countries. Because these countries' cooperation is so important to the effectiveness of the regime, as a part of the transformation process they were able to obtain agreement on the technology transfer fund. But they were only able to do so because the community of nations was convinced by the growing fund of information about the damage to the ozone layer. Because of the nature of the atmosphere, all of the world's nations are vulnerable to any ozone layer damage done by other actors; therefore, without the cooperation of Third World countries, the regulatory regime would be ineffective.

The potential for further regime transformation still exists. With the developing countries now on board, the regime can be further strengthened by speeding up the timetable for phaseout. Transformation can also take the form of regime weakening, and the developing countries or any other large country or group of countries can render the regime ineffective by forcing the countries to delay the final phaseout date.

Conclusion

The pattern of accession to the agreements indicates the changing salience of the ozone layer protection regime for developing countries. The Third World's low level of interest in the early phase of regime evolution is indicated by the fact that during the year[44] the Vienna Convention was open for signature, only 7 of the 28 signatories were Third World countries, and these did not include the most populous countries, which were potentially large users and producers of CFCs. The Third World signatories were Argentina, Burkina Faso, Chile, Egypt, Mexico, Morocco, and Peru. In contrast, all of the members of the Group of Seven, except for Japan, were signatories. The industrialized countries had a clear understanding of how this issue would affect their economic interests. As Table 4.2 shows, the Third World states were also slow to ratify the convention. By the time the Vienna Convention entered into force three and a half years after its adoption, only eight Third World states had ratified it, and this group did not include China, India, and Indonesia—the Third World states with the largest populations. These early ratifiers are equally divided between low- and middle-income states, but with the exception of Mexico and Venezuela, they are primarily exporters of services and nonfuel primary products.[45]

By the time of the Montreal Protocol, there was increased Third World interest, but the protocol was still unsatisfactory to that group's major actors. Consequently, at the time of its entry into force, only 6 of the 30 state parties were from the Third World. Once again, the parties were a mix of low- and middle-income states. With the exception of Uganda and Nigeria, they were primarily exporters of services and diversified exporters.[46]

With the London Amendment, we see a change of pattern among the Third World states. Ten of the 30 states that ratified the agreement before its entry into force were from that group of states. Because of the concessions made regarding the establishment of the fund, China, India, and Indonesia—the world's most populous countries—were among the early ratifiers. Most of the early ratifiers were low-income countries, and half were primarily diversified exporters.[47]

As Table 4.2 shows, the early ratifiers of the ozone protection agreements are drawn from a small group of 18 Third World states, less than 14 percent of that group. All are low- and middle-income states. High-income states are not represented; nor did they play high-profile roles in the negotiations. The largest major export categories represented are diversified exporters and nonfuel primary exporters.[48] China is the only country that is primarily an exporter of manufactures.

Finally, this group represents some of the Third World states for which the ozone issue is clearly salient, because of either circumstances or choice. For China and India, it is particularly relevant because of their large populations and growing industrial sectors. These two states, along with Egypt, Kenya, Mexico, and Venezuela, also chose to assertively represent the

Table 4.2 Third World States That Ratified the Ozone Protection Agreements Before Their Entry into Force

State	Vienna Convention	Montreal Protocol	London Amendment
Cameroon			x
Chile			x
China			x
Egypt	x	x	
Equatorial Guinea	x		
Ghana			x
Guatemala	x		
Guinea			x
India			x
Indonesia			x
Kenya		x	
Maldives	x		x
Malta	x	x	
Mexico	x	x	x
Nigeria		x	
Thailand			x
Uganda	x	x	
Venezuela	x		

Third World position in the negotiations. Additionally, the early ratifiers included states—such as China, Egypt, and Mexico—for which the issue had acquired salience because of their investment in alternate technologies.

Since the ozone issue had not acquired high salience for the Third World countries in the early stages of regime evolution, they were not involved in the definition of the ozone depletion problem; nor did they have leading roles in the evolution of the regime. They had very little input in the early negotiating sessions; however, as they began to become aware of the interests at stake, they gradually directed their energy toward modifying the regime.

Because of the unique characteristics of the atmosphere, developing countries were able to modify the evolution of the ozone protection regime. Ozone depletion involves the atmosphere, which is a common property resource. It is impossible to exclude users, and a situation of open access exists. This property and access arrangement had significant implications for negotiations and implementation. A proper perception of the common-property nature of the resource heightened the sense of interdependence and had implications for the nature of the bargaining. Developing countries have the ability to sabotage efforts to reverse the damage to the ozone layer; thus, the decisions could not be based simply on the international distribution of power. Consequently, parties and interests that wanted a successful ozone layer protection regime had to take the Third World's demands and interests into account.

The globalized nature of the biosphere also has significant implications for implementation. Given the nature of the ozone issue, regime implementation is dependent on the cooperation of all nation-states. It is crucial that the parties carry through with the fund provisions and with other commitments; otherwise, some developing countries may be unable to switch to technology that is not ozone-depleting.

The ozone layer protection regime has evolved gradually. In its early stages, the progress of the Toronto Group and its supporters was slowed by nations that perceived that their economic interests were threatened. Reluctance to set up a fund for the Third World also slowed the regime's progress. However, the dynamic nature of the Vienna Convention allowed the participants to react quickly to advances in scientific knowledge. The end result has been an environmental regime that is generally regarded as effective and viable. The perception of viability springs from the fact that the regime has responded to a technological problem with a technological solution. Because the ozone issue is primarily technological, it can be effectively addressed through the cooperation of the state and industrial sectors. Unlike other environmental problems, it does not require significant socioeconomic change.

Notes

1. Joseph G. Morone and Edward J. Woodhouse, *Averting Catastrophe: Strategies for Regulating Risky Technologies* (Berkeley: University of California Press, 1986).

2. Mario Molina and Sherwood Rowland, "Stratospheric Sink for Chlorofluoromethanes: Chlorine Atom Catalyses Destruction of Ozone," *Nature* 249 (June 1974): 810–812.

3. Peter M. Haas, "Banning Chlorofluorocarbons: Systemic Community Efforts to Protect Stratospheric Ozone," *International Organization* 46, no. 1 (Winter 1992): 199.

4. Mostafa K. Tolba and Osama A. El-Kholy, *The World Environment 1972–1992* (London: Chapman and Hall, 1992), 34.

5. Gareth Porter and Janet Welsh Brown, *Global Environmental Politics* (Boulder: Westview Press, 1991), 74–75.

6. Peter H. Sand, "Protecting the Ozone Layer," *Environment* 27 (June 1985): 18–20, 40–43; cited in Haas, "Banning Chlorofluorocarbons," 201.

7. Porter and Brown, *Global Environmental Politics,* 76.

8. Patrick Szell, "Negotiations on the Ozone Layer," in Gunnar Sjostedt, ed., *International Environmental Negotiation* (Newbury Park: Sage Publications, 1993), 33.

9. Porter and Brown, *Global Environmental Politics,* 77.

10. The 24 nations were Belgium, Canada, Denmark, Egypt, Finland, France, Germany (FRG), Ghana, Italy, Japan, Kenya, Mexico, the Netherlands, New Zealand, Norway, Panama, Portugal, Senegal, Sweden, Switzerland, Togo, the United Kingdom, the United States, and Venezuela. See United Nations, *Multilateral Treaties Deposited with the Secretary-General: Status as at 31 December 1992* (New York: UN, 1993), 827–828.

11. Tolba and El-Kholy, *World Environment,* 47

12. William K. Stevens, "Peril to Ozone Hastens a Ban on Chemicals," *New York Times,* November 26, 1992, A1.

13. World Resources Institute, *World Resources 1992–93* (New York: Oxford University Press, 1992), 152.

14. World Resources Institute, *World Resources 1994–95* (New York: Oxford University Press, 1994), 78.

15. Richard E. Benedick, "The Ozone Treaty: Acting Before the Disaster," *Washington Post,* January 4, 1988, A13.

16. World Resources Institute, *World Resources 1992–93,* 152–153.

17. Craig R. Whitney, "20 Nations Agree to Join Ozone Pact," *New York Times,* March 8, 1989, Section 1, 12.

18. Haas, "Banning Chlorofluorocarbons," 194–195.

19. The Toronto Group received that name because of a meeting held in Toronto at a critical stage in the negotiations on the Vienna Convention.

20. Szell, "Negotiations on the Ozone Layer," 36.

21. Ibid., 39.

22. Ibid.

23. Testimony of Richard Barnett, in U.S. Congress, Senate Committee on the Environment and Public Works, *Ozone Depletion, the Greenhouse Effect, and Climate Change: Joint Hearings Before the Subcommittee on Environmental Protection and Hazardous Wastes and Toxic Substances,* 100th Congress, 1st sess., 1987.

24. "DuPont Position Statement on the Chlorofluorocarbon-Ozone-Greenhouse Issues," *Environmental Conservation* 13 (Winter 1986): 363–364.

25. James K. Sebenius, "Challenging Conventional Explanations of International Cooperation: Negotiation Analysis and the Case of Epistemic Communities," *International Organization* 46, no. 1 (Winter 1992): 358.

26. David Doniger, "Politics of the Ozone Layer," *Issues in Science and Technology* (Spring 1988): 89.

27. Barbara J. Bramble and Gareth Porter, "Nongovernmental Organizations and the Making of US International Environmental Policy," in Andrew Hurrell and Benedict Kingsbury, eds., *The International Politics of the Environment: Actors, Interests and Institutions* (Oxford: Clarendon Press, 1992), 336–337.

28. Bramble and Porter, "Nongovernmental Organizations," 337–340.

29. Ibid., 336–339.

30. Haas, "Banning Chlorofluorocarbons," 194.

31. Ibid., 193.

32. Ibid., 196.

33. Szell, "Negotiations on the Ozone Layer," 32.

34. Porter and Brown, *Global Environmental Politics,* 75.

35. Ibid., 76.

36. Ibid.

37. Ibid.

38. Porter and Brown, *Global Environmental Politics,* 77.

39. Jonathan C. Randal, "Third World Seeks Aid Before Joining Ozone Pact," *Washington Post,* March 17, 1989, Section A, 16.

40. Craig R. Whitney, "20 Nations Agree to Join Ozone Pact," *New York Times,* March 8, 1989, Section 1, 12.

41. Porter and Brown, *Global Environmental Politics,* 78.

42. Szell, "Negotiations on the Ozone Layer," 35.

43. Ibid., 42–43.

44. The Vienna Convention was opened for signature from March 22, 1985, to March 21, 1986.

45. United Nations, *Multilateral Treaties Deposited with the Secretary-General,* 824–825.

46. Ibid., 827–828.

47. Ibid., 829.

48. According to the World Bank (*World Development Report 1993* [New York: Oxford University Press, 1993], 328–329), China, Egypt, Equatorial Guinea, Ghana, Guinea, India, Indonesia, Kenya, the Maldives, Nigeria, Thailand, and Uganda are low-income countries and Cameroon, Chile, Guatemala, Malta, Mexico, and Venezuela are middle-income countries. They fall into the following major export categories—services: Egypt, the Maldives, Malta; nonfuel primary products: Chile, Equatorial Guinea, Ghana, Guatemala, Guinea, and Uganda; diversified exports: Cameroon, India, Indonesia, Kenya, Mexico, and Thailand; fuel exports: Nigeria and Venezuela; manufactures: China.

5
THE HAZARDOUS WASTE TRADE REGIME

In the late 1980s, the media published a spate of news stories about the dumping of hazardous wastes in the developing world. In the wake of these incidents, hazardous waste trade moved near the top of the international environmental agenda. UNEP accelerated talks addressing the regulation of this trade, and the world's nations debated the issue, usually from a North-South perspective. These negotiations resulted in the 1989 Basel Convention, which established a "prior informed consent" system.

States were not the only actors that had an active interest in the talks. Nongovernmental organizations such as environmental groups and business organizations also played a role in the regime's evolution.

The convention, adopted in March 1989, entered into force in May 1992. It was strengthened in March 1994, when the contracting parties agreed to a complete ban on the shipping of hazardous waste from OECD states to non-OECD states.[1]

The Hazardous Waste Trade Problem

The term *hazardous waste* is flexibly defined, but it generally refers to material that poses a threat to human health and the environment, especially if it is not properly managed.[2] Waste materials usually described as hazardous waste include polychlorinated biphenyl, radioactive wastes, pesticides, toxic incinerator ash, chemical sludge, and organic solvents. Modern industry is the principal source of these wastes, with the major portion coming from the chemical industries.[3]

An estimated 90 percent of the world's hazardous wastes is generated by industrialized market economies.[4] The United States alone produces approximately 80 percent of the world's total output.[5] In many of the industrialized countries landfills and incinerators have been the major disposal options for these wastes, but producers are finding stricter regulations and fewer disposal options. As legislative efforts to regulate hazardous waste disposal have increased in these countries, and as citizen scrutiny of waste disposal has intensified, individual firms have sought disposal sites in other countries.

The main exporters of hazardous wastes in Western Europe have been the Netherlands, Belgium, France, Italy, and the Federal Republic of Germany.[6] All of these countries export significant percentages of the hazardous wastes they generate. The United States handles the major proportion of its wastes domestically, exporting only 1 percent—90 percent of this to Canada and the rest to Mexico.[7]

Most of the trade in hazardous wastes has occurred between industrialized countries, but it is estimated that as much as one-fifth of the total annual global trade in wastes goes from industrialized countries to developing countries.[8] Most Third World countries lack the technology or administrative capacity to dispose of the wastes safely, but this has not deterred industrialized country firms from continuing to export their wastes to these countries. One attraction of developing countries has been the low cost of disposal. According to one 1988 estimate, it cost up to US$2,500 per ton to dispose of highly toxic waste in the United States[9]; at that same time, this waste could be disposed of in some developing countries for as little as US$3 per ton.[10]

The countries targeted as cheap dumping grounds share the costs and not the benefits of industrialization. Some Third World governments have been tempted by offers of millions of dollars, but public opposition has been strong. As one example, in 1988 European toxic traders offered Guinea Bissau a sum four times its gross national product for taking 15 million tons of toxic wastes.[11] Although the waste shipments have sometimes followed contracts negotiated legally with developing country officials, in a number of cases the trade has proceeded without the approval of the host states, and it has sometimes involved bribing officials.

During the 1980s, some notorious instances of dumping in the Third World caught the public attention. One such case was the dumping of Italian waste in Koko, Nigeria, which occurred following an illegal arrangement between Italian businesspeople and Nigerian officials. A Nigerian citizen rented his backyard to an Italian businessman for about $100 per month, and the backyard became the dumping ground for five shipments of hazardous waste stored in more than 8,000 drums. The wastes included polychlorinated biphenyl, which is highly carcinogenic and toxic; in addition, some of the drums were leaking. Although the scheme was uncovered and the Italian government directed the removal of the wastes, there were significant health and environmental consequences for the workers who assisted in the removal and for the people who lived in the vicinity of the dump.[12] Many other such schemes were implemented in the 1980s, resulting in waste dumping in other Third World countries such as Namibia, Guinea, Haiti, and Sierra Leone.

The voyage of the *Khian Sea* illustrates the problem of finding disposal sites, and the story of its odyssey has some elements of farce. The ship carried 14,000 tons of incinerator ash from the United States. It wandered the oceans for 27 months, visiting five continents, in the attempt to find a country willing to take the ash. During the voyage, the ship's name was changed several times. Attempts to find a willing recipient proved futile, and the ash is believed to have been dumped somewhere in the Indian Ocean.[13]

Unlike the ozone issue, hazardous waste trade is considered a transboundary issue and is not seen as having the same commons implications as ozone depletion. This no doubt has affected the level of cooperation of some of the major industrial nations.

Evolution of the Hazardous Waste Trade Regime

Although the bulk of the hazardous waste trade has occurred between developed countries, the issue gained prominence on the international agenda because of the increasing numbers of illegal hazardous waste shipments to developing countries. As a result of numerous reports of illegal shipments, in 1982 UNEP decided to address the issue.

The framing of the problem as a North-South issue shaped the debate and set the tone for the ensuing negotiations. The focus of concern was the toxic nature of the substances and materials. The impression was that developed countries were exporting the costs of their own development. Issues of both private and state responsibility and liability stoked public interest and opinion. Until the start of the negotiations on the international convention, there was little regulation of transboundary movement of hazardous wastes. This was convenient since it allowed governments and industries to avoid incurring major cost increases and causing concern among local populations.

As a result of concerns over the illegal traffic, the UNEP Governing Council initiated regulations at the global level. In 1985, a working group produced the Cairo Guidelines and Principles for Environmentally Sound Management of Hazardous Wastes, which were adopted by the UNEP Governing Council in June 1987. The Cairo Guidelines represented the first attempt to address the issue from a global perspective. The guidelines established procedures for managing and disposing of hazardous wastes, specifying prior notification of the state receiving any export, consent by the receiving state prior to export, and verification by the source state that the receiving state's disposal requirements were at least as stringent as those of the source state.

However, the guidelines' declarations were soft-law instruments and therefore were considered nonbinding.[14] In addition, many of the recipient states—notably some of the African states—did not feel the Cairo Guidelines properly addressed their concerns. They wanted hazardous waste trade banned rather than regulated because from their perspective, this trade was a form of exploitation.

At the regional level, some states had already begun to address the issues of the transboundary movement and disposal of hazardous wastes. At Switzerland's initiative, efforts then moved to negotiations on a global convention. A working group of legal and technical experts was established to organize the convention's work, and the organizational meeting of this working group took place in Budapest, Hungary. These initial meetings were followed by a series of meetings that led to a plenipotentiary conference in Basel, Switzerland, in March 1989, at which participants adopted the Basel Convention on the Control of Transboundary Movements of Hazardous Wastes and Their Disposal.[15]

Concurrent with the negotiations, discussion of the issue was also taking place between Third World and industrialized states outside of UN forums. In 1988 the EC joined with representatives from the 68 former colonies in Africa, the Caribbean, and the Pacific in demanding a ban on international trade in wastes.[16]

In theory, the developing states should have been able to deny waste-exporting states access to their countries, but their internal administrative weaknesses made this difficult. The exporting states demanded an informed consent regime, which would require waste exporters to notify their governments of any exports and to notify receiving countries of any shipments prior to their arrival.[17] The developing countries were unable to effect any significant changes in the developed countries' position. At the final meeting in Basel, Switzerland, in March 1989, the veto coalition—led by the United States—gave the waste-importing states an ultimatum: They had to either accept an informed consent regime or settle for the status quo. The Organization of African Unity (OAU) tried to modify this regime. The OAU's amendments would have prevented the export of wastes to countries that did not have the same level of facilities and technology as the exporting nations and would also have required inspection of disposal sites by UN inspectors. But the veto coalition stood its ground, and the industrialized countries rejected the amendments.[18]

The principal provisions of the Basel Convention include the following:

1. Hazardous waste generation is to be reduced to a minimum.[19]
2. The convention provides for prior informed consent, requiring that an importing state and any transit state be notified by, and give consent to, the exporting state before transboundary movement of waste may take place.[20]
3. As a prerequisite to any transboundary movement, the convention requires environmentally sound disposal of hazardous waste. However, "environmentally sound" is not defined in the convention.[21]
4. Under convention rules, any state has the sovereign right to ban

imports, and other parties are prohibited from exporting to states which have notified the secretariat of such import bans.[22] States belonging to an economic and/or political integration organization with legislation prohibiting all waste imports are also protected by this prohibition.[23]

5. Convention obligations apply to both recycling and disposal operations, since recycling also has the potential for environmental damage.[24]
6. Transboundary movements carried out in violation of the convention are considered illegal.[25]
7. Developing countries are entitled to receive technical assistance from developed countries that are parties to the convention, whether or not the former accept or ban imports.[26]

Many environmental groups and developing country governments see the Basel Convention's informed consent system as either inadequate or a step backward. This system allows hazardous wastes to be exported to countries whose facilities for storage are less advanced than those of the exporting country as long as the importing state has received detailed information on the waste shipment and given prior written consent. Agreements between signatory states and nonsignatory states are permitted. Critics charge that the convention goes no further than existing regulations in industrialized countries, which have failed to curb legal or illegal waste trade. Moreover, the enforceability of the convention is weakened by the lack of precision on key definitions, such as "environmentally sound" and "hazardous wastes," and by inadequate enforcement and liability provisions.

A major concern of some interested parties is that the Basel Convention will institutionalize the hazardous waste trade. Greenpeace, for example, has denounced the Basel Convention for the following reasons.[27]

1. The convention does not ban the trading of hazardous waste. Instead, it provides a legal framework within which to trade this waste.[28]
2. Since industrial interests are still able to export their waste problems cheaply, the convention does not discourage waste generation.[29]
3. Given the national and international power asymmetries, the prior informed consent procedures of the convention cannot adequately address the double standards inherent in waste trade.[30]
4. Article 1 can be interpreted as excluding radioactive waste from the scope of the convention.[31]
5. The convention allows exports to nonparties.[32]
6. It contains no liability provisions.[33]
7. The narrow definition of waste management excludes waste prevention measures.[34]

This perception of the convention is also seen in the contempt expressed by industry representatives. A lobbyist for the U.S. Chamber of Commerce remarked that the convention would have little impact on the international waste trade because "no real countries have ratified the Basel Convention."[35]

Developing countries and environmental NGOs continued to press for a total ban on exports of hazardous wastes and products. They took the position that regulating the trade was a way of legitimizing it. Some exporting countries argued, however, that bans violated an importer's sovereign right to make a decision regarding accepting the wastes in exchange for financial or other benefits. As it turned out, in the debate over the Basel Accord the developed countries were more concerned with the sovereign rights of receiving states than were the Third World countries themselves. Many countries have acted on their dissatisfaction with the Basel Accord by adopting stronger regional or national measures.

Ninety-four Third World countries[36] adopted complete unilateral bans on hazardous waste imports; however, China and India, the world's most populous states, were not among this group. Some industrialized countries were also in favor of transforming the Basel Convention from an agreement that merely regulated the hazardous waste trade to one that imposed a complete ban.[37] In March 1990, as part of the Lome Agreement, the EC agreed to stop exporting waste to the 69 countries in Africa, the Caribbean, and the Pacific that are former colonies of EC members; the former colonies agreed not to accept any waste imports. However, a 1992 EC redefinition of the term *hazardous waste* has made the agreement less meaningful than it seemed at first.

Regional agreements were concluded in Africa and Latin America. For example, the Bamako Convention, signed in 1991 by 10 African countries, bans waste imports to the African continent. Central American governments also united against hazardous waste trade. In December 1992 the presidents of Guatemala, El Salvador, Honduras, Nicaragua, Costa Rica, and Panama signed an Agreement on Transboundary Movements of Hazardous Wastes in the Central American Region as part of the regional effort to stop waste export schemes. According to Greenpeace Central America, the region faced at least 54 schemes to import foreign wastes between 1985 and 1993.[38] The Pacific region also started to move toward imposing a regional waste ban. The South Pacific Forum[39] planned to begin negotiations on a convention in 1994, with an agreement completed by the group's 1995 meeting.[40]

In early 1992, at the final preparatory meeting for the United Nations Conference on Environment and Development in New York, government representatives and environmental activists from Africa, Asia, Latin America, and the Pacific proposed a ban on hazardous waste trade from the industrialized to the less industrialized regions of the world. However, this initiative was blocked by the United States and other industrialized countries.

The first meeting of the 35 parties to the Basel Convention occurred in Uruguay from November 30 to December 4, 1992. Six months after the convention entered into force, the polarization between the industrialized countries that were trying to expand the waste trade and the countries that were trying to ban this trade was still evident. UNEP executive director Mostafa Tolba used this opportunity to try to strengthen the convention. Noting that the Basel Convention had done little to halt "toxic terrorism," he proposed a complete ban on waste shipments to developing countries and Eastern Europe. Hazardous wastes were following the path of lower costs and lower standards, and Basel's rules requiring prior notification had had little impact.

Tolba's proposal would have effectively halted exports of wastes from OECD to non-OECD countries, and it received strong support from developing countries and a few industrialized countries. For example, Finland, Denmark, Norway, Switzerland, Italy, and Sweden endorsed a complete ban on waste exports from OECD to non-OECD countries. But a group of industrialized countries managed to block this trade ban. Particularly strong opposition came from the United States, Germany, Canada, Australia, the United Kingdom, and Japan.[41] The meeting's final resolution merely requested that industrialized countries stop disposing of hazardous wastes in developing countries; however, exports for "recovery operations"—which include use as fuel, treatment of land for agricultural purposes, and reuse of previously used oil—are exempted from this request. Developing countries, represented by the Group of 77, expressed their dissatisfaction with the compromise decision.[42]

The exception made for recovery operations has been particularly troubling for the developing countries since exporters used it to justify most of their 1992 waste trade schemes that targeted developing countries. Many industrialized country actors are proponents of "free trade" in everything, including hazardous waste, and some industrialists are trying to make the practice more palatable by renaming it "recycling trade." More than 90 percent of the 1992 waste schemes claimed some sort of "recycling," "reuse," or "humanitarian" benefit.

Some developing countries, including Bolivia and Mexico, that do not accept waste for disposal do accept it for recycling or recovery. Although this may appear to be a somewhat more benign practice, the by-products of the recycling and recovery operations can be dangerous to public health. The facilities in the Third World are often ill equipped to handle these toxic products; some plants keep no inventory of toxic emissions and have no air emissions filters.[43]

Greenpeace investigations discovered that in 1992 alone, Western Europe and the United States shipped toxic wastes to Albania, Bangladesh, Brazil, China, Egypt, Estonia, Georgia, Indonesia, the Marshall Islands, Mexico, Namibia, Palau, the Philippines, Romania, Slovenia, Turkey, and the

Ukraine.[44] Bangladesh was the target of one particularly underhanded scheme. The government purchased more than 3,000 tons of fertilizer from a U.S. company. The company allegedly mixed 1,000 tons of toxic copper-smelting furnace dust into the fertilizer before shipping it to Bangladesh. Much of the fertilizer had been spread on fields before the toxic components were discovered. Tests by the South Carolina Department of Health and Environmental Control revealed hazardous levels of lead and cadmium.[45] Given the flexibility of the "recovery operations" concept, this particular export could possibly be considered to be recovery use for agricultural purposes.

By March 1994, the veto coalition had eroded enough to allow a formal strengthening of the Basel Convention. As Table 5.1 indicates, the contracting parties were able to agree on a complete ban on hazardous waste trade from OECD to non-OECD countries. If effectively enforced, this regulation was to protect the developing world, the countries of Eastern Europe, and the former Soviet Union. The ban, which took effect immediately, prohibited OECD states from sending hazardous wastes for final disposal in any nonmember country. A grace period was allowed for the export of wastes for recycling or recovery, which will become illegal after December 31, 1997. The United States, the only OECD country that is not a party to the convention, lobbied vigorously against the ban. Initially, the United States had support from Australia, Canada, and Germany, but eventually these states decided to support the total ban.[46]

Table 5.1 International Policy Actions on the Regulation of Hazardous Waste Trade

1985	Working group produces the Cairo Guidelines and Principles for the Environmentally Sound Management of Hazardous Wastes.
June 1987	Cairo Guidelines adopted by UNEP Governing Council, and working group is convened to organize global convention.
March 1989	The Basel Convention is adopted.
January 1991	The Bamako Convention is adopted. It bans waste imports to the African continent.
May 1992	The Basel Convention enters into force.
December 1992	The Central American states of Guatemala, El Salvador, Honduras, Nicaragua, Costa Rica, and Panama agree to ban imports of hazardous waste into their region.
March 1994	Parties to the Basel Convention agree to place a complete ban on the shipping of hazardous wastes from member nations of the OECD to non-OECD states. The ban is to be fully in effect by December 31, 1997.

Actors and Interests

Although states were the principal actors in the negotiations, this issue was also of major interest to other national and transnational actors. For example, many major enterprises are involved in the transboundary movements of hazardous wastes. Representatives of these enterprises were allowed to participate in negotiating sessions as nongovernmental organizations. Environmental organizations such as Greenpeace also played a prominent lobbying role.

At the start of the negotiations, most of the actors seemed to share common interests. However, during the course of the negotiations, this basic consensus eroded, and some parties began to feel they would be better off without the proposed agreement. Because last-minute compromises could not accommodate all interests, some countries were reluctant to sign the agreement.[47]

The Nation-States

Because of the issue's strong political profile and its relevance to sovereignty issues, as stated previously, states were the major actors in the negotiations. Although the lines of demarcation were primarily North-South, not all of the participants held strong positions on one side or the other. Some delegations, including those from Lebanon, Egypt, Finland, Sweden, Norway, and Austria, had no stated positions on the disputed issues.[48]

The Third World. Most Third World states took the position that no transboundary movement of wastes should be allowed, except when such movement took place simultaneously with the transfer of adequate and environmentally sound technology. This position was put forward forcefully by the African states, many of which had been the targets of hazardous waste schemes. Their position was also actively supported by Brazil, India, and China.[49] Although participation in such trade would provide these countries with the opportunity to earn badly needed foreign exchange, their experience during the past decade had made them aware of the dangers involved. In addition, there was significant public sentiment against being the dumping ground for the refuse of the developed world's industrialization.

Although there was general agreement among the Third World states on this issue, there was not complete unanimity. For example, Mexico was associated with the industrialized states' position, which favored management of the trade rather than an outright ban.[50] This stance was probably influenced by the operation of Mexico's maquiladora zone, which is a major producer of toxic waste.[51]

Third World countries did not focus on the fact that they were on occasion the sources of hazardous waste. In 1990, the Bahamas, Brazil, Jordan, Mexico, Panama, the Philippines, Singapore, and Uruguay exported hazardous wastes to a mix of industrialized and Third World countries,[52] but even these source states generally opposed the trade. The primary beneficiaries were the trading corporations, not the states themselves.

The industrialized states. Many developed countries saw the hazardous waste trade as merely another component of global trade. Consistent with the dominant philosophy of free trade, they wanted as few restrictions as possible. For them, there were two major advantages to exporting hazardous wastes to poor countries, one primarily economic and the other political. The economic advantage was that disposal was markedly cheaper in the Third World. From the political perspective, disposal in the Third World also meant that the developed countries would be spared the difficult and contentious task of selecting new disposal sites within their own borders. Well-publicized hazardous waste incidents such as Love Canal made this task increasingly difficult.[53]

Major waste exporters, producers, and transit countries had particularly strong interests in maintaining the hazardous waste trade. This group included the United States, the member states of the EC (especially the United Kingdom, France, the Netherlands, Belgium, and the Federal Republic of Germany), Canada, Switzerland, the former German Democratic Republic, and Romania, as well as the former Soviet Union. Although these countries were willing to accept some regulations to manage the trade, they were against a total ban.

Nongovernmental Organizations

Although NGOs did not have voting privileges, they used every opportunity to advance their interests. They were present at the negotiating sessions, and they lobbied for their viewpoint as the circumstances allowed.

Transnational corporations. TNCs were concerned that strict regulations or total bans would result in increases in the cost of doing business. Since public law regulations were at stake, they played an important role in the negotiations. They wanted to retain access to the lower-cost disposal options that were possible in the Third World.

TNCs also had an interest in retaining waste sinks for chemical wastes, contaminated plastics, pesticides, nuclear wastes, and incinerator ash. Major corporations involved in hazardous waste trade include Siemens of West Germany, Boeing of the United States, and Ciba-Geigy of Switzerland.[54]

Environmental NGOs. Major environmental NGOs set high goals and pursued an aggressive course of action throughout the negotiations. Greenpeace, for example, tracked waste shipments and attempted to influence regime evolution through the compilation of data in periodicals and books.[55] These NGOs wanted to see a ban on transboundary waste shipments imposed, but they also wanted the agreement to address the issues of waste generation and disposal standards.[56]

The Third World in the Regime's Evolution

Prior to 1984 the hazardous waste issue had not been considered a major problem; nor did it seem to be politically difficult. As the negotiations on the Basel Convention got underway, however, that began to change. Although the first session, in 1987, revealed some of the problems inherent in developing a solution for the problem, the participants did not become polarized over the issue until early 1988. With this change, the talks shifted from a focus on technical and administrative details to a political North-South confrontation.

Defining the Problem

An integral part of the problem definition process is a determination of the scope of the problem. Was the essence of the problem the trade itself, or was the issue the fact that the trade was poorly managed? An answer to that question would determine whether regime negotiations should be addressing the management of the hazardous waste trade or whether the intent should be a total trade ban.

Many of the recipient states wanted hazardous waste trade banned rather than regulated. They saw it as a form of exploitation of the poor states by industrialized countries and transnational corporations. There was some support for the position of these states by European officials and EC parliamentarians.[57] For example, the Dutch minister of the environment characterized the hazardous waste trade as "waste colonialism." However, major developed world interests, including the United States, insisted that the problem should be defined as the regulation of the hazardous waste trade. Therefore, the Third World countries were not able to redefine the issue to suit their interests, and although they still pressed for a ban, the bargaining focused on the regulation of the waste trade.

Neither the Third World countries nor the developed states pressed for a definition that would address the major problem underlying the hazardous waste trade: the polluting and toxic nature of many industrial processes. Although NGOs such as Greenpeace identified the existence of dirty industries as a significant problem to be addressed, the priority for the developing countries was the issue of the hazardous waste trade.

Bargaining

The bargaining process began in 1987 when the working group started to frame a global convention on the control of the international trade in hazardous wastes. In the series of meetings held over the next year and a half, major differences emerged between the African states and the industrialized countries: The African states continued to press for a total ban on hazardous waste exports, and the source states wanted to be able to continue exporting their wastes.[58]

By early 1988 coalitions had begun to form. Developing countries aligned themselves according to their special interests. Industrialized countries were slower to form similar coalitions; they tended instead to coordinate their strategies on an ad hoc basis. The coalition of socialist countries played a minimal role; only a few participated in the negotiations, and they ultimately joined forces with the industrialized countries.

As stated previously, some prominent members of the negotiating group had no stated positions on negotiating issues.[59] In some cases these delegations had not received detailed instructions from their governments; in other cases their countries became aware of the political significance of the negotiations only at a late date. This lack of a position allowed them the latitude to play important roles in the negotiations. The Third World countries' negotiating position was that no transboundary waste shipments were to be allowed except simultaneously with the transfer of adequate and environmentally sound technology; industrialized countries found this position unacceptable. In turn, developed countries wanted to expand the scope of the convention to control all wastes and ensure their environmentally sound disposal, but developing countries found this unacceptable.[60]

A number of strategic negotiating techniques were used to influence the negotiations, including press leaks and the manipulation of the rules of procedure. Because of the ad hoc nature of some meetings, the rules of procedure became increasingly important, and decisions were made in the meetings as to which of these were to be followed. The chair of the negotiations and the members of the secretariat were able to influence the choice of rules, and the rules changed from meeting to meeting. In the early meetings, the rules of procedure allowed a proposal to be adopted as long as five country delegations did not oppose it. Later, if five country delegates supported a proposal, it was adopted.[61] Consequences of these changing rules included intensive informal consultations, regular meetings of the coalitions, and regular bureau meetings with the participation of the secretariat.

In spring 1988 developing countries raised several new issues for inclusion in the convention, consequently widening the scope of the undertaking. Although these countries formally advanced the issues, NGOs such as Greenpeace assisted with the drafting of proposals for the convention text. Environmental NGOs wanted the hazardous waste issue to be addressed in a more comprehensive manner, and they aired their positions through public relations campaigns and media coverage. They also lobbied developing country representatives and intervened in the capitals of the chief negotiating delegations, particularly the Western countries such as the United States, the United Kingdom, the Federal Republic of Germany, and Austria.

This lobbying led to a change in the original position of some developing countries. For example, the initial negotiating goal of the OAU members was to control transboundary movements of hazardous wastes, but they changed their position to encompass issues such as minimizing waste generation at the source; disposing of wastes within the territory of the waste-generating country, with a few exceptions for environmental or economic reasons; limiting exports of hazardous wastes to countries with at least the same disposal standards as the source country; and instituting "inclusion" of disposal standards. The North-South issues introduced at this phase remained a concern until the end of the negotiations the following year.[62]

Because of the implications of the regulations for the conduct of business, industry representatives lobbied against the imposition of stringent control regulations. These representatives had full access to the delegations of developed countries, but after the focus shifted from technical and administrative details to a political North-South confrontation, their interests were not at the center of the negotiations.[63]

The UNEP secretariat also had a prominent role in the negotiations. The executive director, Mostafa Tolba, played a key role in several ways: He prepared proposals for each negotiating session; he intervened orally in the ongoing negotiations; he attempted to influence the positions of active negotiators; he provided statements to the media; and he successfully pushed for small changes in the rules of procedure, consequently influencing the course of action. On many occasions, Tolba took on the role of mediator in order to facilitate the adoption of compromise solutions, which in principle favored developing country interests.[64]

Negotiators and lobbying groups sometimes changed their positions when they gained a new perspective on how they would be affected by specific provisions. One example involves provisions relating to illegal traffic and state responsibility. Initially, developing countries presumed that this language applied only to industrialized countries. Late in the negotiations, however, Third World participants realized that the provisions were likely to apply to their own countries and citizens. They then proposed language that would have restricted some obligations to developed countries only, but the new language was not included in the final text of the convention.[65]

By playing to the media and adopting aggressive negotiating tactics, developing countries acquired a dominant role in the negotiation process. They were able to put developed countries on the defensive by overstating the level of illegal wastes being transported from developed to developing countries. Television coverage also underlined the North-South dimension of the problem. Developing countries' aggressive negotiating tactics were aimed at maximum protection of their interests. Because they constituted an overall majority, their compromise proposals were widely adopted. The bulk of hazardous waste trade took place between industrialized states; thus in the early stages these countries were primarily concerned with regulations relating to transboundary movements among themselves, and they initially left large areas of the negotiations to developing countries. However, when each side realized that it would be affected by all of the provisions, every issue was reviewed.[66]

In order to gain the support of the industrialized countries, the Third World countries had to settle for a prior informed consent regime. The veto coalition stood its ground and rejected the amendments that would have provided for adequate and safe disposal in the Third World.

Developing states and NGOs continued to press for regime strengthening both at meetings of the parties to the convention and outside the official forums. This eventually resulted in the ban announced in March 1994. Although the concession led to a formal strengthening of the regime to manage hazardous waste trade, it did little to change the existing situation. In fact, most non-OECD destinations were already closed to the OECD states, and some OECD states had already decided not to engage in the hazardous waste trade. The concessions made by the major OECD states that were parties to the convention were merely an acceptance of the status quo. The OECD states were formally recognizing that the developing countries did not want to be dumping grounds, and they were making a commitment not to seize advantages that were not willingly proffered.

Regime Transformation

As regimes go, the hazardous waste trade regime is a young regime that is undergoing rapid transformation. The signing of the Basel Convention began a new phase of bargaining for a stronger regime; at the same time, however, some industrialized countries began to work toward weakening the already weak agreement.

For their part, the Third World countries achieved success in their aim to strengthen the regime with the ban on the export of hazardous wastes to non-OECD countries. Whether the strengthening is apparent rather than real depends on whether it can be implemented successfully.

Industrialized states have also begun a series of actions that could result in the weakening of the Basel Convention. In April 1992 the OECD[67] adopted a regulation that allows uncontrolled trade in wastes as long as the wastes are bound for recycling facilities.[68] Since the amended Basel Convention allows export of wastes for recycling or recovery until December 31, 1997, this OECD regulation has significant implications for the nature and volume of the continuing hazardous waste trade. The OECD has switched to a three-tiered approach to recyclable wastes known as the "red, amber, green" system. Only red-listed wastes were to be regulated according to Basel Convention provisions. Items on the amber list could be put on a fast track that allows preconsent for particular facilities.

This regulation has effectively removed several well-known poisons—including lead, cadmium, and chromium—from the hazardous waste list by green-listing them,[69] which undercuts Basel Convention provisions. The OECD's new definition of hazardous wastes thus contradicts its own previously established definitions, which were embodied in the convention.

This decision gained greater significance later that year. When the EC drafted its regulation dealing with waste shipments in October 1992, it exempted the green-listed wastes from much of the regulation, which applies to non-OECD countries as well. The EC is also a party to the Lome IV Convention and the Basel Convention, and the new OECD definition is inconsistent with both. Article 39 of the Lome Convention forbids any Basel waste from being exported from the EC to the 69 African, Caribbean, and Pacific states.[70] Consequently, the EC would be in violation of both the Basel Convention and the Lome IV Convention if it exported green-listed wastes to a non-OECD Basel party or an ACP country without adopting any controls.[71] The concern is that the OECD countries will weaken the Basel Convention to make it consistent with the new OECD definition of hazardous wastes.

Ongoing changes in the global division of labor might render the Basel Convention meaningless within a few decades. Developed country industries are shifting complete operations to parts of the world where environmental regulations are relatively lenient. The finished products are then shipped back to the head office's home country, where consumers get the benefit of the product while shifting the environmental costs of production onto others. For example, Greenpeace is tracking a shift of new plant investment for organochlorides from the developed world to the developing world. Organochlorides are highly toxic and cause a broad range of damage to a wide array of species. Greenpeace has identified 50 new chlorine-related facilities in Brazil, India, Indonesia, and Thailand, with startup dates ranging from 1993 to 1996.[72] The shift of dirty industries would have occurred with or without the hazardous waste regulations because of both the prevailing global economic logic and the social and political pressure within industrialized nations. This industrial transformation will change the basis of the debate from the management of the hazardous waste trade to the transition to cleaner production methods.

Conclusion

The ratification process for the Basel Convention was slow, with more than three years elapsing between adoption and entry into force. This was largely because the final agreement was satisfactory for neither the Third World nor the industrialized states. Developed countries were looking for an agreement that would manage transboundary movements of hazardous wastes without imposing negative consequences through strict controls. Developing countries saw the negotiations as an opportunity to impose a ban on the hazardous waste trade; failing that, they wanted a transfer of technology for activities related to waste disposal.[73] The product of the negotiations—the Basel Convention—was an unsatisfactory compromise; however, continued pressure by the Third World and environmental NGOs finally led to its strengthening.

By the time the convention entered into force in May 1992, 22 states had ratified it, including 11 Third World states: Argentina, China, El Salvador, Jordan, the Maldives, Mexico, Nigeria, Panama, Saudi Arabia, the Syrian Arab Republic, and Uruguay. They had proceeded with ratification in spite of the convention's shortcomings; major industrialized countries were slow to join them. The fact that France was the only early ratifier from the Group of Seven is an indication of the regime's salience for the major industrialized states. The early ratifiers from the Third World represented all five major export categories, with the largest group being primarily exporters of services. There is less diversity with regard to income group: Eight of the 11 are middle-income states.[74] Most also share the distinction of being targeted for hazardous waste exports; a Greenpeace inventory for 1990 indicated that Argentina, China, El Salvador, Mexico, Nigeria, Panama, the Syrian Arab Republic, and Uruguay were such targets.[75] In addition, Jordan, Mexico, Panama, and Uruguay were identified as exporting countries in 1990.[76] Although there was dissatisfaction with the Basel Convention and, consequently, no rush to ratify, most of the early ratifiers from the Third World were states for which the issue had salience.

The Third World countries were actively and aggressively involved in the issue definition process, but they were unsuccessful at getting their definition of the problem accepted as the basis for the negotiations. Throughout the bargaining process, they continued their efforts to redefine the problem. In spite of both their strong negotiating stance and the supporting media campaign conducted by environmental NGOs, the Third World countries had to be satisfied with a prior informed consent regime. However, as a part of the regime transformation process, the problem was eventually redefined from one of managing the trade to one of banning it.

In the years since Basel, there has been some erosion in the unity of the industrialized states. Some of these states accept the fact that the trade is waste colonialism; others bow to the inevitability of the growing numbers of unilateral bans. But there are still some holdouts, including the United States. When a major producer of waste does not become a party to the waste trade convention, implementation becomes more difficult.

The globalized economy has conditioned the decisions corporations make about the hazardous waste trade. Companies want access to the lowest-cost waste sinks, and many of these happen to be in the Third World. Corporate actors have been able to find ways of thwarting the intent of the Basel Convention, including the use of loopholes such as export for recycling or recovery operations. The consequence of this activity is that the industrialized countries continue to pass on some of the costs of their development to the Third World. Unlike the case of the ozone layer protection regime, the reality of a globalized environment imposes no constraints on industrialized countries' hazardous waste policies because the hazardous waste problem is not a commons problem; as a result, no sense of interdependence and shared vulnerability exists. The waste trade is a transboundary issue, and industrialized countries can distance themselves from the costs of their actions.

The ban will not be completely in effect until December 1997, so the Third World's best option at this stage seems to be to retain unilateral bans on the import of wastes. According to Greenpeace, states that moved quickly to ban waste imports in the late 1980s have rarely been targeted for waste disposal; those without bans have been more likely targets.[77] But the imposition of an import ban is no panacea for the hazardous waste trade. Measures for implementation and monitoring have to be in place, and they must be effective. The fact that a state has acceded to the treaty does not necessarily result in convention compliance. The bulk of the waste is shipped by private corporations rather than by public entities. Although these corporations are legally subject to the states, many powerful corporations are not easily regulated. In addition, many Third World states do not have the technical and administrative personnel to properly enforce import bans.

When the complete hazardous waste trade ban comes into effect, the Third World countries will receive the remedy they sought. Whether this remedy eventually effects a cure depends on two things: how effectively the ban is enforced, and how dramatic the shift of dirty industry to the Third World becomes. After all, the essential problem is the use of polluting production methods. Industries have found it less expensive to shift to areas of lower production cost and less restrictive regulations than to clean up or transform their industrial processes. This shift is an effort to delay addressing these externalities in a coherent manner. If the short- and medium-term impact of the strengthened Basel Convention is to hasten the transfer of dirty industries to the non-OECD countries, the parties to the Basel Convention may well find that their focus on trade was misplaced. Within the Third World, this shift of industries will fuel the ongoing debate regarding the extent to which environmental compromises should be made in the service of economic growth.

Notes

1. Paul Lewis, "Western Lands, Except U.S., Ban Export of Hazardous Waste," *New York Times*, March 26, 1994, Section I, 3.

2. The United States Environmental Protection Agency bases its determination of whether waste is hazardous on the presence of certain characteristics, such as ignitability, reactivity, corrosivity, and toxicity.

3. Mostafa K. Tolba and Osama A. El-Kholy, *The World Environment 1972–1992* (London: Chapman and Hall, 1992), 261.

4. Gareth Porter and Janet Welsh Brown, *Global Environmental Politics* (Boulder: Westview Press, 1991), 85. Also Greenpeace, *Toxic Trade Update* 5, no. 2: 5–6 (1992), cites Mostafa Tolba as saying that about 98 to 99 percent of all hazardous waste is produced by the developed countries, if this group is seen as including the Commonwealth of Independent States.

5. Tolba and El-Kholy, *World Environment*, 264; also, Charles E. Davis (*The Politics of Hazardous Waste* [Englewood Cliffs: Prentice Hall, 1993], 4) cites a study by the Congressional Budget Office that concluded that approximately 266 million metric tons of hazardous wastes are generated in the United States annually.

6. With the reunification of the Federal Republic of Germany and the German Democratic Republic, the waste exports are now from the state of Germany.

7. Porter and Brown, *Global Environmental Politics*, 85.

8. Ibid. Other estimates have placed this at 10 percent. This is the estimate of the UNEP Environmental Law and Institutions Unit, cited in Greenpeace International, "Annotations by Greenpeace International on the Agenda of the Meeting, Prepared for the First Conference of Parties to the Basel Convention 30 November–4 December 1992, Piriapolis, Uruguay" (published by Greenpeace International), 2.

9. Philip Shabecoff, "Irate and Afraid, Poor Nations Fight Efforts to Use Them as Toxic Dumps," *New York Times*, July 5, 1988, C4.

10. James Brooke, "Waste Dumpers Turning to West Africa," *New York Times*, July 17, 1988, A1.

11. Jim Vallette and Heather Spalding, eds., *The International Trade in Wastes: A Greenpeace Inventory* (Washington, D.C.: Greenpeace USA, 1990), 5.

12. Ibid., 94–95.

13. Ibid., 21–25.

14. Tolba and El-Kholy, *World Environment*, 747. They describe soft-law instruments as "nonbinding guidelines and principles adopted as guidance at the regional and global level—which foster more uniform standards and practices among nations and which may ultimately be incorporated into either binding international legal agreements or national law."

15. Willy Kempel, "Transboundary Movements of Hazardous Wastes," in Gunnar Sjostedt, ed., *International Environmental Negotiation* (Newbury Park: Sage Publications, 1993), 50. Kempel represented Austria at the negotiations on the Basel Convention.

16. Porter and Brown, *Global Environmental Politics*, 86; also Vallette and Spalding, *International Trade*, 10.

17. Porter and Brown, *Global Environmental Politics*, 86–87.

18. Ibid., 87.

19. United Nations Environment Programme, *Basel Convention on the Control of Transboundary Movements of Hazardous Wastes and Their Disposal*. Final Act. March 1989, Article 4, paragraph 2(a).

20. Ibid., Articles 6 and 7.
21. Ibid., Article 4, paragraph 8.
22. Ibid., Preamble, paragraph 6; Article 4, paragraph 1(a) and 1(b).
23. Ibid., Article 4(e).
24. Ibid., Annex 4.
25. Ibid., Article 9.
26. Ibid., Article 10.
27. "Basel Convention Now in Force," *Toxic Trade Update* 5, no. 2 (1992): 5–6.
28. United Nations Environment Programme, *Basel Convention,* Article 4.
29. Ibid., Article 6.
30. Ibid.
31. Ibid., Article 1.
32. Ibid., Article 11.
33. Ibid., Article 12.
34. Ibid., Article 2.
35. "Notable Quote," *Toxic Trade Update* 5, no. 2 (1992): 5. Based on the timing of the remarks, the states dismissed as not being "real countries" include Argentina, Mexico, Norway, Saudi Arabia, Sweden, and Switzerland.
36. According to *Toxic Trade Update* ("The 94 Countries Which Strictly Prohibit Waste Trade," 6, no. 2 [1993]: 7), as of June 1993 the countries strictly prohibiting hazardous waste were the following: Algeria, Angola, Antigua and Barbuda, the Bahamas, Barbados, Belize, Benin, Botswana, Burkina Faso, Burundi, Cameroon, Cape Verde, the Central African Republic, Chad, Chile, Colombia, Comoros, the Congo, Costa Rica, Côte d'Ivoire, Djibouti, Dominica, the Dominican Republic, Ecuador, Egypt, El Salvador, Equatorial Guinea, Ethiopia, Fiji, Gabon, Gambia, Ghana, Grenada, Guatemala, Guinea, Guinea Bissau, Guyana, Haiti, Honduras, Indonesia, Jamaica, Kenya, Kiribati, Latvia, Lebanon, Lesotho, Liberia, Libya, Lithuania, Madagascar, Malawi, Mali, Mauritania, Mauritius, Mozambique, Namibia, Nicaragua, Niger, Nigeria, Panama, Papua New Guinea, Peru, the Philippines, Poland, Portugal, Romania, Rwanda, St. Kitts and Nevis, St. Lucia, St. Vincent and Grenadines, Sao Tome and Principe, Senegal, Seychelles, Sierra Leone, the Solomon Islands, Somalia, Sudan, Surinam, Swaziland, Tanzania, Togo, Tonga, Trinidad and Tobago, Tunisia, Turkey, Tuvalu, Uganda, Uruguay, Vanuatu, Venezuela, Western Samoa, Zaire, Zambia, and Zimbabwe.
37. "US Pushes Waste Dumping at Basel Meeting," *Toxic Trade Update* 6, no. 2 (1993): 6.
38. "New Central American Agreement Halts Waste Import Schemes in Honduras, Nicaragua, and El Salvador," *Toxic Trade Update* 6, no. 2 (1993): 6–7.
39. Member states of the South Pacific Forum include Australia, the Cook Islands, Fiji, Kiribati, the Marshall Islands, the Federated States of Micronesia, Nauru, New Zealand, Niue, Papua New Guinea, the Solomon Islands, Tonga, Tuvalu, Vanuatu, and Western Samoa.
40. "South Pacific Forum Countries to Negotiate Regional Waste Trade Ban," *Toxic Trade Update* 6, no. 3 (1993): 4–5.
41. Jim Vallette, "Basel 'Dumping' Convention Still Legalizes Toxic Terrorism," *Toxic Trade Update* 6, no. 1 (1993): 2–3.
42. Ibid., 3.
43. Madeleine Cobbing and Kerry Rankine, "Local Activists and Greenpeace Wage Campaign Against U.K. Waste Dumping in Mexico and Bolivia," *Toxic Trade Update* 6, no. 2 (1993): 19–20.
44. Vallette, "Basel 'Dumping' Convention," 2.

45. "U.S. Toxic Waste Sold as Fertilizer in Bangladesh," *Toxic Trade Update* 6, no. 1 (1993): 13.

46. Lewis, "Western Lands."

47. Kempel, "Transboundary Movements," 61.

48. Ibid., 51.

49. Ibid., 50.

50. Ibid.

51. See Terry L. Anderson, ed., *NAFTA and the Environment* (San Francisco: Pacific Research Institute, 1993), 97–98. The maquiladora region is a 250,000-square-mile area located inside Mexico, near its border with the United States. Established in 1965 as a free trade zone, it contains nearly 2,000 manufacturing plants, most of which are U.S. owned. Most of the plants pose severe health and environmental risks, and inadequate waste disposal has damaged the aquifers and rivers. Although there are legal provisions for returning toxic and hazardous wastes to the country of origin, the law is not adequately enforced.

52. Vallette and Spalding, *International Trade,* AE-1–AE-2.

53. Love Canal was a residential neighborhood in Niagara Falls, New York, that had been built on an old hazardous waste dump. Chemicals began to leach from the ground and into basements. Information collected by the residents suggested that the incidence of cancer and birth defects was unusually high in those areas with the highest concentration of pollutants. The residents were eventually relocated.

54. See Vallette and Spalding, *International Trade,* AA1, AA2, AA6.

55. Greenpeace publishes a quarterly, *Toxic Trade Update,* and an inventory, *The International Trade in Wastes: A Greenpeace Inventory*.

56. Kempel, "Transboundary Movements," 51.

57. Porter and Brown, *Global Environmental Politics,* 86.

58. Ibid.

59. Kempel, "Transboundary Movements," 51.

60. Ibid., 50–51.

61. Ibid., 52.

62. Ibid., 53–54.

63. Ibid., 52.

64. Ibid.

65. Ibid., 59.

66. Ibid., 60.

67. The following twenty-four industrialized countries make up the OECD: Australia, Austria, Belgium, Canada, Denmark, Finland, France, Germany, Greece, Iceland, Ireland, Italy, Japan, Luxembourg, the Netherlands, New Zealand, Norway, Portugal, Spain, Sweden, Switzerland, Turkey, the United Kingdom, and the United States.

68. See Organization for Economic Cooperation and Development, *Decision of the Council Concerning the Transfrontier Movements of Wastes Destined for Recovery Operations* (Paris, April 6, 1992).

69. Paul Johnston, Ruth Stringer, and Jim Puckett, *When Green Is Not.* Technical Note 07/92 (Amsterdam: Greenpeace International, 1992).

70. The ACP states are all Third World states.

71. Johnston, Stringer, and Puckett, *When Green Is Not,* 3.

72. Lisa Finaldi, "Chlorine Chemistry: Coming Soon to a Factory Near You!" *Toxic Trade Update* 6, no. 3 (1993): 27–28.

73. Kempel, "Transboundary Movements," 61.

74. According to the World Bank (*World Development Report 1993* [New York: Oxford University Press, 1993], 328–329), China, the Maldives, and

Nigeria are low-income countries, and Argentina, El Salvador, Jordan, Mexico, Panama, Saudi Arabia, the Syrian Arab Republic, and Uruguay are middle-income countries. They fall into the following major export categories—services: El Salvador, Jordan, the Maldives, and Panama; nonfuel primary exports: Argentina; diversified exports: Mexico, the Syrian Arab Republic, and Uruguay; fuel exports: Nigeria and Saudi Arabia; and manufactures: China.

75. Vallette and Spalding, *International Trade,* AE-1–AE-2. Other Third World targets listed were Angola, the Bahamas, Bangladesh, Belize, Benin, Bermuda, Botswana, Brazil, Chile, Colombia, the Congo, Costa Rica, Djibouti, the Dominican Republic, Equatorial Guinea, Ethiopia, Gabon, Guatemala, Guinea, Guinea Bissau, Guyana, Haiti, Honduras, India, Indonesia, Jamaica, Lebanon, Liberia, Malaysia, Mauritania, Mozambique, Namibia, Nicaragua, Niger, Pakistan, Paraguay, Peru, the Philippines, Senegal, Sierra Leone, the Solomon Islands, Somalia, Sudan, Tonga, Tunisia, Venezuela, Zambia, and Zimbabwe.

76. Ibid. The other Third World source countries listed were the Bahamas, Brazil, the Philippines, and Singapore.

77. Greenpeace International, *Annotations by Greenpeace International on the Agenda of the Meeting*. Prepared for the First Conference of Parties to the Basel Convention, November 30–December 4, 1992, Piriapolis, Uruguay, Attachment C, 2–3.

6
The Biodiversity Regime

As with the ozone issue, negotiations addressing biological diversity were framed by the perception of an integrated, interdependent ecosystem, a perception that mandated that both developed and developing countries give attention to this issue. However, in spite of this common interest, the formation of the biodiversity regime has highlighted many of the issues that separate the industrialized countries and the Third World countries in global environmental politics. These conflicting interests were played out in the regime negotiations; in the process, the Third World countries were able to modify the biodiversity agenda. The Convention on Biological Diversity was signed by most of the world's states in June 1992 and entered into force on December 29, 1993.

The Threat to Biodiversity

Biodiversity, or biological diversity, refers to the variety of life on earth. The term encompasses three categories: genetic diversity, species diversity, and ecosystem diversity. Genetic diversity describes the variation of genes within a species; species diversity describes the variety of species within a region; and ecosystem diversity refers to the number and distribution of ecosystems. The increasing interest in biodiversity is a result of concerns regarding species extinction, depletion of genetic diversity, and disruptions to the atmosphere, water supplies, fisheries, and forests. This growing awareness on the part of both governments and the general public has resulted in a desire to protect the world's natural heritage. Biodiversity brings together a variety of constituencies including forestry, agronomy, biotechnology, pharmaceuticals, and international trade. Although these groups may have different perspectives on biodiversity, they all regard it as an important resource.

Approximately 1.4 million species of plants and animals have been identified, but scientists believe between 10 million and 80 million species actually exist.[1] Species are disappearing rapidly, and there is growing consensus within the international community that a system should be put in place to slow or halt the process of extinction. Arguments in favor of species preservation include the perspective that a species has a right to exist because of its unique nature. But self-interest is also a strong motive: Given the interdependent nature of the ecosystem, the extinction of some species diminishes the well-being of the remaining species, including human beings. Consequently, it is important to protect species and threatened ecosystems such as forests, wetlands, and coastal waters.

Central to the concern about biological diversity is the shrinking genetic pool. It is estimated that tropical forests contain "at least 50 percent and perhaps 90 percent of the world's species."[2] According to one estimate, 20 to 75 species are becoming extinct each day because of deforestation in the tropics.[3] Traditionally, the genetic character of the many species of plants and animals have been considered a part of the common heritage of humankind, but increasingly they have become the objects of an enclosure movement that is seeking to enclose, privatize, and reduce the building blocks of life to marketable products.

Clearly, this is a common-property resource concern; a decrease in biodiversity has consequences for all species. But this common-property resource issue has some distributional characteristics that make it different from the ozone depletion issue. The bulk of the world's biological diversity is found in tropical forests, which are located in the Third World. The common-property and distributional aspects of this issue therefore have implications for both the negotiation strategy and the regime's implementation prospects.

Regulations addressing the issue of biodiversity have relevance for a wide range of national and transnational actors, including nation-states and agricultural and pharmaceutical interests. Concerns in this area include both the protection of biodiversity and the use of biotechnology. Gene technology has implications for fields ranging from medicine to agriculture: The United Nations has estimated that medicines from plants are worth about US$40 billion per year, and a single gene from an Ethiopian barley plant has been used to protect California's $10 million annual barley crop.[4] Recent advances in biotechnology research could lead to increases in the production of energy, food, and pharmaceutical products. A rich pool of genes is important to the continued development of such research.

Pharmaceutical companies are exploring plants, microbes, algae, and fungi for possible leads for products. Some are also investigating the medicines used by traditional communities. This is a lucrative field; about 25 percent of the prescription drugs used in the United States have active ingredients extracted or derived from plants. The market for herbal drugs in the industrialized world could be worth US$47 billion by the year 2000.[5] A variety of small and large companies and institutions are involved in the process of collecting and screening plant and other natural material.[6] They use a variety of institutional and independent collectors; some of these are Third World institutions such as the Chinese Academy of Sciences, the National Biodiversity Institute of Costa Rica, and the Central Drug Research Institute of India.[7]

The odds of obtaining a marketable product from collected samples are seen as ranging from 1 in 1,000 to 1 in 10,000.[8] One particularly successful project involved the rosy periwinkle from Madagascar's tropical rain forest. The plant has a rare genetic trait that has been used to develop pharmaceuticals to treat childhood leukemia. Whereas the pharmaceutical companies are making windfall profits, Madagascar has received nothing from the use of this resource.[9] Eli Lilly developed two drugs from this same plant, which led to sales amounting to approximately US$100 million per year worldwide.[10] Although these sales were a result of traits inherent in the rosy periwinkle plant, the development of the drug was a capital-intensive process, so the plant by itself cannot be seen as being worth $100 million annually.[11] The research added value to the product.

However, not all of the research and development in projects of this kind is done by industrialized country firms. These companies often benefit from centuries of indigenous experimentation as well as local scientific research. The neem tree (*azadirachta indica*) in India illustrates this point. For centuries products from the tree have been used locally for medicine, contraception, toiletries, timber, fuel, and insecticide. Its chemical properties have never been patented in India, but since 1985 U.S. and Japanese firms have taken out more than a dozen U.S. patents for a variety of neem compounds.

W. R. Grace owns at least four of these patents and has begun to set up production in India. The company has based its patents on what it regards as an innovative method of extraction. However, over the centuries complex processes had been used to make neem available for specific uses. Its insecticidal uses and properties were a part of India's common lore, which was one reason the Indian Central Insecticide Board did not register neem products under the 1968 Insecticides Act. The patenting of neem products has caused considerable concern among farmers and scientists in India, particularly since the Uruguay Round of GATT seeks to standardize intellectual property rights. TNC involvement with neem is already having economic consequences for local farmers, who now have to compete with transnational firms for access to neem seeds. It is estimated that from the early 1970s to the early 1990s the price of neem seeds rose from 300 rupees per ton to more than 8,000 rupees per ton.[12]

Loss of biological diversity has tremendous implications for agriculture. The range of food resources has declined over time, although this trend has long been ignored. One estimate is that more than 3,000 plant species have been used for food throughout human history; however, there has been a significant reduction in variety. Now, most of the world's food comes from 20 species. This reduction is primarily a function of conquest and domination, which were usually associated with the suppression of local crops and the introduction of "exotic" varieties, and plant breeding programs, which have focused on a narrow range of crops.[13]

A look at the potential consequences of the biotechnology revolution for developing countries' agriculture is instructive. Many developing countries depend on agricultural products not just for food for their populations but also for a major portion of their foreign exchange earnings. The biotechnology revolution has the potential to affect both plant crops and livestock production since genetic engineering is an increasingly important tool for breeders. Before this revolution, technology development and dissemination were carried out primarily by public or semipublic institutions, and patents and plant variety protection were generally not major issues. With the revolution, technology development and dissemination will primarily be the province of the private sector, and processes and products will be patentable and protectable.[14]

The issue of patents is at the core of the debate over the equity issues related to germ plasm. Over time, farmers and scientists in the industrialized world have altered the genetic structures of plants through selective breeding; consequently, researchers have looked to the Third World as a source of free primitive germ plasm. They assume that, as with the high seas, this primitive germ plasm is the common property of humankind. These genetic resources are used to produce genetically altered seeds for the international market. Since these are now patented and are private property, they can then be sold back to Third World consumers.[15] The genetically altered seeds often need expensive additives such as chemical fertilizers and pesticides, which are often environmentally as well as financially costly. The picture for Third World agriculture deteriorates further when developing country farmers focus on hybrid varieties to the detriment of, and at the risk of causing the disappearance of, the old varieties.

Third World resistance to the institutionalization of this practice was illustrated through a demonstration by more than 1,000 Indian farmers against the transnational company Cargill in 1992. This action was part of their campaign to press the Indian government to not change the Indian Patents Act to conform to the terms of the Uruguay Round of GATT. The farmers were concerned about the encroachment of transnational corporations into India's national seed resources and also about the loss of farmers' rights to produce, sell, and modify seeds. As part of their protest, they stormed the Cargill offices in Bangalore, took files and seed samples that represented four years of research, and burned them in the street.[16]

Evolution of the Biodiversity Regime

The Stockholm Conference was not the first occasion at which issues related to biodiversity were placed on the international agenda. A variety of legal instruments already existed. Some of these were regional, such as the Convention on Nature Protection and Wildlife Preservation in the Western Hemisphere (Washington, D.C., 1940) and the African Convention on the Conservation of Nature and Natural Resources (Algiers, 1968). Other measures dealt with specific species, such as birds and marine and polar-region species. Prior to Stockholm, the only major international legal instrument for conserving biodiversity was the 1971 Convention on Wetlands of International Importance Especially as Waterfowl Habitat. The 61 parties to this convention pledged to make an inventory of designated wetlands, to promote their conservation, and to establish nature reserves in the important wetlands.

But no comprehensive international treaty addressed the problem of biological diversity. Although Stockholm did not produce such a document, it was the first time the issue was addressed in such a holistic manner. The issue of biodiversity was debated, and the conference documents included provisions aimed at protecting biodiversity.

The area of genetic resources and biotechnology was already controversial in 1972, at the time of the Stockholm Conference. Developing countries were concerned about their lack of access to the biotechnology that was developed from the use of their resources, and they tried to use linkage politics to gain access to this technology. They pressed their demand for the transfer of technology on noncommercial terms. This demand was rejected by the developed countries, and the final statement of the conference diluted the language that addressed this linkage between economics and the environment.

Both the Declaration of the United Nations Conference on the Human Environment and the Action Plan for the Human Environment include language that addresses biodiversity. Principles 2, 4, and 6 of the declaration include provisions for safeguarding flora and fauna and preserving ecosystems.[17] The action plan generally addresses the importance of protecting forests, which, among other things, are important habitats for wildlife;[18] it recommended that wildlife be monitored to assess the impact of pollutants[19] and that the economic value of wildlife be assessed.[20] Governments were asked to take steps to protect ecosystems that have international significance.[21] Recommendations 39 through 45 deal generally with the issue of preserving genetic resources.[22]

In the period between the Stockholm and Rio conferences, the body of legislation concerning biodiversity continued to grow. Relevant major international legislation included the Convention Concerning the Protection of the World Cultural and Natural Heritage (1972), the Convention on International Trade in Endangered Species of Wild Fauna and Flora (1973), and the Convention on Conservation of Migratory Species of Wild Animals (1979).

In the aftermath of Stockholm, developing countries continued their push for greater access to the biotechnology that resulted from their biological wealth. A nonbinding International Undertaking on Plant Genetic Resources (Resolution 8/33) was passed by the FAO in 1983. It stated that access to genetic resources should not be restricted, and it declared that all seed resources were the common heritage of humanity; therefore, both primitive stocks and those developed by proprietary means should be free to all. Some developed world producers were opposed to this declaration, and many industrialized countries were not parties to it because it was incompatible with their patent rights.[23] Third World members, however, accepted its provisions.[24]

In 1989 the FAO Commission proposed the concept of farmers' rights, thereby implying that the international community was the trustee for present and future farmers. This concept was intended to be the basis for helping farm communities all over the world to benefit from the improvements in genetic plant resources. But no funding mechanism was set up to transfer resources to the developing countries, and these countries also no longer endorsed the common heritage concept with regard to their plant resources. They wanted access to their resources to be based on bilateral arrangements.

A 1991 Costa Rican deal is considered one possible model for future bilateral arrangements. The parties to the deal were the National Biodiversity Institute, a nonprofit Costa Rican research center, and Merck & Co., the world's largest pharmaceutical company. Merck agreed to pay the institute US$1.1 million, as well as royalties from any product developed, in return for plant, insect, and microbe samples from all over Costa Rica.[25] (Costa Rica is estimated to have about 5 percent of all plant and animal species on the planet.) Ten percent of the up-front money and 50 percent of any royalties go directly into conservation. Although this agreement provides for compensation, some critics say it gives away Costa Rican resources for too little money. Nevertheless, many developing countries are studying this arrangement with interest.[26]

The years between Stockholm and Rio saw incremental progress with regard to the items on the Third World's biodiversity agenda. Developing states wanted to make their own arrangements concerning resource access, and, as the Merck deal illustrates, the slow process of norm change had begun. But the progress of these states in the campaign for transfer of technology and financial assistance is more difficult to assess. Although developing countries continued to push for changes in these areas, developed countries maintained their determined resistance. These conflicting perspectives were reflected in the preparatory negotiations for the Rio Conference.

Unlike Stockholm, Rio produced a separate document addressing biodiversity. Negotiations on the Convention on Biological Diversity began in 1991. The complexity of issues such as access, financial assistance, and technology transfer made negotiations difficult. The convention provides a comprehensive framework for the conservation of biodiversity, including the following commitments.

1. National identification and monitoring of biological diversity.[27]
2. The development of national strategies and programs for conserving biological diversity.[28]
3. National in situ and ex situ conservation measures.[29]
4. Environmental assessment procedures to take into account the effects of projects on biological diversity.[30]
5. National reports from parties on measures taken to implement the convention and the effectiveness of the measures.[31]

The language of the convention is general. It is liberally sprinkled with qualifiers such as "as far as possible and as appropriate" and "in accordance with its particular conditions and capabilities." In spite of the general language and the qualifiers, the specific issues of interest to developing countries proved to be controversial.

The Biodiversity Convention was adopted in May 1992, a few weeks before the Rio Conference. Probably because of the high political profile of the Rio meeting, the convention drew more signatures than did the agreements on hazardous waste and the protection of the ozone layer. At the Rio Conference, which ran from June 3 to June 14, 1992, 157 parties signed the convention. Although the United States did not sign the convention at that time, in 1993, after a change of administration, it became a signatory. As Table 6.1 indicates, the Biodiversity Convention entered into force in December 1993, within eighteen months of its adoption. It had a speedier ratification process than did either the Basel Convention or the Vienna Convention.

Table 6.1 International Policy Actions on Conserving Biodiversity

1971	Convention on Wetlands of International Importance Especially as Waterfowl Habitat.
1972	Convention Concerning the Protection of the World Cultural and Natural Heritage.
1973	Convention on International Trade in Endangered Species of Wild Fauna and Flora.
1979	Convention on Conservation of Migratory Species of Wild Animals.
1987	Governing Council of UNEP established the ad hoc Working Group of Experts on Biological Diversity.
May 1992	Text of Convention on Biological Diversity adopted at Nairobi.
June 1992	Convention on Biological Diversity signed at UNCED.
December 1993	Convention on Biological Diversity enters into force.

In the period between the Stockholm and Rio conferences, the countries of the Third World made uneven progress with regard to their major biodiversity concerns. This is reflected in a review of the progress made on the issues of sovereignty, technology transfer, and financial assistance.

The Sovereignty Issue

The Stockholm Conference addressed the issue of sovereignty in a general manner. Principle 21 of the declaration recognizes that states have sovereignty over their own resources and that they should manage the resources in keeping with their own environmental policies. This right of sovereignty is restricted only by states' responsibility not to "cause damage to the environment of other States or of areas beyond the limits of national jurisdiction."[32]

The Biodiversity Convention (Article 15) also recognizes the sovereign rights of states over their natural resources. But it goes farther than the Stockholm Declaration; its language indicates that states have the authority to grant access to their resources on mutually agreed terms.[33] Developed countries and their institutions are concerned about the implications of this article. It might indicate that the days of free scientific and commercial access are ending and that foreign enterprises will have to come to terms with developing country institutions before collecting specimens. The Merck deal in Costa Rica illustrates the kind of arrangement that can be made.

Access to Technology

The declaration and the action plan from the Stockholm Conference contain several references to transfer of technology or the use of technology to address environmental concerns. In the action plan, the relevant parts are principles 12, 18, and 20. These principles deal generally with the use of science and technology "for the common good of mankind,"[34] they encourage the free flow of up-to-date scientific information, and they address the issue of making environmental technologies available to developing countries on terms they can afford.[35] Numbers 26 and 27 of the action plan recommend that the United Nations Food and Agriculture Organization coordinate research and information exchange and transfer on forest-related issues, whereas number 108 recommends studies "to find means by which environmental technologies may be made available for adoption by developing countries under terms and conditions that encourage their wide distribution without constituting an unacceptable burden to developing countries."[36]

At Rio, technology transfer is dealt with in more detail. The Rio Declaration encourages exchanges of scientific and technological knowledge and the development, adaptation, diffusion, and transfer of technologies, including new and innovative technologies.[37] However, the articles that address science and technology are ambiguous, with some provisions seeming to be aimed at satisfying the interests of the developing countries and others seeming to target developed countries' concerns.

Articles 15, 16, 17, 18, and 19 address exchange and cooperation with regard to science and technology. Scientific research based on genetic resources is to be carried out with the full participation of the countries providing the resources. These states should also share equitably in the results and benefits of the research;[38] however, access to these benefits should occur on mutually agreed terms.[39] Technologies should be transferred under fair and favorable terms, including concessional and preferential terms when mutually agreed. However, if patents and intellectual property rights are involved, access and transfer should be provided on terms consistent with the protection of these rights.[40] Article 17 calls for the exchange of information, including results of technical, scientific, and socioeconomic research;[41] and Article 18 states that technical and scientific cooperation should occur in conservation and sustainable use of biological diversity.[42] The language in these articles tries to do the difficult task of satisfying the interests of both the developing and the developed countries; the language that calls for transfer of technology was intended to satisfy the interests of the developing countries, and the qualifiers that deal with mutual agreement and intellectual property rights were included to satisfy the developed countries.

Financial Assistance

The Stockholm documents made several references to the issue of financial assistance for developing countries.[43] Recommendation 45 of the action plan was the only one that made specific reference to financial assistance for the purpose of conserving genetic diversity.[44] The declaration recognized that because of their underdevelopment and the "costs which may emanate from their incorporating environmental safeguards into their development planning,"[45] developing countries would need assistance. The action plan made the point that developed countries' preoccupation with their own environmental problems should not be an excuse to slow the flow of assistance.[46]

Nevertheless, at the Rio Conference two decades later, this preoccupation did contribute to the contentious nature of the debate over financial assistance. The Biodiversity Convention had to address two primary issues related to financial assistance: the amount of money to be contributed by the developed nations, and the financial mechanism to be used to administer the funds. Article 21 addressed the second issue, and Article 20 addressed the first.

According to Article 20, the developed country parties should fund the "agreed full incremental costs" developing countries incur in meeting the obligations of the convention. It states that developing countries need this assistance in order to meet these additional commitments since these countries' priorities are "economic and social development and eradication of poverty."[47] Arriving at the figure for the "agreed" costs is likely to be challenging.

Article 21, which addresses the financial mechanism, is controversial. The mechanism, policy, strategy, program priorities, and eligibility criteria were to be determined by "the Conference of Parties"[48] within a year of the time the treaty entered into force. A major concern of the parties was whether the financial institution would be run by majority rule or be donor controlled. Although developing countries would prefer the former, the developed countries would be less willing to contribute funds to an institution they did not control. Until the convention's entry into force, the financial mechanism was to be administered by the Global Environment Facility (GEF) of the United Nations Development Programme, the United Nations Environment Programme, and the World Bank.[49] This interim financial arrangement was weighted toward donor control. However, under the terms of the convention, the GEF was to function "under the authority and guidance of, and be accountable to," the conference of parties.[50] The GEF has been restructured to use a double majority voting system, giving each side a veto, since decisions require a majority based on both the number of countries and the amount of contributions.

Actors and Interests

Early in the debate, it was clear that significant convergent and divergent interests both united and divided the stakeholders in the evolving biodiversity regime. These groups were interested in biodiversity for reasons ranging from the spiritual to the material: Some saw the earth as the Great Mother or Great Spirit and for that reason wanted to keep it as inviolate as possible; others saw the preservation of biodiversity as important for the strength of the agricultural industry or as the source of needed foreign exchange through ecotourism; for others it was crucial to the very survival of humankind, which was but another species; still others saw biodiversity as a veritable treasure trove for pharmaceuticals. But this common concern with conserving biodiversity did not mean there was consensus on the strategy and policies for conservation.

Third World Nation-States

At Stockholm, the nation-states of the South began to link the issue of technology transfer with that of biodiversity and the related genetic resources and also to push for financial assistance. From their perspective, if the Third World's concerns regarding sovereignty, financial assistance, and technology transfer were not appropriately addressed, the resulting regime would be weak and ineffective.

The sovereignty issue. For developing countries, the recognition of sovereign rights over all of their natural resources, including genetic resources, is important. This recognition underscores their right to control access to these resources and legitimizes demands for reimbursement for both the use of these resources and the products of research resulting therefrom. Recognition can establish the basis on which countries can charge commercial users for prospecting for biodiversity resources within their territory, although industrialized countries, corporate interests, and sectors of the scientific community have perceived this interest as conflicting with their interests in having continued access to developing countries' natural resources. Developing countries also want legal recognition of their rights to indigenous knowledge of their local plant and animal species.

Access to technology. Technology transfer has long been an issue for developing countries. In the 1970s it was an important item on the agenda of the New International Economic Order, and in the 1980s and 1990s it became an integral part of the debate over environmental regimes. In exchange for allowing the nations of the North access to their plant and animal species, the Third World wants access to the resulting biotechnologies and also to technology that might help it better conserve its biological diversity. Almost all advanced technology originates in industrialized countries; consequently, nearly all of the world's patents are registered in those states and are in the hands of the transnational corporations.[51] The issue of access to science and technology has been under international discussion for years, mostly in UN bodies. Countries of the South have adopted a common position in negotiating with the North on technology matters, an issue on which the interests of developed countries and corporations conflict with those of the developing world.

It is the Third World's position that its claim to the transfer of biotechnology is particularly strong when the technology product depends on raw materials acquired in the Third World. But beyond this, these nations see that biotechnology could be used to address problems in the Third World in areas such as agriculture, health, and industrial development. The obstacle to this is restricted access to biotechnology. Step by step with the development of biotechnology has been the privatization of knowledge, caused in part by the fact that commercial firms and universities have obtained patents on the fruits of their research. Some critics argue that the industrialized world is in the process of gaining almost complete control of biotechnology because of its possession of the bulk of the patents for biotechnology and bioprocesses.[52]

Lack of access to technology was addressed in a series of negotiations in the 1970s and 1980s. Considerable progress toward facilitating the South's access to technology was made during the 1970s in negotiations during the United Nations Conference on Trade and Development on an International Code of Conduct on the Transfer of Technology and on a revision of the intellectual property system. There was also some progress on changing the Paris Convention for the Protection of Industrial Property, but stalled negotiations prevented its revision.[53]

Although developing countries have formed a common front on this issue, not all are at the same stage of biotechnology development. Several have begun to build biotechnology infrastructures; India, Brazil, and Mexico, for example, have devoted considerable resources to institution building for biotechnology research. India was one of the first Third World states to establish a long-term biotechnology program, and Mexico's research community is working in a number of areas, including genetic engineering and nitrogen fixation. Through its Centre for Biotechnology Development, China is building its capability in the field of enzyme restriction. It has even become involved in a joint venture with a U.S.-based firm. Increasingly, Third World countries are entering into joint ventures with other Third World countries, as Brazil, for example, has done with Argentina and Cuba.[54] Other developing countries, including Thailand and Venezuela, have also begun to establish biotechnology programs.[55]

Financial assistance. Developing countries see pulling their countries out of poverty as their first priority. In their opinion, poverty is a significant cause of environmental degradation. They believe it would be counterproductive to pull resources away from basic needs projects in order to use them for the conservation of biodiversity; therefore, they need financial assistance for their conservation projects. They argue that since conservation of their biodiversity will benefit the entire community of nations, developing countries should not have to bear the entire financial burden.

However, the interests of the developing states are directly at odds with those of other parties and stakeholders. In the industrial age, the political and economic forces that control access to fossil fuel have been able to exert tremendous economic control; in the new age of biotechnology, the forces that control access to genetic resources will exercise tremendous power over the world economy. Whereas at one level the Third World countries can control access, most lack the technological resources needed to unlock the genetic secrets of their biological diversity.

Industrialized Nation-States

The sovereignty issue. Industrialized country interests have been rushing to gain access to the shrinking gene pool. Since developing countries are the repositories of the bulk of these genetic resources, the industrialized countries want to be assured of continued access. It is these interests that have the capital and technological capability to transform that wealth into commercial products, and they want to retain the scientific and economic benefits of access to Third World biodiversity.

Access to technology. The industrialized countries did not favor giving the developing countries access to technology on concessional terms, even if the technology was the result of Third World resources. They took the position that these resources only gain value with the application of their technology and that, therefore, compensation was not justified. The developed states and corporations were concerned that any commitment to technology transfer might have negative consequences for the protection of intellectual property rights.

Financial assistance. There was significant resistance to additional financial assistance by the developed countries because they would have to provide the bulk of the money for any fund.

Transnational Corporations

Transnational corporations' interests in biodiversity are similar to those of the industrialized countries. Large transnational firms with interests in oil, chemicals, food, and pharmaceuticals have been playing leading roles in agricultural biotechnology. The companies are developing their own research and development capacities and are engaging in collaborative efforts with other enterprises.[56] They want access to the available resources at the lowest possible cost, and they want to establish and retain property rights over as many related products and processes as possible.

Corporations are searching the gene pool for traits that are commercially valuable. This strategy has increased tensions between actors from the industrialized nations and those from the Third World, as the descriptions of the concerns over the patenting of products from India's neem tree and the storming of Cargill's offices demonstrate.

Environmental NGOs

Environmental NGOs have been actively involved in the conservation of biodiversity since the 1950s. A broad spectrum of national and transnational NGOs are involved in trying to shape biodiversity strategy. They include Conservation International, the Rainforest Alliance, the World Conservation Union, the World Resources Institute, and the World Wildlife Fund. Some of these organizations help to shape biodiversity strategy by investing in debt-for-nature swaps, while others attempt to influence policy through research and publication and through collaboration with UN agencies and the World Bank. Environmental NGOs have tended to focus their efforts on ecosystem protection, but since the 1980s their focus has broadened: More attention has been given to the issue of genetic diversity and to the relationship between poverty and ecosystem destruction.

The Third World in the Regime's Evolution

As the Stockholm proceedings show, the Third World countries were quick to identify the interests they had at stake in the evolving biodiversity regime. They pursued these interests aggressively in the processes of problem definition and bargaining, and they are likely to maintain an active role in the process of regime transformation.

Problem Definition

The industrialized nation-states initially defined the biodiversity issue to focus on conservation; however, over time the Third World countries have been able to modify and broaden the definition and, consequently, the agenda. As a result, issues such as sovereignty, technology transfer, and financial assistance have become significant in the debate.

Regime objectives have changed over the course of the two decades between the Stockholm Conference and the Rio Conference. The objectives have reflected the parties' interests and the salience of the issue by becoming more specific over time as interest in the subject grew. The Stockholm Conference addressed biodiversity within the broader context of environmental protection. As a result, in 1972 the Declaration of the United Nations Conference on the Human Environment examined the importance of safeguarding flora, fauna, and natural ecosystems as part of the general objectives addressing environmental protection.[57] The issue of biodiversity gained salience as biotechnology and genetic resources became major components of the debate.

By the time of the Rio Conference, the issue had become more controversial, and regime objectives had become more specific. They included the protection of biological diversity, the transfer of technology, and access to genetic resources. Article 1 of the Convention on Biological Diversity expressed the objectives as follows.

> The objectives of this Convention, to be pursued in accordance with its relevant provisions, are the conservation of biological diversity, the sustainable use of its components and the fair and equitable sharing of the benefits arising out of the utilization of genetic resources, including by appropriate access to genetic resources and by appropriate transfer of relevant technologies, taking into account all rights over those resources and to technologies, and by appropriate funding.[58]

Bargaining

Third World countries have used linkage politics in the negotiations dealing with biological diversity. They see global environmental negotiations as opportunities to advance a broader agenda of change in the structure of North-South economic relations.

As the biodiversity regime has evolved since 1972, a major demand by developing countries has been to link the North's access to biological resources in developing countries to the South's access to the resulting biotechnology. In addition, they want reimbursement for the use of their natural resources, and increased financial assistance to help them conserve their biological diversity.

The outcome of the Rio Conference regarding the Third World's biodiversity agenda has been mixed. Of the three agenda items under discussion, the sovereignty issue is the one on which there has been the most progress. The convention underscores the sovereignty of countries over their resources and legitimizes restrictions of access to those resources. The implications of this fact are most important with regard to genetic resources, which have been increasing in economic value as the genetic pool shrinks. Merck's arrangement with the Costa Rican institute is a recognition of these changes. The combination of new patterns of behavior and the language of the convention is likely to help usher in new norms regarding access and reimbursement.

Developing countries were less successful with regard to the issue of technology transfer. At Rio, they tried to use access to plant genetic resources to bargain for technology transfer. They did achieve limited success in this area: According to the Biodiversity Convention, research, profits, and technology should be shared with the nations whose resources are used. But the language is not strong enough to make this mandatory; it can be interpreted to mean that companies do not have to turn over technologies or pay royalties unless they agree to. Even this weak language, however, can help to establish new norms for the relationship between companies and developing countries in the area of genetic resources.

The United States was especially critical of the treaty provisions that addressed technology issues. It was the only major country not to sign the biodiversity convention at Rio. President George Bush claimed accession to the convention was impossible because the United States could not make commitments for private industry to transfer protected technology. He took the position that accession would retard biotechnology and undermine the protection of ideas. That concern, however, did not prevent other OECD countries from becoming signatories.[59] They were aware that, because of its ambiguity, the language addressing technology transfer would not constrain them unduly.

It is too early to assess Third World countries' success with regard to financial assistance. On the face of it, they received a commitment for a biodiversity fund to enable them to meet the costs of the conservation obligations assumed under the Biodiversity Convention.[60] The fund is to be administered by the GEF. Much depends on how the reconstituted GEF operates and how well it responds to the needs of the Third World countries. They did not receive a commitment for the transfer of a specific amount of funds, and it is likely that any financial assistance will be less than the Third World's perceived need. In addition, since the double majority voting system provides the donor countries with veto power, it is also likely that those countries will ultimately determine funding policy.

Regime Transformation

The biodiversity regime is not as strong as the ozone layer protection regime. It contains more general, ambiguous language. However, it deals with a more complex issue, and the regime will depend on the cooperation of a wider network of actors for its success. In addition, it is at an earlier stage of evolution than the ozone regime, and there is the prospect for regime strengthening. Because this is a common-property resource issue, any party with access to or control of components of biological diversity can deny the regime its objective of conserving biodiversity. The Third World, with its large stores of biodiversity, can have a significant impact on regime effectiveness.

As a part of the regime implementation process, biodiversity strategies have been prepared. In 1992 a Global Biodiversity Strategy was released, and a companion document followed in 1993. The latter outlines a Global Marine Biodiversity Strategy and was prepared jointly by UNEP, the World Conservation Union, the World Bank, the World Wildlife Fund, and the Center for Marine Conservation. The strategy provides a framework for marine resource management to the year 2000 and beyond. It compiles recommendations from Agenda 21, from the 1992 World Parks Congress, and from a variety of other organizations and sources. As a part of the implementation process, a network of private and government institutions and individuals is being formed. The International Marine Conservation Network will review recommendations and make suggestions for relevant actions.[61]

Conclusion

The Third World was able to affect the problem definition process and to modify the agenda of the negotiations on biodiversity. The developing countries were also able to exert a modest influence on the bargaining process.

Third World countries also moved expeditiously to ratify the Biodiversity Convention, making up about 60 percent (14 out of 23) of the states that ratified the Biodiversity Convention by October 1993. Developing countries included Burkina Faso, China, Ecuador, Fiji, Guinea, India, Jordan, Mexico, Peru, the Philippines, Tunisia, Uganda, Uruguay, and Zambia.[62] They were almost evenly divided into middle- and low-income groups and were spread over all the major export sectors, except for the fuel-exporting sector.[63] Once again, there were no high-income developing countries in the group of early ratifiers. For some members of this group, biodiversity has particular salience because they have invested substantially in biotechnology research programs. Early ratifiers such as China, India, Mexico, Peru, and the Philippines do have biotechnology research programs, but this was not a significant indicator of who the early ratifiers would be since other major biotechnology investors such as Brazil, Thailand, and Venezuela were not among this group.[64]

The Third World's success in influencing the regime outcome was modified by the globalization of both economies and the environment. The perception of a globalized environment meant the biodiversity issue was seen as a commons problem; as such, action by any country has implications for any other country. A Third World country's treatment of its natural resources can have significant implications for the citizens of other countries with regard to food supply, weather, and medicine, which gives developing countries some leverage. In addition, with most of the world's biodiversity found within their territories, some of these countries have asymmetrical possibilities for affecting the world's biodiversity and potentially have the means to control access. However, the biodiversity issue does not carry the same sense of vulnerability and sensitivity that is attached to ozone depletion, which somewhat modifies the developing countries' influence. Their leverage is also modified by their role in the global economy, which further limits their options with regard to biodiversity.

The convention does recognize these countries' sovereignty over their biodiversity, but given their economic constraints, there is the danger that, for most of them, biodiversity will merely become one more set of resources to sell. At most, developing countries can regulate access to their natural resources. They are also faced with increased privatization of resources and the patenting of genetic resources, which modifies the advantages they would gain from any concessions regarding technology transfer. Finally, with regard to the limited concessions on financial assistance, given developing countries' economic position, donor countries are likely to use financial transfer as a tool to encourage preferred policies.

The outcome is reflective of the Third World's short-term and medium-term prospects in global environmental negotiations. These countries are at a disadvantage because global environmental politics largely reflects the structure of the global economy, which is clearly controlled by the industrialized interests; but because of both the nature of the environmental issue and their adoption of a common position, Third World countries have been able to induce incremental changes in these politics. Although they fell short of their goals, they clearly succeeded in making the issue of development as prominent as that of environmental protection.

Notes

1. John C. Ryan, "Conserving Biological Diversity," in Lester R. Brown, *State of the World 1992* (New York: Norton, 1992), 9.

2. World Resources Institute, *World Resources 1992–93* (New York: Oxford University Press, 1992), 130.

3. Ibid., 128.

4. Mostafa Kamal Tolba, *Earth Audit* (Nairobi: UNEP, 1972), 15.

5. J. A. McNeely, *Economics and Biological Diversity: Developing and Using Economic Incentives to Conserve Biological Diversity* (Gland: IUCN, 1988); cited in Mostafa K. Tolba and Osama A. El-Kholy, *The World Environment 1972–1992* (London: Chapman and Hall, 1992).

6. As listed in World Resources Institute (*Biodiversity Prospecting* [Baltimore: World Resources Institute, 1993], 8–13), these include Abbot Laboratories, Boehringer Ingelheim, Bristol-Myers Squibb, Ciba-Geigy, Eli Lilly, Glaxo Group Research, Inverni della Beffa, Merck & Co., Inc., Miles, Inc., Monsanto, National Cancer Institute, Pfizer, Pharmagenesis, Phytopharmaceuticals, Rhone-Poulenc Rorer, Shaman Pharmaceuticals, Inc., SmithKline Beecham, Sphinx Pharmaceuticals, Sterling Winthrop, Syntex Laboratories, and Upjohn Co.

7. Ibid., 8–13.

8. Peter P. Principe, personal communication, 1993; cited in ibid., 47.

9. Jeremy Rifkin, *Biosphere Politics* (New York: Crown Publishers, 1991), 66–67.

10. Tolba and El-Kholy, *World Environment*, 202.

11. Norman R. Farnsworth, "Screening Plants for New Medicines," in E. O. Wilson and Francis M. Peters, eds., *Biodiversity* (Washington, D.C.: National Academy Press, 1988), 83–97.

12. Vandana Shiva and Radha Holla-Bhar, "Intellectual Piracy and the Neem Tree," *The Ecologist* 23, no. 6 (November–December 1993): 223–227. Shiva and Holla-Bhar drew the information on the price for neem seeds from two sources: a letter to Professor Nanjundaswamy, convenor of the Karnataka Rajya Raitha Sangha farmers' organization; and R. Stone, "A Biopesticidal Tree Begins to Blossom," *Science*, (February 28, 1992): 1070–1071.

13. Calestous Juma, *The Gene Hunters: Biotechnology and the Scramble for Seeds* (Princeton: Princeton University Press, 1989), 14.

14. M. Kenney and F. Buttel, "Biotechnology: Prospects and Dilemmas for Third World Development," *Development and Change* 16 (1985): 70.

15. J. Kloppenburg, Jr., *First the Seed: The Political Economy of Plant Biotechnology 1492–2000* (New York: Cambridge University Press, 1988); cited in Thomas C. Wiegele, *Biotechnology and International Relations: The Political Dimensions* (Gainesville: University of Florida Press, 1991), 112.

16. "Angry Indian Farmers Destroy Cargill's Seeds," *Ecologist Campaigns* (March–April 1993): 1.

17. United Nations, *Report of the United Nations Conference on the Human Environment Held at Stockholm 5–16 June 1972;* reprinted in *International Legal Materials* 11 (1972): 1418.

18. Ibid., *Report,* Recommendations 24–25, 1431–1432.
19. Ibid., Recommendation 29, 1433.
20. Ibid., Recommendation 30, 1433.
21. Ibid., Recommendation 38, 1435.
22. Ibid., 1435–1441.
23. Canada, France, West Germany, Japan, and the United States initially withheld membership in the FAO Commission on Plant Genetic Resources.
24. Wiegele, *Biotechnology and International Relations,* 113.
25. World Resources Institute, *World Resources,* 138.
26. "Chemical Prospecting: Hope for Vanishing Ecosystems?" *Science* 256 (May 22, 1992): 1142.
27. United Nations Environment Programme, *Convention on Biological Diversity* (June 1992), Article 7; reprinted in *International Legal Materials* 31 (July 1992), 825.
28. Ibid., Article 6, 825.
29. Ibid., Articles 8 and 9, 825–826.
30. Ibid., Article 14, 827.
31. Ibid., Article 26, 834.
32. United Nations, *Report,* 1420.
33. United Nations Environment Programme, *Convention on Biological Diversity,* Article 15, 828.
34. United Nations, *Report,* 1420.
35. Ibid.
36. Ibid., 1463–1464.
37. United Nations Environment Programme, *The Rio Declaration on Environment and Development* (June 14, 1992), Principle 9; reprinted in *International Legal Materials* 31 (July 1992): 877.
38. United Nations Environment Programme, *Convention on Biological Diversity*, Article 15; reprinted in *International Legal Materials* 31 (July 1992): 828.
39. Ibid., *United Nations Conference,* Article 19, 830.
40. Ibid., Article 16, 829.
41. Ibid.
42. Ibid., 829–830.
43. These references were contained in Principles 9 and 12 of the Stockholm Declaration and in Recommendations 45, 107, and 109 of the Action Plan.
44. United Nations, *Report,* 1439–1441.
45. Ibid., 1419.
46. Ibid., 1464.
47. United Nations Environment Programme, *Convention on Biological Diversity,* Article 20, 830–831.
48. Ibid., Article 21, 831–832.
49. United Nations Environment Programme, *Resolutions of the Conference for the Adoption of the Agreed Text of the Convention on Biological Diversity* (May 22, 1992); reprinted in *International Legal Materials* 31 (July 1992): 843.
50. United Nations Environment Programme, *United Nations Conference,* Article 21.1, 831.
51. Willy Brandt, *North-South: A Program for Survival* (Cambridge: MIT Press, 1980), 194.
52. Wiegele, *Biotechnology and International Relations,* 105.
53. The South Commission, *The Challenge to the South* (Oxford: Oxford University Press, 1990), 254.
54. Juma, *The Gene Hunters,* 117–124.

55. Wiegele, *Biotechnology and International Relations,* 119; and Henk Hobbelink, *Biotechnology and the Future of World Agriculture* (London: Zed Books, 1991), 120–129.

56. Lawrence Busch, William B. Lacy, Jeffrey Burkhardt, and Laura R. Lacy, *Plants, Power, and Profit: Social, Economic, and Ethical Consequences of the New Biotechnologies* (Cambridge: Basil Blackwell, 1991), 25. The authors identified the following as leading corporations in this area: American Cyanamid, Campbell Soup, Ciba-Geigy, DuPont, Eli Lilly, Hershey Foods, Lubrizof, Monsanto, Rhone-Poulenc, RJR Nabisco, Rohm and Haas, Sandoz, Shell, Standard Oil, and W. R. Grace.

57. United Nations, *United Nations Conference on the Human Environment: Final Documents* (June 16, 1972): Principles 2, 4, and 6; reprinted in *International Legal Materials* 11 (November 1972): 1416–1471.

58. United Nations Environment Programme, *Convention on Biological Diversity,* Article 1; reprinted in *International Legal Materials* 31 (July 1992): 823.

59. United Nations, *Multilateral Treaties Deposited with the Secretary-General: Status as at 31 December 1992* (New York: United Nations, 1993), 840.

60. United Nations Environment Programme, *Convention on Biological Diversity,* Article 20.2.

61. "Global Marine Biodiversity Strategy," *CEPNEWS* (June–July 1993): 3.

62. World Resources Institute, *World Resources 1994–95* (New York: Oxford University Press, 1994), 374–375, 382.

63. According to the World Bank (*World Development Report 1993* [New York: Oxford University Press, 1993], 328–329), Burkina Faso, China, Guinea, India, Uganda, and Zambia are low-income countries, and Tunisia, Jordan, the Philippines, Mexico, Ecuador, Peru, Uruguay, and Fiji are middle-income countries. They fall into the following major export categories—services: Burkina Faso, Jordan, and Fiji; primary nonfuel exports: Guinea, Uganda, Zambia, and Peru; diversified exports: Tunisia, India, the Philippines, Mexico, Ecuador, and Uruguay; and manufactures: China.

64. Hobbelink, *Biotechnology,* 120–129.

PART 3

THE THIRD WORLD AND ENVIRONMENTAL GOVERNANCE

7
THE THIRD WORLD IN ENVIRONMENTAL REGIME FORMATION

Most of the world's population and territory are contained in the Third World; therefore, by either omission or commission, Third World policies will have significant consequences for the global environment. In addition, environmental policy enacted in global forums will have significant consequences for plant and animal life in the Third World. However, given the locus of economic power, the Third World countries play limited roles in the development of environmental regimes. The examination of the three environmental regimes conducted in Part 2 of this volume shows that only in specific circumstances can Third World country interests substantially modify the regime evolution process.

Regime formation is dependent on the convergence of interests among individual governments, the power distribution among those governments, and the relative salience of the issue involved. For each of the regimes examined, it was clear that the issue was salient enough to draw states to the bargaining table, although not all issues had the same relative salience for all parties. For example, the hazardous waste trade issue appeared to have greater relative salience for the Third World countries than for the industrialized states. Nation-states' perception of their interests was informed by their domestic circumstances, but it was even more reflective of the global economy. As a consequence, there was generally substantial divergence of interests between the industrialized countries and the Third World. Within a context of conflicting interests, the distribution of power conditions how states perceive and pursue their interests; therefore, it is important to examine the international context in which these actors function.

This context is one of globalization, a globalization of economies and of the environment. Industrialized economies find they are sensitive to changes in the global economy, and Third World countries have long been vulnerable to the ravages of global capitalism. Awareness of the globalization of the environment is inescapable, given the consequences of issues such as ozone depletion or nuclear fallout. The traditional concept of the environment focused on resource concerns and national needs in areas such as energy, food, and local pollution. But there is a growing awareness of the environment as one integrated system—a single biosphere. In this integrated, interdependent system, each actor is becoming increasingly aware of a sensitivity and vulnerability to the actions of others.

The present study has assessed the impact of globalization on Third World countries' capacity to influence environmental politics. It questions whether the regime process will inevitably be determined by the traditional patterns of power within the global economy. Generally, one can argue that the globalization of economies has worked in the favor of industrialized countries, which have the preponderance of power. They control institutions such as the World Bank, the IMF, and the GATT; they also have many more interests in common with the powerful TNCs than do the Third World countries.

However, the cases examined here suggest that, under certain circumstances, the growing perception of the environment as an integrated system can modify the way power is wielded within the global system. The Third World can exercise a measure of influence even if in most cases it is negative power—power to deny the regime its objectives. Therefore, although the Third World countries are constrained by their position in the world economic system, characteristics peculiar to the global environment have enhanced their ability to influence environmental regime outcomes.

Reviewing the Cases

The study found that the Third World countries can exercise this modest influence only in specific contexts. The mere fact that an issue is environmental does not automatically constitute a difference in the influence these countries are able to exercise. Issues of property and access are important. Key questions, then, are whether an environmental problem deals with a common-property resource issue and also whether the resource is held in open access or alternative arrangements. These factors have important implications for the negotiation process and for regime implementation. An examination of the evolution of the ozone layer protection regime, the hazardous waste trade regime, and the biodiversity regime is illustrative. The Third World's role in problem definition, bargaining, and regime transformation varied depending on the issue's characteristics.

The Ozone Layer Protection Regime

The ozone depletion problem addresses a common-property resource concern, the atmosphere. Thus, each user is capable of subtracting from the welfare of others. In addition, it is impossible to control access to this particular resource.

Problem definition. The Third World played no role in this phase of the process. The issue was defined and the agenda set primarily by individuals, organizations, and nations of the industrialized world. A transnational epistemic community, drawn primarily from industrialized countries, played a major role in the definition of the issue. The major producers of CFCs are First World corporations, which were aware that the way the problem was defined could have negative impacts on their economic interests. Consequently, they attempted to modify the definition. At the beginning of the process, Third World countries did not identify an interest in the evolving regime. They saw the issue primarily as a concern of the producer states, so they let the industrialized countries determine the agenda.

Bargaining. By 1987 the Third World countries had become more aware of the interests they had at stake in the process. The focus of the negotiations was on phasing out ozone-depleting chemicals, and the developing countries' concern was that a phaseout would impede their development and industrialization process. In order to advance their interests, they employed linkage politics, tying their accession to the agreement to the establishment of a fund to help them make the transition to new ozone-friendly technology. Although the United States opposed the establishment of such a fund, it finally gave in under pressure from both industrialized and Third World states.

Industrialized country actors realized that Third World countries had the ability to deny the regime its objective. Scientific evidence suggested that the consequences of a failed regime would include damage to human health, agriculture, and ecosystems. If China, India, Indonesia, and Mexico—all with large populations—were to industrialize using the old CFC technology, they would defeat the purpose of the regime. In fact, China, India, and Brazil initially refused to sign the Montreal Protocol and did not sign until after commitments were made regarding the establishment of a fund.

Regime transformation. This regime has undergone rapid transformation. The pace of regime change is a testament to the issue's high salience for the community of nations. However, the Third World has not played a major role in the transformation process, which has been spurred primarily by the series of revelations about the damage to the ozone layer. As a result, the ozone layer protection regime is a strong regime that includes specific commitments.

Overall, then, the only stage at which the Third World exerted any significant influence in the formation of this regime was at the bargaining stage, when the countries used linkage to gain the concession of a fund. This provision set an important precedent for later environmental negotiations.

The Hazardous Waste Trade Regime

This issue was perceived as a transboundary problem rather than a common-property resource concern; it also had greater relative salience for the importing states. The fact that the hazardous waste trade transferred environmental costs to the importers, while the exporters—primarily the developed states—received environmental, political, and economic benefits, made it difficult to get developed states' support for significant change. They reaped the environmental benefit of not having to dispose of these wastes on their own territory; they also enjoyed the political benefit of not having to make difficult siting decisions regarding a landfill or an incinerator; and they obtained the economic benefit from the industrial process that had generated the waste. The importing states also stood to gain economic advantages from accepting the waste, but in many cases they preferred not to bear the associated environmental and political costs.

Because this was a transboundary problem rather than an open access commons problem, industrialized states did not perceive the same kind of interdependence and vulnerability they did with regard to the ozone depletion issue. However, access considerations did become a part of the developing countries' strategy. Since importing states could formally control access to their territories, they could take unilateral action against waste imports, which is what many did because of their frustration with the inadequacy of the Basel Convention provisions. The problem with this option is that it is extremely difficult to monitor the activities of corporate networks, especially when there is limited cooperation from the source states.

Problem definition. Third World nations and major environmental NGOs such as Greenpeace played a significant role in publicizing the hazardous waste problem, but the Third World countries were initially unsuccessful in defining the issue to reflect their own interests. Some of these states wanted to define the problem as the existence of the trade itself; therefore, the solution would be to completely ban the hazardous waste trade. However, the problem was eventually defined in a manner more consonant with the interests of the developed states—that is, as a matter of regulating the hazardous waste trade. Later in the regime transformation process, the problem was redefined to allow a complete banning of such trade.

Bargaining. The bargaining process began before the problem definition process was complete. As bargaining proceeded, developing countries continued to press for the complete banning of the hazardous waste trade, whereas the developed countries argued for loose controls so they could continue to conduct the trade as they wished. Although the developing countries and the environmental NGOs were part of a high-profile media campaign during this stage, at the conclusion of the Basel Convention they remained unsuccessful in influencing the industrialized countries on this issue.

Regime transformation. Efforts at transformation have been aimed at weakening as well as strengthening the regime. The developed states and the transnational corporations have moved to weaken the regime, whereas the Third World states and environmental NGOs have focused on strengthening it. Developed country interests, through changes in OECD and EC regulations, have modified their definition of the hazardous wastes that should be handled under the Basel Convention regulations; in addition, the TNCs are continuing to ship waste illegally to the Third World. For their part, the Third World countries, aided by environmental NGOs, have succeeded in obtaining a total ban on the movement of hazardous wastes. Individual countries and regions have also imposed bans on the import of waste.

The reversal by some industrialized states with regard to the imposition of a ban largely represented a formal recognition of the fact that most of the world's nations had already initiated unilateral bans. However, a ban is extremely difficult to enforce, especially in the face of recalcitrant exporters. As the Bangladesh example shows (see Chapter 5), waste exporters will resort to subterfuge. Therefore, a major concern is whether the states can successfully monitor the activities of corporations that are often powerful global actors in their own right. The legislative trend, as illustrated by GATT, is toward moving away from regulating the actions of corporations.

With regard to the hazardous waste trade issue, although the Third World states were influential in placing the issue on the agenda, they were not able to control the definition process. The evolution of this regime was also substantially determined by the power asymmetry that exists between the two nation-state groups. Since the hazardous waste trade is not perceived as a commons problem, the developed states did not see themselves incurring costs from a "free trade" in hazardous wastes. Although developing countries were finally able to secure an agreement to stop the trade, it is not clear how the ban can be effectively implemented without the cooperation of the TNCs. Consequently, the regime is weak, and the Third World states will have to bear the brunt of the burden of regime implementation.

The Biodiversity Regime

Destruction of biodiversity is a commons issue, but it is somewhat different from the ozone depletion problem. Whereas the atmosphere is held in an open access regime, biodiversity is held in mixed property arrangements in which all four types of property arrangements—open access, private property, communal property, and state control—are relevant. This situation affects perceptions of interdependence and vulnerability. Another complicating factor is the concentration of biodiversity in the Third World.

Problem definition. The developed country interests initially defined the problem: They saw the regime's focus as the conservation of diversity.

However, the Third World countries were able to broaden the scope to address issues such as sovereignty and technology transfer. Their biological wealth gave them the leverage to modify the agenda.

Bargaining. The industrialized countries came into the negotiation process wanting to protect biological diversity and to be assured of continued access to Third World diversity. Considerable economic interests were at stake in the area of genetic resources. For its part, the Third World demanded sovereignty, access to technology, and financial assistance. These countries took the position that biodiversity was a resource like oil and lumber and that they had the right to control access and receive reimbursement. They also wanted access to technology—to the biotechnology developed from the use of their resources as well as to the technology that would help them conserve their biodiversity. Finally, they continued their press for financial resources, claiming that the environment and natural resources could only be conserved under conditions of sustainable global development.

The bargaining tactic of Third World countries was to link accession to the treaty and access to their biological resources to financial and technical assistance. They were successful in having their sovereignty formally recognized; however, they were less successful with regard to the technology transfer issue, and it is difficult to assess their success regarding financial assistance. There are provisions for technology transfer and the sharing of research, but these are substantially modified by language that addresses intellectual property rights and patents. And although there is a commitment to provide financial assistance, it is not yet clear how effectively the proposed funding mechanism will address the Third World's interests.

Regime transformation. The biodiversity regime is still relatively weak, but the convention does allow for regime strengthening. Third World countries did not receive everything they wanted, but the language regarding both sovereignty and control of access and the sharing of the profits of technology might indicate a shift in norms. Because so much global biodiversity is within the sovereign control of Third World countries, individual countries can act effectively to protect biodiversity.

But such action requires much more than merely passing statutes. The predation of the economic elite must be controlled, and the local population must be given more control of its economic and social circumstances; only then will conservation be more likely to be seen by citizens as a viable option. When people have severely reduced options, they are less likely to be concerned about conservation. Conservation of biodiversity, then, cannot be effectively addressed in isolation from the socioeconomic contexts of the global community and of the individual nation-state.

The Third World's Role

An examination of these three cases suggests that the Third World's impact on regime formation is greater when the matter under debate is a common-property resource concern. Under commons circumstances other actors are willing to make compromises to obtain Third World cooperation, as was the case with the ozone protection regime. Linkage politics becomes moderately successful in this context, and it was used by developing countries to secure some economic and technical assistance. However, even when a situation is not purely one of open access, if the Third World countries control access to resources of significant economic interest to the industrialized world, some concessions will be made, as was the case in the biodiversity regime. These two situations can be compared to the hazardous waste regime, in which no real concessions were made. The complete ban was only agreed to under protest after most Third World countries had already formally closed their borders to hazardous wastes. In the case of the hazardous waste trade regime, the Third World had nothing to bargain with. This trade was not a common-property resource concern, so they could not offer the developed countries environmental goods in order to obtain their cooperation; the ban would, in fact, deprive the exporting states of environmental goods. And few Third World countries were in the position to offer scarce economic goods in exchange for cooperation.

In all three cases, developed country interests defined the issues, although the Third World was able to modify the agenda of the biodiversity regime. Even in the case of the hazardous waste trade, in which the developing countries played a key role in bringing the problem to the public's attention, the developed country interests had a large role in the definition process and, therefore, in the content of the agenda and the nature of the bargaining process. In terms of bargaining, the developed countries held the preponderance of power and exercised the greater amount of influence. But this study suggests that in spite of the differences in economic and political power, common-property resource issues allow Third World countries to exercise some influence in environmental regime formation. Property and access relations, because of their impact on perceptions of vulnerability and economic interests, are likely to determine the further transformation of these regimes and to condition the evolution of other environmental regimes.

Convergence and Divergence of Interests

The Third World is a diverse group of countries, linked by the common experience of colonialism and imperialism. In spite of the many economic and political differences within the group, its members exhibited a remarkable convergence of interests as they participated in the evolution of the three regimes discussed here. Although there was little divergence, there was substantial differentiation in levels of interest within the group because not all countries felt these regimes had the same degree of salience. An examination of their roles in, and responses to, the development and evolution of the three regimes illustrates this point.

The ozone layer protection regime. This issue acquired salience for Third World countries only midway through the regime's evolution. Once the issue gained salience, China and India, with their populous states and growing industrial sectors, had a particular interest. The Third World case was also well represented by Argentina, Brazil, Egypt, and Kenya. For Brazil, China, Egypt, and Mexico, the issue had particular relevance because they had already begun to invest in alternate technologies.

The early ratifiers of the agreements, as we have seen, were all low- and middle-income countries representing all of the major export sectors, especially the diversified and nonfuel primary goods categories. However, an examination of the early ratifiers does not necessarily identify the countries for which the regime had the greatest salience. Some states delayed signing the Vienna Convention and the Montreal Protocol because they found those documents did not adequately address their interests. Consequently, China, India, and Indonesia only signed after the London Amendment had made provisions for financial concessions.

The hazardous waste trade regime. Although the bulk of the Third World states were in favor of a waste trade ban, there was some divergence of interests. Mexico sided with the industrialized states in preferring trade management over a ban, and some states were willing to accept waste for recycling. An examination of the early ratifiers reveals that most were either targets of waste trade schemes or were identified as source states; consequently, these were states for which the issue had particular salience.

The early ratifiers represented a wide range of major export categories, but about 70 percent were middle-income states. Third World countries also initiated several regional responses to the Basel Convention, but, since these actions were complementary, they represented a convergence of interests.

The biodiversity regime. This was a high-profile matter, with the convention drawing ready signatures in June 1992 from most of the world's states. No significant divergence of interests was apparent, but there were substantial differences in levels of salience. As noted previously, the regime had particular relevance for states that were making their resources available to biodiversity prospectors, as well as for countries such as China, India, Mexico, Peru, and the Philippines, which had invested in biotechnology research programs. Again, the early ratifiers were spread over the five major export sectors and were low- and middle-income countries.

An examination of the Third World actors involved in all three regimes shows that China, India, and Mexico were key actors for which the regimes had great salience. A study of the major export categories of the early ratifiers shows no recognizable pattern, but the income group data do reveal a pattern. No high-income country was either an early ratifier or a key player in the negotiations.[1] Perhaps, because of their economic circumstances, these countries did not see their well-being as significantly affected by the outcome of the negotiations. Additionally, they were not eligible for some of the concessions wrung from the industrialized states; for example, they could not qualify for grants from the Global Environment Facility since GEF grants are only available to countries with annual per capita incomes below $4,000.[2]

The Global Environment Facility and Regime Implementation

In the process of bargaining over environmental regimes, Third World countries have consistently argued that a necessary condition for environmental protection in their countries is financial assistance. For example, they need assistance to make the transition to chemical substitutes that will not damage the ozone layer as well as to protect their biodiversity. They argued that they could not be expected to divert resources from survival needs to take care of important, but less pressing, environmental matters. With financial assistance they would be able to accede to the convention and fulfill its provisions.

Industrialized country interests created a funding institution to address these concerns, but the institution is being criticized because of its policy decisions and its structure. At issue is whether this institution will serve the industrialized country interests and possibly those of the Third World elites or whether it will indeed serve the interests of the Third World population and the environment.

The institution, the Global Environment Facility, was established in 1990. Fiscal year 1993 was the second full year in which it operated as a pilot project to provide grants for environmental protection in developing countries. Its funds are intended to cover the increased costs of protecting the global environment in four areas: global warming, international waters, biological diversity, and the ozone layer. Agenda 21 of the Rio Conference listed GEF as the source of funds for projects intended to provide global environmental benefits. The Convention on Biological Diversity also designated GEF, on an interim basis, as the source of funds for activities aimed at protecting biodiversity.

The facility is run by the World Bank, UNEP, and the United Nations Development Programme (UNDP). Participants have pledged $1.3 billion for the initial pilot phase. At the end of fiscal year 1993, GEF had 63 members, two-thirds of which were from the Third World. The facility is expected to eventually have universal membership. Eligibility for grants is dependent on income levels, with countries with annual per capita incomes of less than $4,000 qualifying for grants. By 1993 32 projects, with a value of $250 million, had been approved, and 79 others were being processed.[3]

The GEF was established as a partnership among the World Bank, UNEP, and UNDP, but the World Bank acted as the managing partner.[4] There was concern among environmental NGOs that the World Bank, which had funded ecological devastation throughout the Third World, was poorly suited to manage an institution that had been put forward as part of the solution to the global environmental crisis. In addition, Third World states were concerned that unlike most UN institutions, in which voting is done on a one country–one vote basis, the GEF was donor controlled.

During the facility's pilot period, its stated focus was on projects with substantial global benefits in the four targeted areas. This strategy neglected other crucial Third World concerns such as toxic waste pollution and landlessness. Some analysts have suggested that the projects approved for funding were those that would benefit the industrialized countries and the elites in the Third World. About 60 percent of the funds approved under the first round of GEF funding targeted biodiversity projects. The chair of GEF was particularly interested in targeting important gene pools and economically significant species,[5] which is consistent with the TNCs' interest in biotechnology and the efforts to patent life forms and germ plasm.

Some GEF-funded projects will have destructive environmental consequences. World Bank–funded development projects have been criticized in the past for their associated environmental destruction and displacement of people. But GEF has taken the position that the resulting environmental damage can be mitigated, and it has invested in hydroelectric projects. For example, in the Arun Valley in Nepal, GEF biodiversity money is funding the Arun Hydro-Project and is thereby contributing indirectly to biodiversity destruction.[6] China is trying to raise money for the world's largest dam, and one of the target sources is the GEF. The $20-billion project would create a 375-mile-long lake and displace about 1.6 million people; it would also submerge historic sites and threaten several endangered species.[7] Another controversial use of GEF money is in the Congo, where funds have been used to build roads into areas targeted for protection and to clear riverside vegetation.[8]

GEF is also working in the area of energy, financing projects designed to slow global warming. Initiatives that have been supported include a $7-million photovoltaic project in Zimbabwe. In Mauritius it is funding a $3.3-million project to develop energy from sugarcane residues. GEF has also shown interest in a variety of other projects, including installing efficient lighting, capturing methane gas from coal mines, and developing biomass-fueled gas turbines.[9]

As the pilot phase drew to a close, criticism about the decisionmaking structure of GEF increased. Negotiations over the future of the funding mechanism were concluded in March 1994, and the participating countries made some determinations. GEF would be a permanent structure and would receive an infusion of $2 billion during the period from 1994 to 1997.[10] It was decided that instead of creating a new institution for environmental funding, GEF would build on the institutional structure provided by the World Bank, UNEP, and UNDP. It would be available to function as the funding mechanism for environmental conventions at the parties' request.[11]

A new governance structure was developed in an attempt to address the concerns of both the developed and the developing countries. The GEF will be administered by an independent secretariat. The secretariat's CEO will report to a 32-seat Governing Council made up of representatives of recipient as well as donor countries. The facility will use a double majority voting system. Each decision will require two separate votes: In one, voting strength will be weighted according to financial contributions, and the other will be conducted on a one country–one vote basis. This system will give recipients some choices, but donor countries will retain enough control so they will be willing to contribute money to the facility.[12] GEF has expanded its project areas to include land degradation and will fund programs that are country driven as long as they are consistent with sustainable development.[13]

The results of an independent evaluation raise questions about GEF's suitability for its assigned task. The assessment identified serious flaws in the facility's performance during its pilot phase. These were problems typically associated with World Bank projects, including secrecy, difficulties working with local communities, and an inordinate rush to lend money. It remains to be seen whether GEF's restructuring will help it shed the World Bank's style of operation.

Conclusion

When there is a shared perception of environmental vulnerability, the Third World is able to gain a modest bargaining advantage. Although developing countries are generally at an economic disadvantage in the global system, within specific environmental contexts they can win concessions from the industrialized countries, concessions they see as being crucial to their participation in environmental regimes. An important component of the concessions has been provision for financial assistance.

The current funding arrangement, GEF, is under the aegis of the World Bank. Problems inherent in the functioning of the GEF call into question the value of the financial concessions won by the Third World. Some GEF projects follow the pattern of World Bank development projects, thus raising the concern that developing countries might have expended their leverage for the sake of a false victory. Given the structure of the GEF, the financial concessions could well be Trojan horses to be used by the industrialized country interests to steer Third World resource policies in the directions they prefer. Although this might serve the interests of some Third World elites, the environment and the majority of the population may not be well served. As it is currently structured and administered, the GEF might delay rather than hasten the achievement of regime objectives.

Notes

1. According to the World Bank (*World Development Report 1993* [New York: Oxford University Press, 1993], 328–329), the high-income Third World countries are the Bahamas, Brunei, Cyprus, Kuwait, Qatar, Singapore, and the United Arab Emirates. They have annual per capita incomes of $7,911 or more.

2. World Bank, *Annual Report 1993* (Washington, D.C.: World Bank, 1993), 51.

3. Ibid.

4. Oliver Tickell and Nicholas Hildyard ("Green Dollars, Green Menace," *The Ecologist* 22, no. 3 [May–June 1992]: 82) quote the GEF administrator, Ian Johnson, as admitting that in the GEF, "the World Bank is judge, jury and executioner."

5. Ibid.

6. Ibid., 83.

7. "China to Lobby on Three Gorges at GEF," *The Ecologist Campaigns* (May–June 1993): 1.

8. Tickell and Hildyard, "Green Dollars," 83.

9. Nicholas Lenssen, "Providing Energy in Developing Countries," in Lester R. Brown, ed., *State of the World 1993* (New York: Norton, 1993), 118.

10. Hilary French, "GEF Replenishment," *World Watch* 7, no. 4 (July–August 1994): 7.

11. World Bank, *Annual Report 1993,* 51.

12. Hilary French, "GEF Replenishment," *World Watch,* 7, no. 4 (July–August 1994): 7.

13. World Bank, *Annual Report 1993,* 51.

8

Global Environmental Politics and Sustainable Development

International environmental regimes are seen as crucial components in the effort to protect the biosphere, but few environmental agreements can be implemented using a top-down strategy; they will depend on cooperation at all levels of the global society.[1] It will not be enough to have the agreement of the major global actors; implementation of these policies and agreements will also depend on cooperation at the national and local levels. An issue such as the conservation of biodiversity is dependent on the actions of the poorest peasant as well as on those of the heads of governments and corporations.

But it is difficult to obtain the required cooperation when, on the one hand, significant destitution is found in the society and, on the other, a small class is ready to exploit the available natural and human resources. The growing globalization of society might make the task even more difficult because with globalization, the rich have greater freedom to exploit the poor. With its attendant economic asymmetry, the globalization of the economy has clear consequences for environmental health and sustainable development.

The Environmental Cost of Structural Inequality

Structural inequality is reflected at both the global and national levels. Although governments wield power at the national level, they are generally becoming less powerful at the global level. Nation-states, for the most part, are artificial structures with decreasing power and legitimacy. They will not determine the environmental future by themselves, in part because transnational actors will play major roles. Power is shifting increasingly from nation-states to transnational actors such as TNCs, international financial markets, multilateral banks, and international media groups such as the Cable News Network (CNN).[2] Local and national bureaucracies no longer control information or the important sectors of the economy; these are now controlled by international oligarchies composed of business executives, financiers, and image makers.

To the extent that power continues to shift from local communities to centralized global actors, it will become that much more difficult to properly address major environmental issues. Local communities will have less control over the disposition of their resources. The move toward greater concentration and centralization of power will result in decreased accountability to any nation or community. This is consistent with the trend that shows power shifting away from workers and from local and national governments toward huge corporations, thereby freeing them from local and national regulations. Changes in information, communication, transportation, and manufacturing technologies have enhanced the ability of TNCs to relocate their facilities around the world. The resulting competition among workers, communities, and countries is likely to have a depressing effect on wages and the social environment; it is also likely to be deleterious for the natural environment as environmentally damaging industries continue their shift from the industrialized countries to the poorer countries.

When there is a separation of producer from consumer, employer from employee, and investor from investment, the decisionmaking process is freer to ignore the externalities that might otherwise be factored in. This kind of decisionmaking process justifies the hazardous waste trade and the establishment of hazardous waste landfills and incinerators in poor communities. In this economic environment, businesses and individuals are seizing the opportunity to separate themselves from the costs of their actions. The focus is often on extracting the benefits and passing the cost on to other actors; in this way, a firm can profit from investments that turn out to be very costly for the community. An activity such as clear-cut logging can register positively on a company's balance sheet and in a country's GNP without the community being compensated for the resulting damage, which can include increased flooding, drought, soil loss, and the cost of replanting. Truly sustainable environmental development depends on the opposite trend—toward decentralization and the distribution of economic power.

National governments have lost much of their power to choose their own economic paths. Their actions have been constrained by the power of capital to pick up and leave. Transnationals are now the world's preeminent economic actors, yet there are no international institutions that provide a countervailing force to these powerful actors and no systematic efforts to bring them to account for the harmful by-products or consequences of their activities. Power has also passed from national actors to international institutions such as the International Monetary Fund, the World Bank, and the General Agreement on Tariffs and Trade. Although the decisions of these institutions have an enormous impact on the global economy and ecology, they are able to carry on much of their business away from public scrutiny.

National governments are tied to geography and are motivated to satisfy enough interests so they can remain in power. TNCs recognize fewer constraints; they transcend geography and are driven by the logic of profit.[3] These corporations are supported in their quest by instruments such as GATT and NAFTA, whose primary goal is to increase the mobility of resources, including capital. In order to achieve this objective, these organizations work to reduce the safeguards that get in the way of the TNCs' business—including environmental provisions. Under the provisions established in the Uruguay Round of GATT, any member country has the right to challenge another country's environmental laws as constituting illegal trade barriers. Three World Trade Organization experts then hear the case in closed session, and countries found in violation face trade sanctions if they do not repeal the offending laws.

Third World governments' efforts to carve out a niche in the global economy can also have costly environmental consequences. One approach has been to establish export-processing zones. Although these provide a number of low-wage jobs, they have also been associated with negative social impacts and environmental damage. The corporations enjoy special privileges such as tax breaks, the use of valuable land, influence in local government decisionmaking, and priority access to local water supplies and power generation; in addition, local taxpayers pay for the infrastructure these enterprises need. Sometimes these businesses add to the cost by contaminating local land and water supplies with their toxic wastes. All of these costs seem disproportionate to the benefits received, especially when the primary benefit is low-wage jobs. In addition, Third World countries do not usually enjoy the investment benefits of the profits earned by these enterprises since the firms usually export the profits.

Structural inequities distort societies and economies and threaten the development of a global consensus on issues such as the environment and development. Consequently, they present significant obstacles to the successful implementation of environmental regimes, and they jeopardize the transition to sustainable development.

Prospects for Sustainable Development

The concept of sustainable development suggests that it is possible to achieve sound environmental planning "without putting a brake on human aspirations for economic and social improvement."[4] However, this concept has many shades of meaning. Some definitions emphasize the sustainable component of the term and focus on the protection and conservation of living and nonliving resources. Other definitions focus on the development component of the term, targeting changes in technology as a way to enhance growth and development. Still others posit that sustainable development is a contradiction in terms and that the focus should be on redistribution instead of growth.[5] A definition proposed by the World Conservation Union (IUCN) highlights the constraints of the biosphere. The IUCN defines sustainable development as "improving the quality of human life while living within the carrying capacity of supporting ecosystems."[6]

Missing from these definitions, but becoming increasingly recognized as an important prerequisite to sustainable development, is the issue of equity—equity for future generations and equity for those of the present generation who have little or no access to natural resources and economic goods.[7] An adequate response to the threat to the global environment will therefore have to address issues of equity; it will also have to be based on an awareness of the variety of ways in which the environment is socially constructed in different parts of the world. For example, in much of the industrialized world the focus is on aesthetics and conservation; in the Third World, because of its position in the global division of labor, the environment and its resources are more likely to be regarded as means of increasing material well-being. In many of these countries, earning a livelihood involves working in agriculture, forestry, and mining—to a greater extent than is the case in the industrialized world. Capital accumulation is dependent on the exploitation of labor and natural resources.[8]

The premise of the global economy is endless growth, and that is clearly unsustainable. The industrialized countries want to keep growing because with growing economies they can pacify the less affluent members of their societies by promising them better economic times without having to deal with redistributive issues. The Third World countries also want their economies to grow; to that end, many have embraced the Western model of development.

However, the planet cannot support everyone in such a resource-intensive lifestyle. For example, if China and India were to adopt the unsustainable Western economic model, the global system would collapse long before even a small fraction of their citizens had made the lifestyle transition. Related to lifestyle is the issue of culture. Globalization has a cultural component, with the end result likely to be cultural homogeneity. But if such homogeneity means that everyone must adopt the globally dominant Western culture, this would also work against a culture of sustainability. For example, it might mean the abandonment of local norms, such as the injunction in some cultures that "when a tree is harvested, two must be planted."[9]

Because of the global communication network, the Third World elites and the people of the industrialized world now share some of the same values, so education for sustainability has to be worldwide. The people of the industrialized world need to learn to destroy fewer resources, and those in the Third World must aspire to be less resource consuming than the people of the industrialized countries. A change in economic logic is clearly necessary for sustainable development to occur.

Lawrence Summers, former chief economist at the World Bank, took the position that growth created "both the way and the will to improve the environment."[10] But before such an assumption can be made, one must determine who benefits from growth. If economic growth benefits only a small sector, this will have little positive impact on the protection of the environment; in addition, the economic activity expended in generating that growth may have been costly for the environment. Although growth does not have to result in environmental degradation, in a context in which the objective is to cut costs at any point possible, growth is likely to have negative implications for the environment.

At the Rio Conference in 1992, one objective of the proposals before the conference was to merge the UN environmental and developmental capacities into a new institution in order to take advantage of the linkages between them and to promote sustainable development. The conference did devise a plan for a Commission on Sustainable Development, which was approved by the General Assembly in December 1992 and was established by the UN Economic and Social Council in February 1993. Its task is to monitor and oversee the implementation of Agenda 21, including progress toward the achievement of the UN target of providing 0.7 percent of industrialized countries' gross national products for official development assistance.[11] But a new commission and the provision of aid will go only a short way toward achieving sustainable development. Global regimes provide a valuable context, but they need to be supported by changes at the global, regional, national, and local levels.

Strategies at the Global Level

Sustainable development is often addressed as a Third World concern, but given the globalization of the environment and the economy, sustainable development will be a global project or it will fail. Although its achievement might require different actions in the Third World than in the industrialized world, it is a goal that requires action in all of the world's nations.

Sustainable development would be greatly assisted by a series of international policy changes. Debt relief is one such area of concern. The debt burden increases the impoverishment of Third World countries, in part because in situations of destitution, people are unlikely to want to focus on longterm environmental commitments. The large debts owed by Third World countries mean that future generations of people in these countries will be working to repay future generations of industrialized country residents; further, natural resources are likely to be sacrificed in the push to earn foreign exchange.

It might be impossible to put a monetary value on the ecological damage that has been done by the industrialized countries. But one could argue that although the Third World countries owe an enormous economic debt to the developed country institutions, the developed world owes the

Third World an even more enormous ecological debt. Unfortunately, an argument for debt forgiveness on these grounds is not likely to be taken seriously by the industrialized countries.

A code of conduct for TNCs is even more necessary today than it was when the environmental issue was first considered in UN forums decades ago. Nation-states may formulate environmental agreements, thereby ceding some of their sovereignty, but this will not accomplish the desired ends if transnational corporations continue their activities unconstrained. Since many TNCs do not adhere to an environmental or any other code of ethics, restraints must be placed on their activities. This is difficult in an environment that tends to see corporate freedom of action as crucial to economic growth.

Many major corporations are exhibiting a new environmental awareness; this has led more than 1,100 firms from all over the world to endorse the Business Charter for Sustainable Development, which sets out environmental principles for corporate conduct.[12] For some firms, adhering to codes of this nature is a matter of embracing the form and not the substance. But even a superficial greening can help in making the transition to new norms of corporate behavior. In order to assist in this behavioral change, the United Nations should continue its work on a code of conduct for TNCs as well as on a means of monitoring such a code.

The imposition of a global green tax on TNCs would modify corporate behavior. The tax could also solve two additional problems. First, it would provide some of the resources needed to implement Agenda 21. A Third World spokesperson observed that the Commission on Sustainable Development's mandate to implement Agenda 21 was being hampered by the meager flow of resources.[13] Tax money could be used to fund research on cleaner production methods and more forgiving energy technologies. The research products could be patented by the United Nations and then be made freely available to all nations. Second, the tax would also encourage TNCs to internalize some of the environmental costs of their activities and to make a more rapid transition to less polluting technologies. Any rational strategy to address sustainable development must face the fact that global resources need to be targeted to the development of new sources of energy and to new technologies for transportation, agriculture, housing, and manufacturing.

Efforts to reform multilateral institutions such as the World Bank and GATT should also continue. Although this is a difficult challenge, the environmental regime process has shown that the industrialized world is not a monolith. Industrialized country coalitions did break apart in the bargaining over the ozone layer protection regime and the biodiversity regime. In addition, although they are reluctant to change policy, these institutions are not impervious to pressure for change. For example, the World Bank has made small, limited changes in response to public pressure. Two new policies have been instituted to make the Bank more responsive to the public: One makes documents more accessible, and the other establishes an independent appeals panel.[14]

One issue of concern as we try to institute global governance is whether a shared idea of progress exists among the world's nations. If there is no sense of a global community, there will be no global consensus as to whose consumption or progress should be sacrificed in the effort to address the environmental crisis. In the context of global limits, should the poor give up their meager share to accommodate the rich, or should the rich curb their consumption to accommodate the poor? We have a situation in which the nations of the Third World emphasize the values of equity and justice and countries of the industrialized world emphasize the values of efficiency and technological progress. Yet regardless of the perspectives on shared progress and shared values, a single biosphere imposes a shared destiny on the earth's citizens. The challenge, then, is to increase global awareness of this common destiny.

Strategies at the Regional Level

Regional environmental institutions represent an important strata of environmental governance. They provide support for global regimes and often involve fewer transactions costs than global institutions because the participants more readily identify common interests. One example involves the series of conventions on regional seas that has emerged out of the UN Regional Seas Program. These regional arrangements support, and are designed to be consistent with, the United Nations Convention on the Law of the Sea, which contains provisions for the environmentally sound management of the oceans. The Regional Seas Program is based on the assumption that the countries of each region share a common interest in safeguarding their marine environment and have a mutual need for sustainable development of marine resources. Regional arrangements have also proved to be efficient means of addressing transboundary issues, such as the issue of atmospheric pollution from industries in neighboring countries.

It is also noteworthy that when the developing countries felt shortchanged by the Basel Convention, one of their strategies was to develop regional responses to the hazardous waste trade. Regional organizations are in the position to monitor and support both global and national initiatives.

Strategies at the National Level

In spite of the challenges of the global community, Third World governments do not really have the option of delinking from the global economy; nor can they depend on the ethics or beneficence of other global actors. They must seek and create their own opportunities. Developing countries need to adopt a twofold strategy for their participation in global environmental politics. One plank of this strategy should be the continued use of linkage politics. These countries have had some modest success with this approach, and they should continue to use it when the circumstances are propitious, such as to target global institutions and to lobby for structural change.

Achieving sustainable development can be aided by access to financial assistance and technology, but Third World countries need to weigh the terms of the assistance carefully. Their linkage politics should target the institutions that make the funding decisions. The objective is that the projects funded should be those that benefit the majority of the people affected and not just a small elite and global capital. Developed country actors will not be inclined to dispense large amounts of charity to developing countries. Significant change in developed country behavior is dependent on a perception of self-interest, which in turn is dependent on two factors: a recognition that the transfer of resources is necessary in order to maintain a healthy world environment, and the assurance that the resources will indeed be used either toward that end or in the interests of global capital.

The second component of the Third World strategy is increasing cooperation among the developing countries. The success of this approach depends on the extent to which they can identify a common interest in the area of sustainable development. It would mean putting more effort into South-South cooperation. Third World countries' strategies should focus on the development of their own capabilities, which could be facilitated by pooling and sharing scientific and technological resources. For example, in the area of biodiversity, Brazil, Venezuela, and Thailand—all of which have established a biotechnology infrastructure—could cooperate with other developing countries that are just beginning to establish the requisite infrastructure.[15] A Centre for Science and Technology of the Non-Aligned and Other Developing Countries has been set up in India.[16] This organization could work with other Third World scientific institutions to coordinate joint research and development. Such a strategy could increase developing countries' capacity to benefit from and manage their own resources. Even more important, it would increase their ability to set the terms of their own development.

Although much government power has been ceded to or seized by global entities, national governments still make decisions that have important consequences for sustainable development. For example, their investment decisions are likely to have significant impacts on sustainable development in individual states. Even if these decisions do not involve direct government investment, governments can use policy instruments to encourage or discourage certain types of investments. Government decisions also help to determine the internal distribution of costs and benefits.

The distribution of costs and benefits reflects the socioeconomic profile of the society. States are not necessarily representative of citizens' interests.

Although the Third World governments' position might represent a broad spectrum of national interests, it sometimes reflects the narrow interests of a small group such as business or the military, which might use political and economic power to enrich itself. In the case of natural resource–rich countries, such use of power might involve the exploitation of minerals, forests, and marine resources—ignoring the interests of the communities in which these resources are located. But local and community management systems are imperative in the quest for sustainable development; consequently, activities at the local level are crucial to its achievement.

Strategies at the Local Level

Local and community forces have two major roles to play in the push for sustainable development. They must provide a counterforce to global forces that serve to devalue and discount them, and they need to support environmental and development strategies that maintain or improve their quality of life.

The formation of global networks of community organizations has been part of an attempt to counter the internationalization of capital, labor, and other resources. Although these local organizations have roots in the community, some are also part of a transnational network that will facilitate their efforts to work on a global level for objectives such as minimum human, labor, and environmental rights. One example of these transnational networks based on common interests was seen during the anti-NAFTA campaign when national and community organizations in Canada, the United States, and Mexico consulted and communicated with each other regarding their concerns about the impending agreement.

Third World NGOs have begun to challenge government and corporate practices, and they are also using sustainable development strategies. The Chipko Movement in India is only one of many thousands of such movements in the Third World. These community-based NGOs want to ensure that people at the bottom of the socioeconomic ladder have the opportunity to participate in shaping their own destinies. As a part of this process, they want communities to be consulted on local development projects. Many Third World citizens are poor, and because of their lack of economic power they often have development policies imposed upon them. But attempts to implement development schemes need to be informed by an understanding of the people who are participating in the development process. If the development is for them, it should occur on their terms and incorporate their ideas. Sustainable development depends on decentralization at the local level, and a crucial consideration is the control of the resources. Aid may or may not help the poor in the Third World, depending on how well it is targeted. If the aid is poorly targeted, it may be used to perpetuate the existing inequities in the society instead of being used to ameliorate them.

In order to address the environmental impacts of business activities, community-based accounting is necessary. This would ensure the internalization of the social and environmental costs of economic activity. The emphasis on free trade and the globalization of the economy works against such an accounting system. If the costs had to be internalized, however, investment proposals would be assessed differently. There would be greater accountability than is the case with the present emphasis on the global market.

Finally, it is futile to attempt to implement international or regional agreements local communities are unlikely or unable to support. No global consensus exists on the concept of progress or a vision of the future, and some Third World countries are so riven by inequity that no national consensus exists either. Without such a consensus, each local or national actor is likely to see any sacrifices made as benefiting the other actor disproportionately, and each is less likely to identify a common stake in environmental protection. It is difficult to envisage the achievement of sustainable development in an environment of severe inequity, yet if strategies for such development are not supported at the local or community level, the efforts to formulate environmental institutions will be for naught.

Conclusion

Addressing environmental problems calls for global strategies. But global action is futile unless it is supported by action at all levels, especially at the community level. Inequities at the global, national, and local levels, however, present obstacles to the support of the regimes and constitute a real threat to adequate implementation and enforcement of international environmental institutions.

As important actors in the development and evolution of environmental regimes, Third World states' responsibility does not end at the bargaining table. Often, the pronouncements and posturings of these states in international forums are at odds with their domestic policies, and their push for equi-ty and justice in the global context is not translated to the domestic arena. But achieving sustainable development of the biosphere demands equity and justice in the national and local contexts as well as in the global context. Addressing extreme inequities at the community, national, and global levels is an important prerequisite for the achievement of sustainable development.

Notes

1. Some environmental regimes are moderately successful using a top-down approach. One example is the ozone layer protection regime, which does

not require significant global and national socioeconomic change. Its major requirement is for technological change; consequently, agreement by nation-states, backed up by the relevant industrial sector, will go a long way toward assuring the achievement of the regime's goals. However, success in areas such as biodiversity, global warming, desertification, and deforestation is more dependent on substantial socioeconomic change and on cooperation at global, regional, national, and community levels.

2. Robert Gilman, "What Time Is It?" *In Context* 36 (1993): 14.

3. Richard Barnet, "Inquiries into the Human Prospect," *World Policy Journal* 10, no. 1 (Spring 1993): 95–96.

4. Michael Redclift, *Sustainable Development: Exploring the Contradictions* (London: Routledge, 1987), 33.

5. Herman E. Daly, "Towards Some Operational Principles of Sustainable Development," *Ecological Economics* 2 (1990): 1, 5.

6. IUCN–the World Conservation Union, the United Nations Environment Programme (UNEP), and the World Wide Fund for Nature (WWF), *Caring for the Earth* (Gland, Switzerland: IUCN, UNEP, and WWF, 1991), 10.

7. World Resources Institute, *World Resources 1992–93*, (New York: Oxford University Press, 1992), 3.

8. Redclift, *Sustainable Development,* 200–201.

9. Asian NGO Coalition, IRED Asia, and the People-Centered Development Forum, "Coming Back to Life," *In Context* 36 (1993): 18.

10. "Conference Explores Issues, Obstacles and Support for NAFTA Agreement," *IMF Survey* 21, no. 16 (August 3, 1992): 245.

11. "Assembly Creates Sustainable Development Commission, endorses 'Agenda 21,'" *UN Chronicle* 30, no. 1 (March 3, 1993): 80–81; and "From Words to Deeds: New Commission Builds on Earth Summit Legacy," *UN Chronicle* 30, no. 3 (September 1993): 62–63.

12. World Resources Institute, *World Resources 1994–95* (New York: Oxford University Press, 1994), 214.

13. "From Words to Deeds," 62. This observation was made by Manuel Rodriguez, director of the Environmental Institute of Colombia, who was speaking on behalf of the Group of 77.

14. "Chinks in the World Bank's Armor," *World Watch* 7, no. 2 (March–April 1994): 6.

15. Thomas C. Wiegele, *Biotechnology and International Relations: The Political Dimensions* (Gainesville: University of Florida Press, 1991), 119.

16. South Commission, *The Challenge to the South* (Oxford: Oxford University Press, 1990), 209.

Abbreviations and Acronyms

ACP	African, Caribbean, and Pacific
BCSD	Business Council for Sustainable Development
CFCs	chlorofluorocarbons
EC	European Community
ECOSOC	Economic and Social Council (UN)
EPA	Environmental Protection Agency
FAO	Food and Agriculture Organization
FOE	Friends of the Earth
GATT	General Agreement on Tariffs and Trade
GDP	gross domestic product
GEF	Global Environment Facility
GNP	gross national product
IBASE	Brazilian Institute for Economic and Social Analysis
IBRD	International Bank for Reconstruction and Development
ICC	International Chamber of Commerce
ICP	Industry Cooperative Programme
IDA	International Development Association
IFC	International Finance Corporation
IGO	intergovernmental organization
IMF	International Monetary Fund
ITC	International Technical Conference on the Protection of Nature
IUCN	International Union for Conservation of Nature and Natural Resources (World Conservation Union)
IUPN	International Union for the Protection of Nature
IWC	International Whaling Commission
MMPA	Marine Mammal Protection Act
NAFTA	North American Free Trade Agreement
NEPA	National Environmental Protection Agency
NGO	nongovernmental organization

NIC	newly industrializing country
NRDC	National Resources Defense Council
OAU	Organization of African Unity
OECD	Organization for Economic Cooperation and Development
OES	Bureau of Oceans and International Environmental and Scientific Affairs
TFAP	Tropical Forestry Action Plan
TNC	transnational corporation
TWG	technical working group
UN	United Nations Technical Working Group
UNCED	United Nations Conference on Environment and Development
UNDP	United Nations Development Programme
UNEP	United Nations Environment Programme
UNESCO	United Nations Educational, Scientific, and Cultural Organization
UNSCCUR	United Nations Scientific Conference on the Conservation and Utilization of Resources
U.S.	United States
WHO	World Health Organization
WMO	World Meteorological Organization
WTO	World Trade Organization

Bibliography

Adams, W. M. *Green Development: Environment and Sustainability in the Third World*. London: Routledge, 1990.

Aldous, Tony. *Battle for the Environment*. London: Fontana Books, 1972.

Altieri, Miguel. *Agroecology: The Scientific Basis of Alternative Agriculture*. Boulder: Westview Press, 1987.

Amin, Samir. *Unequal Development: An Essay on the Social Formation of Peripheral Capitalism*. New York: Monthly Review Press, 1976.

Anderson, D., and R. Fishwick. *Fuelwood Consumption and Deforestation in African Countries*. Washington, D.C.: World Bank, 1984.

Anderson, Terry L. (ed.). *NAFTA and the Environment*. San Francisco: Pacific Research Institute, 1993.

Andresen, Steinar, and Willy Ostreng (eds.). *International Resource Management: The Role of Science and Politics*. London: Belhaven Press, 1989.

Ascher, William, and Robert Healy. *Natural Resource Policymaking in Developing Countries*. Durham: Duke University Press, 1990.

Asian NGO Coalition, IRED Asia, and the People–Centered Development Forum. "Coming Back to Life." *In Context* 36 (1993): 18–23.

Asimov, Isaac, and Frederik Pohl. *Our Angry Earth*. New York: Tom Doherty, 1991.

Attwood, Donald W., Thomas C. Bruneau, and John G. Galaty (eds.). *Power and Poverty: Development Projects in the Third World*. Boulder: Westview Press, 1988.

Axelrod, Robert. *The Evolution of Cooperation*. New York: Basic Books, 1984.

Ayres, Robert. *Banking on the Poor*. Cambridge, Mass.: MIT Press, 1984.

Ball, George W. *Global Companies: The Political Economy of World Business*. Englewood Cliffs: Prentice–Hall, 1975.

Bank Information Center. *Funding Ecological and Social Destruction: The World Bank and International Monetary Fund*. Washington, D.C.: Bank Information Center, 1990.

Baran, Paul. *The Political Economy of Growth*, 2d ed. New York: Monthly Review Press, 1956.

Barde, Jean-Phillipe, and David Pearce (eds.). *Valuing the Environment: Six Case Studies*. London: Earthscan Publications, 1991.

Barkun, Michael. *Disaster and the Millennium*. New Haven: Yale University Press, 1974.

Barnet, Richard. "Inquiries into the Human Prospect." *World Policy Journal* 10, no. 1 (Spring 1993): 91–96.

Barnet, Richard, and Robert Muller. *Global Reach: The Power of Multinational Corporations*. New York: Simon and Schuster, 1974.
Bartelmus, Peter. *Environment and Development*. Boston: Allen and Unwin, 1986.
"Basel Convention Now in Force." *Toxic Trade Update* 5, no. 2 (1992): 5–6.
Benedick, Richard Elliot. *Ozone Diplomacy: New Directions in Safeguarding the Planet*. Cambridge, Mass.: Harvard University Press, 1991.
Berg, Robert, and Jennifer Seymour Whitaker (eds.). *Strategies for African Development*. Berkeley: University of California Press, 1986.
Bergsten, C. Fred. "Interdependence and the Reform of International Institutions." *International Organization* 30 (Spring 1976): 361–372.
Berkes, Fikret (ed.). *Common Property Resource: Ecology and Community-Based Sustainable Development*. London: Belhaven Press, 1989.
Berkes, F., D. Feeny, B. J. McCay, and J. M. Acheson. "The Benefit of the Commons." *Nature* 340 (July 13, 1989): 91–93.
Birnie, Patricia. "The International Organization of Whales." *Denver Journal of International Law and Policy* 13 (Fall–Winter 1984–1985): 309–333.
Birnie, Patricia, and Alan Boyle. *International Environmental Law*. Oxford: Oxford University Press, 1992.
Biswas, Asit K., T. N. Khoshoo, and Ashok Khosla (eds.). *Environmental Modelling for Developing Countries*. London: Tycooly Publishing, 1990.
Blackburn, Anne M. *Pieces of the Global Puzzle: International Approaches to Environmental Concerns*. Golden, Colo.: Fulcrum, 1986.
Blaikie, Piers. *The Political Economy of Soil Erosion in Developing Countries*. London: Longman, 1985.
Boardman, Robert. *International Organization and the Conservation of Nature*. Bloomington: Indiana University Press, 1981.
Bookchin, Murray. *The Modern Crisis*. Philadelphia: New Society Publishers, 1986.
Bornschier, Volker, and Christopher Chase-Dunn. *Multinational Corporations and Underdevelopment*. Westport, Conn.: Greenwood, 1985.
Botkin, Daniel B. *Discordant Harmonies: Ecology in the 21st Century*. New York: Harcourt Brace Jovanovich, 1989.
Boulding, Kenneth. *The Three Faces of Power*. Beverly Hills: Sage, 1989.
Bradford, Colin I., Jr. "The Rise of NICs as Exporters on a Global Scale." In Louis Turner and Neil McMullen (eds.), *The Newly Industrializing Countries: Trade and Adjustment*. London: George Allen and Unwin, 1972.
Bramble, Barbara J., and Gareth Porter. "Nongovernmental Organizations and the Making of US International Environmental Policy." In Andrew Hurrell and Benedict Kingsbury (eds.), *The International Politics of the Environment: Actors, Interests, and Institutions*. Oxford: Clarendon Press, 1992.
Brandt, Willy. *North–South: A Program for Survival*. Cambridge, Mass.: MIT Press, 1980.
Broad, R. *Unequal Alliance, 1979–1986: The World Bank, the International Monetary Fund, and the Philippines*. Quezon City, Philippines: Ateneo de Manila University Press, 1988.
Broad, Robin, and John Cavanagh. "Beyond the Myths of Rio." *World Policy Journal*, 10, no. 1 (Spring 1993): 65–72.
Bromley, David W. "Property Relations and Economic Development: The Other Land Reform." *World Development* 17 (1989): 867–877.
Brown, Christopher. *The Political and Social Economy of Commodity Control*. New York: Praeger, 1980.
Brown, Halina S., Patrick Derr, Ortwin Renn, and Allen L. White. *Corporate*

Environmentalism in a Global Economy. Westport, Conn.: Quorum Books, 1993.

Brown, Lester R. *Building a Sustainable Society*. New York: Norton, 1981.

———. *On Global Environmental Issues*. New York: W. W. Norton, 1991.

——— (ed.). *State of the World 1991*. New York: Worldwatch Institute, 1991.

Brown, Seyom, Nina W. Cornell, Larry L. Fabian, and Edith Brown Weiss. *Regimes for the Ocean, Outer Space, and Weather*. Washington, D.C.: Brookings, 1977.

Bruno, Kenny. *The Greenpeace Book of Greenwash*. Amsterdam: Greenpeace International, n.d.

Buchholz, Rogene A., Alfred A. Marcus, and James Post. *Managing Environmental Issues: A Casebook*. Englewood Cliffs: Prentice–Hall, 1992.

Bull, David. *A Growing Problem: Pesticides and the Third World Poor*. Oxford: Oxfam, 1982.

Bunker, Stephen G. *Underdeveloping the Amazon: Extraction, Unequal Exchange, and the Failure of the Modern State*. Urbana: University of Illinois Press, 1985.

Busch, Lawrence, William B. Lacy, Jeffrey Burkhardt, and Laura R. Lacy. *Plants, Power and Profit: Social, Economic, and Ethical Consequences of the New Biotechnologies*. Cambridge: Basil Blackwell, 1991.

Cairncross, Francis. *Costing the Earth*. Boston: Harvard Business School Press, 1992.

"Cakes and Caviar? The Dunkel Draft and Third World Agriculture." *The Ecologist* 23, no. 6 (November–December 1993): 219–220.

Caldwell, Lynton K. *In Defense of Earth: International Protection of the Biosphere*. Bloomington: Indiana University Press, 1972.

———. *Between Two Worlds: Science, the Environmental Movement, and Policy Choice*. Cambridge: Cambridge University Press, 1990.

———. *International Environmental Policy: Emergence and Dimensions*. 2d ed. Durham: Duke University Press, 1990.

"Camdessus Hails Conclusion of Uruguay Round Negotiations." *IMF Survey* 23, no. 1: 1.

"Campaigns." *The Ecologist* 23, no. 1 (January–February 1993): 38–39.

Capra, Fritjhof, and Charlene Spretnak. *Green Politics*. London: Hutchinson, 1984.

Caron, David D. "Protection of the Stratospheric Ozone Layer and the Structure of International Environmental Lawmaking." *Hastings International and Comparative Law Review* 14 (1991): 755–780.

Carroll, John E. (ed.). *International Environmental Diplomacy: The Management of Transfrontier Environmental Problems*. Cambridge: Cambridge University Press, 1988.

Carson, Rachel. *Silent Spring*. Cambridge, Mass.: Riverside Press, 1962.

Cassen, Robert, et al. (eds). *Rich Country Interests and Third World Development*. London: Croom Helm, 1982.

Catton, William. *Overshoot: The Ecological Basis for Revolutionary Change*. Urbana: University of Illinois Press, 1980.

Chase–Dunn, Christopher. "Interstate System and Capitalist World–Economy: One Logic or Two?" *International Studies Quarterly* 25: 19–42

"Chemical Prospecting: Hope for Vanishing Ecosystems?" *Science* 256 (May 22, 1992): 1142.

Chenery, Hollis (ed). *Redistribution with Growth*. Oxford: Oxford University Press, 1974.

"The Chinese Foiled." *The Economist* 243, no. 6722 (June 24, 1972): 28–29.

Clapham, Christopher. *Third World Politics*. Madison: University of Wisconsin Press, 1985.

Cleveland, Harlan. *The Global Commons: Policy for the Planet*. Lanham, Md.: University Press of America, 1990.

Cobbing, Madeleine, and Kerry Rankine. "Local Activists and Greenpeace Wage Campaign Against U.K. Waste Dumping in Mexico and Bolivia." *Toxic Trade Update* 6, no. 2 (1993): 19–20.

Cockburn, Alexander. "Talking Dirty in Private." *New Statesmen and Society* 5, no. 192 (March 6, 1992): 34.

Cogan, Douglas G. *Stones in a Glass House: CFCs and Ozone Depletion*. Washington, D.C.: Investor Responsibility Research Center, 1988.

Cohen, Mark Nathan. *The Food Crisis in Prehistory: Overpopulation and the Origins of Agriculture*. New Haven: Yale University Press, 1977.

Colby, Michael E. *Environmental Management in Development*. Washington, D.C.: World Bank, 1990.

Commoner, Barry. *Making Peace with the Planet*. New York: Pantheon Books, 1990.

Cotgrove, Stephen F. *Catastrophe or Cornucopia: The Environment, Politics and the Future*. Chichester: Wiley, 1982.

Cowling, Keith, and Roger Sugden. *Transnational Monopoly Capitalism*. New York: St. Martin's Press, 1987.

Crosby, Alfred. *Ecological Imperialism and the Biological Expansion of Europe, 900–1900*. Cambridge: Cambridge University Press, 1986.

Dahlberg, Kenneth. *Beyond the Green Revolution: The Ecology and Politics of Global Agricultural Development*. New York: Plenum, 1979.

——— (ed.). *New Directions for Agriculture and Agricultural Research: Neglected Dimensions and Emerging Alternatives*. Totawa, N.J.: Rowman and Allanheld, 1986.

Daly, Herman E., and John B. Cobb. *For the Common Good: Redirecting the Economy Toward Community, the Environment, and a Sustainable Future*. Boston: Beacon Press, 1989.

Davis, Charles E. *The Politics of Hazardous Waste*. Englewood Cliffs: Prentice Hall, 1993.

"Debt Swaps: A Southern View." *The Ecologist* 22, no. 3 (May–June 1992): 102.

De Grazia, Alfred. *A Cloud over Bhopal—Causes, Consequences*. Calcutta: Asia Publishing, 1985.

Deutsch, Karl. *The Nerves of Government*. London: Free Press, 1963.

Dhawan, B. D. *Irrigation in India's Agricultural Development*. New Delhi: Sage Publications, 1988.

"The Dirty Half-Dozen Stand Alone." *Toxic Trade Update* 6, no. 3 (1993): 2.

Dixey, F. "Conservation and Utilization of World Resources: United Nations Conference." *Nature* 164, no. 4176 (November 12, 1949): 813–815.

Doniger, David. "Politics of the Ozone Layer." *Issues in Science and Technology* (Spring 1988): 86–92.

Dos Santos, Theotonio. "The Structure of Dependence." In K. T. Kan and Donald C. Hodges (eds.), *Readings in U.S. Imperialism*. Boston: Extending Horizons, 1971.

Dougherty, James E., and Robert L. Pfaltzgraff, Jr. *Contending Theories of International Relations*. New York: Harper and Row, 1990.

Doyle, Jack. *Altered Harvest: Agriculture, Genetics and the Fate of the World's Food Supply*. New York: Viking, 1985.

Dunning, John H. *International Production and the Multinational Enterprise*. Boston: Allen and Unwin, 1981.

"DuPont Position Statement on the Chlorofluorocarbon-Ozone-Greenhouse Issues." *Environmental Conservation* 13 (Winter 1986): 363–364.

Durning, Alan B. *Action at the Grassroots: Fighting Poverty and Environmental Decline*. Worldwatch Paper 88. Washington, D.C.: Worldwatch Institute, January 1989.

———. *Poverty and Environment: Reversing the Downward Spiral*. Worldwatch Paper 92. Washington, D.C.: Worldwatch Institute, November 1989.

Eckholm, Erik. *Down to Earth: Environment and Human Needs*. New York: Norton, 1986.

Ehrlich, Paul, Anne Ehrlich, and John P. Holdren. *Extinction: The Causes and Consequence of the Disappearance of Species*. London: Victor Gollancz, 1982.

Ehrlich, Paul, Anne Ehrlich, and John P. Holdren. *Ecoscience: Population, Resources, Environment*. San Francisco: W. H. Freeman, 1977.

Elfstrom, Gerard. *Moral Issues and Multinational Corporations*. New York: St. Martin's Press, 1991.

Engel, J. R., and J. G. Engel. *Ethics of Environment and Development*. London: Belhaven, 1990.

Engel, Leonard. "Science Notebook." *The Nation* 169 (September 3, 1949): 226.

Enloe, Cynthia. *The Politics of Pollution in Comparative Perspective*. New York: David McKay, 1975.

Falk, Richard A. "Environmental Policy as a World Order Problem." *Natural Resources Journal* 12 (April 1972): 161–171.

Farmer, B. H. *Agricultural Colonization in India Since Independence*. London: Oxford University Press, 1974.

Finaldi, Lisa. "Chlorine Chemistry: Coming Soon to a Factory Near You!" *Toxic Trade Update* 6, no. 3 (1993): 27.

Findlay, Allan, and Anne Findlay. *Population and Development in the Third World*. New York: Methuen, 1987.

Firor, John. *The Changing Atmosphere: A Global Challenge*. New Haven: Yale University Press, 1990

Fisher, D. E. *Fire and Ice: The Greenhouse Effect, Ozone Depletion and Nuclear Winter*. New York: Harper and Row, 1990.

Fisher, Roger, and William Ury. *Getting to Yes: Negotiating Agreements Without Giving In*. Boston: Houghton Mifflin, 1981.

Fowler, Cary, and Pat Mooney. *Shattering: Food, Politics, and the Loss of Genetic Diversity*. Tucson: University of Arizona Press, 1990.

Frank, Andre Gunder. *Capitalism and Underdevelopment in Latin America*. New York: Monthly Review Press, 1967.

French, Hilary F. *After the Earth Summit: The Future of Environmental Governance*. Worldwatch Paper 107. Washington, D.C.: Worldwatch Institute, March 1992.

———. *Costly Tradeoffs: Reconciling Trade and the Environment*. Worldwatch Paper 113. Washington, D.C.: Worldwatch Institute, March 1993.

———. "GEF Replenishment." *World Watch* 7, no. 4 (July–August 1994): 7.

George, Susan. *How the Other Half Dies: The Real Reasons for World Hunger*. Hammondsworth, U.K.: Penguin, 1977.

Ghosh, Pradip K. *Multi-National Corporations and Third World Development*. Westport, Conn.: Greenwood, 1984.

Gilman, Robert. "What Time Is It?" *In Context* 36 (1993): 11–17.

Gilpin, Robert. *U.S. Power and the Multinational Corporation*. New York: Basic Books, 1975.

Girling, Robert H. *Multinational Institutions and the Third World*. New York:

Praeger, 1985.
Glaeser, Bernhard. *Ecodevelopment: Concepts, Projects, Strategies*. Elmsford, N.Y.: Pergamon, 1984.
Goodman, David, and Anthony Hall (eds.). *The Future of Amazonia: Destruction or Sustainable Development*. London: Macmillan, 1990.
Goulet, Denis. *The Uncertain Promise: Value Conflicts in Technology Transfer*. New York: New Horizons, 1989.
Graham, Frank. *Since Silent Spring*. Boston: Houghton Mifflin, 1970.
Greenpeace International. *Annotations by Greenpeace International on the Agenda of the Meeting*. Prepared for the First Conference of Parties to the Basel Convention November 30–December 4 1992, Piriapolis, Uruguay (published by Greenpeace International), Attachment C, 2–3.
Greenpeace U.S.A. *The International Trade in Wastes: A Greenpeace Inventory*. Washington, D.C.: Greenpeace U.S.A., 1990.
Gupta, Joyeeta. *Toxic Terrorism*. London: Earthscan Publications, 1990.
Gurr, Ted Robert. "On the Political Consequences of Scarcity and Economic Decline." *International Studies Quarterly* 29 (1985): 51–75.
Haas, Ernst B. "On Systems and International Regimes." *World Politics* 27 (January 1975): 147–174.
———. "Words Can Hurt You; or, Who Said What to Whom About Regimes." *International Organization* 36, no. 2 (Spring 1982): 207–243.
———. *When Knowledge Is Power: Three Models of Change in International Organizations*. Berkeley: University of California Press, 1990.
Haas, Peter. "Do Regimes Matter? Epistemic Communities and Mediterranean Pollution Control." *International Organization* 43 (Summer 1989): 377–403.
———. "Obtaining International Environmental Protection Through Epistemic Consensus." *Millennium* 19, no. 3 (Winter 1990): 347–364.
———. *Saving the Mediterranean: The Politics of International Environmental Cooperation*. New York: Columbia University Press, 1990.
———. "Epistemic Communities and International Policy Co-ordination." *International Organization* 46, no. 1 (Winter 1992): 1–35.
———. "Banning Chlorofluorocarbons: Systemic Community Efforts to Protect Stratospheric Ozone." *International Organization* 46, no. 1 (Winter 1992): 187–224.
Hadjor, Kofi Buenor. *Dictionary of Third World Terms*. London: I. B. Tauris, 1992.
Haggard, Stephan, and Beth A. Simmons. "Theories of International Regimes." *International Organization* 41 (Summer 1987): 491–517.
Hardin, Garrett. "The Tragedy of the Commons." *Science* 162 (December 13, 1968): 1243–1248.
———. *Exploring New Ethics for Survival*. New York: Viking, 1972.
Hardin, Garrett, and John Baden (eds.). *Managing the Commons*. San Francisco: W. H. Freeman, 1977.
Harf, James E., and Thomas B. Trout. *The Politics of Global Resources. Population, Food, Energy and the Environment*. Durham, N.C.: Duke University Press, 1986.
Harris, Nigel. *The End of the Third World*. New York: Penguin, 1986.
Hartshorn, Gary S. "Key Environmental Issues for Developing Countries." *Journal Of International Affairs* 44 (1991): 393–402.
Henderson, Hazel. *The Politics of the Solar Age: Alternatives to Economics*. New York: Anchor/Doubleday, 1981.
Hirsch, Fred. *Social Limits to Growth*. Cambridge, Mass.: Harvard University

Press, 1976.
Hobbelink, Henk. *Biotechnology and the Future of World Agriculture*. London: Zed Books, 1991.
Hurrell, Andrew, and Benedict Kingsbury (eds.). *The International Politics of the Environment: Actors, Interests, and Institutions*. Oxford: Clarendon Press, 1992.
"The IMF and the Environment." *IMF Survey* 22, no. 12 (June 14, 1993): 188.
International Union for the Protection of Nature. *Preparatory Documents to the International Technical Conference on the Protection of Nature, August 1949, U.S.A.* Paris: UNESCO, 1949.
IUCN–the World Conservation Union, the United Nations Environment Programme (UNEP), and the World Wide Fund for Nature (WWF). *The World Conservation Strategy*. Gland, Switzerland: IUCN, 1980.
———. *Caring for the Earth*. Gland, Switzerland: IUCN, UNEP, and WWF, 1991.
Jacobson, Jodi L. *Gender Bias: Roadblock to Sustainable Development*. Worldwatch Paper 110. Washington, D.C.: Worldwatch Institute, September 1992.
Jessup, Philip C. *The Price of International Justice*. New York: Columbia University Press, 1971.
Johnson, Brian, and Robert O. Blake. *The Environment and Bilateral Development Aid*. London: International Institute for Environment and Development, 1980.
Johnson, Keith. "A Second Copernican Revolution." *Uniterra* 1 (1982): 4–5.
Johnson, Paul, Ruth Stringer, and Jim Puckett. *When Green Is Not*. Technical Note 07/92. Amsterdam: Greenpeace International, 1992.
Johnson, Stanley. *The Green Revolution*. New York: Harper and Row, 1972.
Joyner, Christopher. "Stockholm in Retrospect: Progress in the International Law of the Environment." *World Affairs* 136, no. 4 (Spring 1974): 347–363.
Juma, Calestous. *The Gene Hunters: Biotechnology and the Scramble for Seeds*. Princeton: Princeton University Press, 1989.
Kamieniecki, Sheldon. "Political Mobilization, Agenda Building and International Environmental Policy." *Journal of International Affairs* 44 (1991) : 339–358.
Kempel, Willy. "Transboundary Movements of Hazardous Wastes." In Gunnar Sjostedt (ed.), *International Environmental Negotiation*. Newbury Park: Sage Publications, 1993.
Kennan, George F. *Realities of American Foreign Policy*. Princeton: Princeton University Press, 1972.
Kenney, M., and F. Buttel. "Biotechnology: Prospects and Dilemmas for Third World Development." *Development and Change* 16 (1985): 61–91.
Keohane, Robert O. *After Hegemony: Co-operation and Discord in the World Political Economy*. Princeton: Princeton University Press, 1984.
Keohane, Robert O., and Joseph S. Nye. *Transnational Relations and World Politics*. Cambridge, Mass.: Harvard University Press, 1971.
———. "Power and Interdependence Revisited." *International Organization* 41, no. 4 (Autumn 1987): 725–753.
———. *Power and Interdependence: World Politics in Transition*. 2d ed. Boulder: Westview Press, 1990.
Kimball, Lee A. *Forging International Agreement: Strengthening Inter-Governmental Institutions for Environment and Development*. Washington, D.C.: World Resources Institute, 1992.
Kloppenburg, J. R. (ed.). *Seeds and Sovereignty: The Use and Control of Plant*

Genetic Resources. Durham, N.C.: Duke University Press, 1988.

Koehler, Jamison, and Scott A. Hajost. "The Montreal Protocol: A Dynamic Agreement for Protecting the Ozone Layer." *Ambio* 19 (1990): 82–86.

Krasner, Stephen D. (ed.). *International Regimes*. Ithaca: Cornell University Press, 1983.

———. *Structural Conflict: The Third World Against Global Liberalism*. Berkeley: University of California Press, 1985.

Kuhn, Thomas. *The Structure of Scientific Revolutions*. Chicago: University of Chicago Press, 1970.

Leonard, David K., and Dale Rogers Marshall (eds.). *Institutions of Rural Development for the Poor: Decentralization and Organizational Linkages*. Berkeley: University of California, Institute of International Studies, 1982.

Leonard, H. Jeffrey (ed.). *Divesting Nature's Capital: The Political Economy of Environmental Abuse in the Third World*. New York: Holmes and Meier, 1985.

——— (ed.). *Environment and the Poor: Development Strategies for a Common Agenda*. New Brunswick: Transaction Books, 1990.

———. *Pollution and the Struggle for the World Product: Multinational Corporations, Environment, and International Comparative Advantage*. Cambridge: Cambridge University Press, 1991.

Leonard, H. Jeffrey, and D. Morrell. "The Emergence of Environmental Concern in Developing Countries: A Political Perspective." *Stanford Journal of Environmental Law* 17 (1985): 281–313.

Lerner, Steve (ed.). *Earth Summit: Conversations with Architects of an Ecologically Sustainable Future*. Bolinas: Commonwealth, 1991.

Lesser, William H. (ed.). *Animal Patents: The Legal, Economic, and Social Issues*. London: Macmillan, 1989.

Lewis, John P. (ed.). *Strengthening the Poor: What Have We Learned?* U.S.–Third World Policy Perspectives No. 10. Washington, D.C.: Overseas Development Council, 1986.

"Lies, Fantasy, Cynicism." *The Ecologist* 22, no. 6 (November–December 1992): 259–260.

Lipschultz, Ronnie D., and Ken Conca (eds.). *The State and Social Power in Global Environmental Politics*. New York: Columbia University Press, 1993.

Little, Peter D., Michael M. Horowitz, and A. Endre Nyerges. *Lands at Risk in the Third World: Local Level Perspectives*. Boulder: Westview Press, 1987.

Lovelock, J. E. *Gaia: A New Look at Life on Earth*. London: Oxford University Press, 1979.

MacDonald, N. *Brazil: A Mask Called Progress*. Oxford: Oxfam, 1991.

MacNeill, Jim, Peiter Winsemius, and Taizo Yakushiji. *Beyond Interdependence: The Meshing of the World's Economy and the Earth's Ecology*. New York: Oxford University Press, 1991.

Mahini, Amir. *Making Decisions in Multinational Corporations: Managing Relations with Sovereign Governments*. New York: Wiley, 1988.

Mahony, Rhona. "Debt-for-Nature Swaps: Who Really Benefits?" *The Ecologist* 22, no. 3 (May–June 1992): 97–103.

Manley, Michael. *The Poverty of Nations: Reflections on Underdevelopment and the World Economy*. London: Pluto Press, 1991.

Martin, Lisa L. "Interests, Power, and Multilateralism." *International Organization* 46, no. 4 (Autumn 1992): 765–792.

Martinussen, John. *Transnational Corporations in a Developing Country: The Indian Experience*. Newbury Park, Calif.: Sage, 1988.

Mathews, Jessica Tuchman. "Redefining Security." *Foreign Affairs* 68 (Spring 1989): 162–177.

——— (ed.). *Preserving the Global Environment: The Challenge of Shared Leadership*. New York: W. W. Norton, 1991.

Mattelart, Armand. *Transnationals and the Third World: The Struggle for Culture*. Westport, Conn.: Greenwood, 1985.

Mayda, Jaro. "Environmental Legislation in Developing Countries: Some Parameters and Constraints." *Ecology Quarterly* 12 (1985): 997–1024.

McClelland, David C. "The Two Faces of Power." *Journal of International Affairs* 24, no. 1 (1970): 29–47.

McCord, William, with Arline McCord. *Paths to Progress: Bread and Freedom in Developing Societies*. New York: Norton, 1986.

McCormick, John. *Reclaiming Paradise: The Global Environmental Movement*. Bloomington: Indiana University Press, 1989.

McKibben, Bill. *The End of Nature*. New York: Doubleday, 1989.

McNeely, J. A., K. R. Miller, W. Reid, R. Mittermeier, and T. Werner. *Conserving the World's Biological Diversity*. Washington, D.C.: World Resources Institute, 1990.

Meadows, Donella H. *Beyond the Limits*. Post Mills, Vt.: Chelsea Green, 1992.

Meadows, Donella, Dennis L. Meadows, Jorgen Randers, and William W. Behrens III. *The Limits to Growth*. New York: Universe Books, 1972.

Mikesell, Raymond F., and Larry Williams. *International Banks and the Environment*. San Francisco: Sierra Club Books, 1992.

Milbrath, Lester W. *Envisioning a Sustainable Society: Learning Our Way Out*. Albany: State University of New York, 1989.

Miller, Lynn H. *Global Order*. 2d ed. Boulder: Westview Press, 1990.

Miller, Marian A.L. "Balancing Development and Environment: The Third World in Global Environmental Politics." *Society and Natural Resources* 5 (1992): 297–305.

Mingst, Karen. "Implementing International Environmental Treaties: The Role of NGOs." Paper prepared for the Annual Meeting of the International Studies Association, Acapulco, March 24–27, 1993.

Mitchell, James K. (ed.). *Global Environmental Change: Human and Policy Dimensions*. Guildford: Butterworth–Heinemann, 1990.

Molina, Mario, and Sherwood Rowland. "Stratospheric Sink for Chlorofluoromethanes: Chlorine Atom Catalyses Destruction of Ozone." *Nature* 249 (June 1974): 810–812.

Morgenthau, Hans J. *Politics Among Nations*. 5th ed. New York: Knopf, 1978.

Morone, Joseph G., and Edward J. Woodhouse. *Averting Catastrophe: Strategies for Regulating Risky Technologies*. Berkeley: University of California Press, 1986.

Morrison, Peter H. *Old Growth in the Pacific Northwest: A Status Report*. Washington, D.C.: Wilderness Society, 1988.

Murdoch, William W. *The Poverty of Nations: The Political Economy of Hunger and Population*. Baltimore: Johns Hopkins University Press, 1980.

Myers, Norman. *The Sinking Ark: A New Look at the Problem of Disappearing Species*. New York: Pergamon, 1979.

———. *The Primary Source: Tropical Forests and Our Future*. New York: Norton, 1986.

Myrdal, Gunnar. *The Challenge of World Poverty*. New York: Pantheon Books, 1970.

Nanda, Ved P. "Stratospheric Ozone Depletion: A Challenge for International Environmental Law and Policy." *Michigan Journal of International Law* 10

(1989): 482–525.
"Narmada Review." *The Ecologist Campaigns* (July–August 1993): 4.
National Academy of Sciences. *Protection Against Depletion of Stratospheric Ozone by Chlorofluorocarbons*. Washington, D.C.: National Academy of Science Press, 1983.
National Research Council. *Ozone Depletion, Greenhouse Gases, and Climate Change*. Washington, D.C.: National Academy Press, 1988.
"New Central American Agreement Halts Waste Import Schemes in Honduras, Nicaragua, and El Salvador." *Toxic Trade Update* 6, no. 2 (1993): 6–7.
Niebuhr, Reinhold. *Christianity and Power Politics*. New York: Charles Scribner's Sons, 1940.
Nielsen, Waldemar. *The Endangered Sector*. New York: Columbia University Press, 1979.
Odum, Howard T. *Environment, Power, and Society*. New York: Wiley, 1971.
Office of Technology Assessment. *Commercial Biotechnology: An International Analysis*. Washington, D.C.: U.S. Congress, 1984.
———. *Intellectual Property Rights in an Age of Electronics and Information*. Washington, D.C.: U.S. Congress, 1987.
Ophuls, William, and A. Stephan Boyan, Jr. *Ecology and the Politics of Scarcity Revisited: The Unraveling of the American Dream*. New York: W. H. Freeman, 1992.
Oppenheimer, Michael F., and Donna M. Tuths. *Nontariff Barriers: The Effects on Corporate Strategy in High-Technology Sectors*. Boulder: Westview Press, 1987.
Organization for Economic Cooperation and Development. *Decision of the Council Concerning the Transfrontier Movements of Wastes Destined for Recovery Operations*. Paris: OECD, April 6, 1992.
Orr, David. "In the Tracks of the Dinosaur: Modernization and the Ecological Perspective." *Polity* 11 (Summer 1979): 562–587.
Ostrom, Elinor. *Governing the Commons: The Evolution of Institutions for Collective Action*. New York: Cambridge University Press, 1990.
Overseas Development Council (ODC), and World Wildlife Fund (WWF). *Environmental Challenges to International Trade Policy: A Conference Report*. Washington, D.C.: ODC and WWF, 1991.
Oye, Kenneth A. (ed.). *Cooperation Under Anarchy*. Princeton, N.J.: Princeton University Press, 1986.
Paul, Samuel. *Community Participation in Development Projects: The World Bank Experience*. World Bank Discussion Papers, No. 6. Washington, D.C.: World Bank, 1987.
Pearce, David W., Edward Barbier, and Anil Markandya. *Sustainable Development: Economics and Environment in the Third World*. London: Edward Elger, 1990.
Pearson, Charles, and Anthony Pryor. *Environment North and South: An Economic Interpretation*. New York: Wiley, 1978.
Pearson, Charles. *Down to Business: Multinational Corporations, the Environment and Development*. Washington, D.C.: World Resources Institute, 1985.
Pirages, Dennis C. *The Sustainable Society*. New York: Praeger, 1977.
———. *Global Technopolitics*. Pacific Grove, Calif.: Brooks/Cole, 1989.
Poore, Duncan. *No Timber Without Trees: Sustainability in the Tropical Forest*. London: Earthscan Publications, 1989.
Porter, Gareth, and Janet Welsh Brown. *Global Environmental Politics*. Boulder: Westview Press, 1991.

"The Power of the Transnationals." *The Ecologist* 22, no. 4 (July–August 1992), 159.

"Power: The Central Issue." *The Ecologist* 22, no. 4 (July–August 1992): 157–164.

Preston, Lewis. "Global Changes Require Quick Response." *IMF Survey* 22, no. 19: 296–297.

Ramakrishna, Kilaparti. "The Emergence of Environmental Law in the Developing Countries: A Case Study of India." *Ecology Law Quarterly* 12, no. 4 (1985): 907–935.

Rawls, John. *A Theory of Justice*. Cambridge, Mass.: Harvard University Press, 1971.

Ray, Dixie L. *Trashing the Planet*. Washington, D.C.: Regnery Gateway, 1990.

Redclift, Michael. *Sustainable Development: Exploring the Contradictions*. New York: Methuen, 1987.

Reed, David. *The Global Environment Facility*. Washington, D.C.: World Wildlife Fund–International, 1991.

Reid, Walter V., and K. R. Miller. *Keeping Options Alive: The Scientific Basis for Conserving Biodiversity*. Washington, D.C.: World Resources Institute, 1989.

Reilly, William K. "Statement on Ozone Depletion." Washington, D.C.: Environmental Protection Agency, April 4, 1991.

Renner, Michael. *National Security: The Economic and Environmental Dimensions*. Washington, D.C.: Worldwatch Institute, 1989.

Repetto, Robert (ed.). *The Global Possible: Resources, Development, and the New Century*. New Haven: Yale University Press, 1985.

———. "Population, Resources, Environment: An Uncertain Future." *Population Bulletin* 42 (1987): 2–44.

Rich, Bruce. *Mortgaging the Earth: The World Bank, Environmental Impoverishment, and the Crisis of Development*. Boston: Beacon Press, 1994.

———. "The Multilateral Development Banks, Environmental Policy and the United States." *Ecology Law Quarterly* 12 (1985): 685–688.

———. "The Emperor's New Clothes: The World Bank and Environmental Reform." *World Policy Journal* 7, no. 2 (Spring 1990): 319.

Richards, Peter, and Wilbert Gooneratne. *Basic Needs, Poverty, and Government Policies in Sri Lanka*. Geneva: International Labour Organisation, 1980.

Rifkin, Jeremy. *Biosphere Politics*. New York: Crown Publishers, 1991.

Rodney, Walter. *How Europe Underdeveloped Africa*. London: Bogle-L'Ouverture, 1973.

Rorty, James. "Growing into World Order." *Commonweal* (October 7, 1949): 623.

Rose, Adam, Brandt Stevens, and Gregg Davis. *Natural Resource Policy and Income Distribution*. Baltimore: Johns Hopkins University Press, 1988.

Rosenau, James N. *Turbulence in World Politics*. Princeton: Princeton University Press, 1990.

———. *The United Nations in a Turbulent World*. Boulder: Lynne Rienner Publishers, 1992.

Ross, Lester. *Environmental Policy in China*. Bloomington: Indiana University Press, 1988.

Rothgeb, John M., Jr. *Defining Power: Influence and Force in the Contemporary International System*. New York: St. Martin's Press, 1993.

Rowland, F. Sherwood. "Stratospheric Ozone Depletion by Chlorofluorocarbons." *Ambio* 19 (1990): 281–292.

Ruggie, John Gerard. "International Responses to Technology: Concepts and Trends." *International Organization* 29 (1975): 557–583.

Ruggie, John Gerard, and Ernst B. Haas (eds.). *International Responses to Technology*. Special issue of *International Organization* 29 (1975).

Ryan, John C. "Conserving Biological Diversity." In Lester R. Brown (ed.), *State of the World 1992*. New York: Norton, 1992.

Sand, Peter H. *Lessons Learned in Global Environmental Governance*. Washington, D.C.: World Resources Institute, 1990.

Sanderson, Steven E. *The Transformation of Mexican Agriculture*. Princeton: Princeton University Press, 1986.

Schachter, Oscar. *Sharing the World's Resources*. New York: Columbia University Press, 1977.

———. *International Law in Theory and Practice*. Boston: Martinus Nijhoff, 1991.

Schiel, Carl-Heinz. "Promoting Indigenous Research Capacities in Developing Countries—The International Foundation for Science (IFS) and Its Work." *Ambio* 19 (1990): 346–348.

Schmidheiny, Stephan. *Changing Course*. Cambridge: MIT Press, 1992.

Schneider, Jan. *World Public Order of the Environment: Towards an International Ecological Law and Organization*. Toronto: University of Toronto Press, 1979.

Schramm, Gunther, and Jeremy Warford (eds.). *Environmental Management and Economic Development*. Baltimore: Johns Hopkins University Press, 1989.

Schumacher, E. F. *Small Is Beautiful: Economics as if People Mattered*. London: Abacus, 1974.

Schwartzman, Stephan. *Bankrolling Disasters: International Development Banks and the Global Environment*. San Francisco: Sierra Club, 1986.

Schwarz, Adam. "Back Down to Earth: Global Summit Fails to Live Up to Ambitions." *Far Eastern Economic Review* (June 25, 1992): 61–62.

Scott, James C. *Weapons of the Weak: Everyday Forms of Peasant Resistance*. New Haven: Yale University Press, 1985.

Sebenius, James K. "Challenging Conventional Explanations of International Cooperation: Negotiation Analysis and the Case of Epistemic Communities." *International Organization* 46, no. 1 (Winter 1992): 323–365.

Seidel, Stephen R., and Daniel P. Blank. "The Montreal Protocol: Pollution Prevention on a Global Scale." *Ambio* 19 (1990): 301–304.

"Seminar Explores Links Between Macro Policy and the Environment." *IMF Survey* 22, no. 12 (June 14, 1993): 177, 187.

Sen, Amartya. *Poverty and Famines*. Oxford: Clarendon Press, 1981.

Shane, Douglas R. *Hoofprints in the Forest: Cattle Ranching and the Destruction of Latin America's Tropical Forests*. Philadelphia: Institute for the Study of Human Issues, 1986.

Shiva, Vandana, and Radha Holla-Bhar. "Intellectual Piracy and the Neem Tree." *The Ecologist* 23, no. 6 (November–December 1993): 223–227.

Simai, Mihaly. *Global Power Structures: Technology and the World Economy in the Late 20th Century*. New York: Columbia University Press, 1990.

Simon, Julian, and Herman Kahn. *The Resourceful Earth*. Oxford: Basil Blackwell, 1984.

Smart, Bruce. *Beyond Compliance: A New Industry View of the Environment*. Washington, D.C.: World Resources Institute, 1992.

Sohn, Louis B. "The Stockholm Declaration on the Human Environment." *Harvard International Law Journal* 14, no. 3 (Summer 1974): 423–515.

Soroos, Marvin S. *Beyond Sovereignty: The Challenge of Global Policy*. Columbia: University of Southern Carolina Press, 1986.

South Commission. *The Challenge to the South*. Oxford: Oxford University Press, 1990.

"South Pacific Forum Countries to Negotiate Regional Waste Trade Ban." *Toxic Trade Update* 6, no. 3 (1993): 4–5.

Sprout, Howard, and Margaret Sprout. *Toward a Politics of a Planet Earth*. New York: Van Nostrand Reinhold, 1971.

Starke, Linda. *Signs of Hope: Working Towards Our Common Future*. Oxford: Oxford University Press, 1990.

Stein, Arthur A. "Coordination and Collaboration: Regimes in an Anarchic World." *International Organization* 36, no. 2 (Spring 1982): 299–324.

Stein, Robert E., and Brian Johnson. *Banking on the Biosphere? Environmental Procedures and Practices of Nine Multilateral Development Agencies*. Lexington, Mass.: Lexington Books, 1979.

Stockholm Group for Studies on Natural Resources Management. *Perspectives of Sustainable Development: Some Critical Issues Related to the Brundtland Report*. Stockholm: Stockholm Group for Studies on Natural Resources Management, 1988.

Stoels, Thomas B., Jacob Scherr, and Diana C. Crowley. *Environment, Natural Resources and Development: The Role of the US Agency for International Development*. Washington, D.C.: Natural Resources Defense Council, 1978.

Stone, Peter. *Did We Save the Earth at Stockholm?* London: Earth Island, 1973.

Stone, R. "A Biopesticidal Tree Begins to Blossom." *Science* (February 28, 1992): 1070–1071.

Stratospheric Ozone Depletion by Halocarbons: Chemistry and Transport Panel on Stratospheric Chemistry amd Transport. Washington, D.C.: National Academy of Sciences, 1979.

Streeten, Paul. *What Price Food: Agricultural Price Policies in Developing Countries*. New York: St. Martin's Press, 1987.

———. *First Things First: Meeting Basic Human Needs in the Developing Countries*. New York: Oxford University Press, 1991.

Susskind, Lawrence. *Environmental Diplomacy: Negotiating More Effective International Agreements*. New York: Oxford University Press, 1992.

Susskind, Lawrence, Esther Siskind, and J. William Breslin (eds.). *Nine Case Studies in International Environmental Negotiation*. Cambridge, Mass.: Program on Negotiation at Harvard Law School, 1990.

Szell, Patrick. "Negotiations on the Ozone Layer." In Gunner Sjostedt (ed.), *International Environmental Negotiation*. Newbury Park: Sage Publications, 1993.

Tessitore, John, and Susan Woolfson (eds.). *A Global Agenda: Issues Before the 46th General Assembly of the United Nations,* New York: University Press of America, 1991.

Testimony of Richard Barnett, in U.S. Congress, Senate Committee on the Environment and Public Works. *Ozone Depletion, the Greenhouse Effect, and Climate Change: Joint Hearings Before the Subcommittee on Environmental Protection and Hazardous Wastes and Toxic Substances*. Washington, D.C.: 100th Congress, 1st session, 1987.

Thomas, Caroline. *The Environment in International Relations*. London: Royal Institute of International Affairs, 1992.

Thurow, Lester. *The Zero Sum Society*. New York: Basic Books, 1980.

Tickell, Oliver, and Nicholas Hildyard. "Green Dollars, Green Menace." *The Ecologist* 22, no. 3 (May–June 1992): 82.

Tolba, Mostafa Kamal. *Earth Audit*. Nairobi: UNEP, 1972.
———. *Development Without Destruction: Evolving Environmental Perceptions*. Dublin: Tycooly International, 1982.
———. *Sustainable Development: Constraints and Opportunities*. London: Butterworths, 1987.
Tolba, Mostafa Kamal, and Osama A. El–Kholy. *The World Environment 1972–1992*. London: Chapman and Hall, 1992.
"Trade Agreement Mandates Board Changes." *IMF Survey* 23, no. 1 (January 10, 1994): 2.
Travis, Lee (ed.). *Multinational Managers and Poverty in the Third World*. South Bend, Ind.: University of Notre Dame, 1984.
Tucker, Robert. *The Inequality of Nations*. New York: Basic Books, 1977.
Tulchin, Joseph. *Habitat, Health, and Development: A New Way of Looking at Cities in the Third World*. Boulder: Lynne Rienner Publishers, 1986.
United Nations. *Report of the United Nations Conference on the Human Environment Held at Stockholm 5–16 June 1972*. Reprinted in *International Legal Materials* 11 (1972): 1416–1471.
———. *Long–Range World Population Projections*. New York: United Nations, 1992.
———. *Multilateral Treaties Deposited with the Secretary-General: Status as at 31 December 1992*. New York: United Nations, 1993.
———. *Report of the United Nations Conference on the Human Environment Held at Stockholm, 5–16 June 1972*. List of Participants, UN Doc. A/Conf. 48/Inf. 5 (1972).
———. *United Nations Conference on the Human Environment: Final Documents* (June 16, 1972): Principles 2, 4, and 6. Reprinted in *International Legal Materials* (November 1972): 1416–1471.
United Nations Conference on Trade and Development. *Review of Maritime Transport 1991*. New York: United Nations, 1992.
United Nations Development Programme. *Human Development Report 1992*. New York: Oxford University Press, 1992.
———. *Human Development Report 1993*. New York: Oxford University Press, 1993.
United Nations Environment Programme. *A Review of the Major Achievements in the Implementation of the Stockholm Action Plan on the Environment*. In UNEP Doc. Na. 81-4960. Nairobi: UNEP, 1981.
———. *Basel Convention on the Control of Transboundary Movements of Hazardous Wastes and Their Disposal*. Final Act. March 1989.
———. *Register of International Treaties and Other Agreements in the Field of the Environment*. Nairobi: UNEP, 1991.
———. *Resolutions of the Conference for the Adoption of the Agreed Text of the Convention on Biological Diversity*, May 22, 1992. Reprinted in *International Legal Materials* 31 (1992): 842–847.
———. *The Rio Declaration on Environment and Development*, June 14, 1992, Principle 9. Reprinted in *International Legal Materials* 31 (1992): 876–880.
———. *Convention on Biological Diversity*, 1992. Reprinted in *International Legal Materials* 31 (1992): 818–841.
United Nations World Food Council. *The Global State of Hunger and Malnutrition and the Impact of Economic Adjustment on Food and Hunger*. Beijing: World Food Council Thirteenth Ministerial Session, 1987.
U.S. Department of State, Council on Environmental Quality. *The Global 2000 Report to the President: Entering the Twenty–First Century*. New York:

Penguin Books, 1982.

U.S. National Research Council. *Proceedings of the Conference on Common-Property Resource Management*. Washington, D.C.: National Academy Press, 1986.

"U.S. Pushes Waste Dumping at Basel Meeting." *Toxic Trade Update* 6, no. 2 (1993): 6.

"U.S. Toxic Waste Sold as Fertilizer in Bangladesh." *Toxic Trade Update* 6, no. 1 (1993): 13.

Vallette, Jim. "Basel 'Dumping' Convention Still Legalizes Toxic Terrorism." *Toxic Trade Update* 6, no. 1 (1993): 2–3.

Vallette, Jim, and Heather Spalding (eds.). *The International Trade in Wastes: A Greenpeace Inventory*. Washington, D.C.: Greenpeace, USA, 1990.

Vig, Norman J., and Michael Kraft (eds.). *Environmental Policy in the 1990's—Toward a New Agenda*. Washington, D.C.: CQ Press, 1990.

Wallerstein, Immanuel. *The Modern World System*. New York: Academic Press, 1974.

———. *The Capitalist World-Economy*. New York: Cambridge University Press, 1979.

———. *The Modern World System II: Mercantilism and the Consolidation of the European World Economy, 1600–1750*. London: Academic Press, 1980.

———. *The Politics of the Capitalist World-Economy*. Cambridge: Cambridge University Press, 1984.

———. "World-System Analysis." In Anthony Giddens and Jonathan H. Turner (eds.), *Social Theory Today*. Stanford: Stanford University Press, 1987.

Ward, Barbara, and René Dubos. *Only One Earth: The Care and Maintenance of a Small Planet*. New York: W. W. Norton, 1972.

Warford, Jeremy J. "Environmental Management and Economic Policy in Developing Countries." In Gunter Schramm and Jeremy Warford (eds.), *Environmental Management and Economic Development*. Baltimore: Johns Hopkins University Press, 1991.

Westing, Arthur (ed.). *Global Resources and International Conflict*. Oxford: Oxford University Press, 1986.

Wiegele, Thomas C. *Biotechnology and International Relations: The Political Dimensions*. Gainesville: University of Florida Press, 1991.

Wilson, E. O. "The Biological Diversity Crisis: A Challenge to Science." *Issues in Science and Technology* 2, no. 1 (Fall 1985): 20–29.

Wilson, E. O., and Francis M. Peters (eds.). *Biodiversity*. Washington, D.C.: National Academy Press, 1988.

World Bank. *The World Bank and the Environment: First Annual Report, Fiscal 1990*. Washington, D.C.: World Bank Publications, 1990.

———. *World Development Report 1990: Poverty*. New York: Oxford University Press, 1990.

———. *Annual Report 1993*. Washington, D.C.: World Bank, 1993.

———. *World Development Report 1993*. New York: Oxford University Press, 1993.

World Bank, and European Investment Bank. *Managing a Common Resource*. Washington, D.C.: World Bank Publications, 1990.

World Commission on Environment and Development. *Environmental Protection and Sustainable Development: Legal Principles and Recommendations*. London: Graham and Trotman, 1987.

———. *Our Common Future*. Oxford: Oxford University Press, 1987.

World Resources Institute. *World Resources 1992–93*. New York: Oxford University Press, 1992.

———. *Biodiversity Prospecting*. Baltimore: World Resources Institute, 1993.
———. *The 1993 Information Please Environmental Almanac*. Boston: Houghton Mifflin, 1993.
———. *World Resources 1994–95*. New York: Oxford University Press, 1994.
World Wildlife Fund. *Amended and Restated Debt-for-Nature Agreement Between WWF (US) and Fundacion Natura,* April 4, 1989.
Young, Oran R. *Resource Management at the International Level: The Case of the North Pacific*. London: Pinter and Nichols, 1977.
———. "Regime Dynamics." *International Organization* 36, no. 2 (Spring 1982): 282–285.
———. *International Cooperation: Building Regimes for Natural Resources and the Environment*. Ithaca, N.Y.: Cornell University Press, 1989.
———. "The Politics of International Regime Formation: Managing Natural Resources and the Environment." *International Organization* 43 (Summer 1989): 349–375.
———. (ed.). "Global Environmental Change and International Governance." *Millennium* 19, no. 3 (Winter 1990).

INDEX

About the Book and the Author

Both the North and the South have significant stakes in the global environment, but they bring differing interests and agendas to the bargaining table. An inequitable global economic system and the internationalization of economies have reduced Third World countries' control over the disposition of their resources and affected their strategies in global environmental negotiations.

Focusing on these issues, Marian A. L. Miller traces the efforts of developing countries to influence evolving environmental regimes. Her analysis centers on four themes: the areas of divergence and convergence in various countries' environmental policies; how these affect common goals and strategies; the negotiation process itself; and the degree to which the strategies of developing countries have succeeded in achieving desired outcomes. Negotiations regarding hazardous waste trade, biodiversity, technology transfer, and atmosphere and climate serve as case studies.

The book concludes with an assessment of the prospects for global environmental cooperation and for sustainable development in the Third World.

Marian A. L. Miller is assistant professor of political science at the University of Akron.